by heart

by heart

Conversations with
Martin Luther's Small Catechism

R. Guy Erwin • Mary Jane Haemig • Ken Sundet Jones

Martin J. Lohrmann • Derek R. Nelson • Kirsi I. Stjerna

Timothy J. Wengert • Hans Wiersma

AUGSBURG FORTRESS

BY HEART
Conversations with Martin Luther's Small Catechism

This book has a corresponding facilitator guide (ISBN 978-1-5064-3149-9) and DVD (ISBN 978-1-5064-3150-5).

Image credits are listed on page 223.

Publication Staff: Suzanne Burke, project editor; Julie O'Brien and Chris Zumski Finke, production managers; Kristofer Skrade, product design; Tory Herman, cover and interior design; Michael Moore, permissions.

The paper used in this publication meets the minimum requirements of American National Standard for Information Sciences—Permanence of Paper for Printed Materials, ANSI Z329.48-1984

ISBN: 978-1-5064-3148-2

Manufactured in the U.S.A.

21 20 19 18   3 4 5

Contents

Abbreviations

BC   *The Book of Concord*, ed. Robert Kolb and Timothy J. Wengert (Minneapolis: Fortress Press, 2000)

LW   *Luther's Works* [American edition], ed. Helmut Lehmann and Jaroslav Pelikan, 55 vols. (Philadelphia: Fortress Press, and St. Louis: Concordia, 1955–1986)

TAL   *The Annotated Luther*, ed. Hans J. Hillerbrand, Kirsi I. Stjerna, and Timothy J. Wengert, 6 vols. (Minneapolis: Fortress Press, 2015–2017)

Introduction

For all the variations later generations made to Martin Luther's Small Catechism, the core texts always included the Ten Commandments, Apostles' Creed, and Lord's Prayer. Along with the chief parts that were often found in late medieval catechisms, Luther also provided explanations of the sacraments, a table of scripture passages for the household (showing biblical warrants for various vocations), prayers, and liturgical orders for baptisms and weddings. Each of these builds on what Luther lays out as the foundations of faith. This book, *By Heart: Conversations with Martin Luther's Small Catechism*, regards Luther's words as already being so clear and profound that nothing more need be added. But understanding the theology and history behind the words can be helpful. Knowing how the Small Catechism reflects Luther's own life and thought can open up its proclamation of the gospel so that you can see how it seeks to surround your own life with the same freeing word.

Portrait of Martin Luther by Lucas Cranach the Elder as he appeared at the time he wrote the Small Catechism in 1529.

Every section of the Small Catechism has the same goal at its core: getting God's work in Christ to penetrate deep inside your heart. As you will see in the story of how the Small Catechism came to be, Luther saw firsthand how far removed the gospel was from his people's experience. So he set about crafting a proclamation of that word by which the Holy Spirit would create faith in sixteenth-century readers, in believers since 1529, and in you. Luther's explanations of the articles of the Apostles' Creed all begin with "I believe" and end with a declaration of that faith: "This is most certainly true." He compares the Lord's Prayer to our coming to God like children who trust a loving parent. In his explanations of baptism and the sacrament of the altar, he tells us that the sacraments give gifts that enable faith to happen and strengthen that faith. Faith shows up in Luther's explanation of the first commandment: "We are to fear, love, and trust God above all things." Faith hovers all through his explanations as we learn and take the catechism to heart. Faith is the hinge that moves us all from sin and unfaith to faith and righteousness as God's word creates a clean heart and right spirit within us. This is the center of what we could call the catechism's "by-heartedness."

Behind the Small Catechism lies Luther's own experience. He knew what it was to move daily from sin to faith, from fear to love of God, from life under the law to true freedom in Christ. Many of the great theologians of prior centuries created vast theological systems. They often used the logic and tools of ancient philosophy to come to some conclusions about theology. In his massive work *Summa Theologica*, Thomas Aquinas tried to answer every possible question connected to faith, God, and the Bible. At the same time, many medieval writers were also producing catechisms and prayer books to help the faithful. Luther took the situation of his people to heart and avoided complicated systems or simple explanations aimed at increasing a believer's meritorious works. More than most, he knew that faith doesn't happen as a result of finely wrought systems addressed to hypothetical people. Faith is given "by heart" when God's word comes to real people.

Luther's good friend Lucas Cranach had arrived in Wittenberg several years before Luther took up his post at the university. Cranach was the court artist to Frederick the Wise. Not only was he a fine producer of paintings, but he was on occasion the town mayor and owned an apothecary shop. Cranach's workshop was just off the Wittenberg town square, where he employed a full complement of workers. Cranach's staff learned the master's style and often carried out the carving and engraving of woodcuts and etchings for use as illustrations (including those in the first editions of the catechism) in the publishing industry, which had slowly developed since Johannes Gutenberg (c. 1398–1468) perfected movable type in the 1450s. When the pages of the catechism were pulled from the local printing presses and the ink dried, Luther handed over more than those individual sheets on which the various

Self-portrait of Lucas Cranach the Elder from 1550.

parts of the catechism were originally printed, and later, a handy booklet that included his preface, the liturgical parts, and the household chart of biblical passages. Luther was handing his readers Christ.

That Luther could do this so succinctly and vividly comes not only from the printing demands to reduce each chief part of the catechism to a single page, but also from his own experience of the gospel. By 1529 he was quite familiar with the daily life of a Christian. Luther, Cranach, and the people they served were on the receiving end of the crushing religious demands of the day. But as a onetime friar who had given his life over to days of prayer, study, and worship in the friary, and then as professor at the university and preacher and pastor at Wittenberg's city church, Luther's experience of the demands was perhaps heightened. Looking back on his earlier religious life in 1545, Luther described what that time had been like:

The Weimar Edition of Luther's Works.

> Although I was living an irreproachable life as a monk, I felt that I was a sinner before God with an extremely distressed conscience. I could not have confidence that it could find peace through my performance of satisfactions. I did not love—I hated!—the righteous God who punishes sinners Secretly, I expressed my anger with God, if not in the form of blasphemy, at least with intense grumbling.[1]

In Moses' final song at the end of Deuteronomy, he declares God's words when God vindicates the chosen people: "There is no god besides me. I kill and I make alive; I wound and I heal, and no one can deliver from my hand" (Deuteronomy 32:39). For long years Luther knew the killing and wounding that came from the constant demands to achieve righteousness and gain salvation.

It wasn't until Luther understood Paul's words about "the righteousness of God" in Romans (1:17) that everything shifted. God's judgment became God's salvation, and Luther's fear of God as judge found a match in the love of God as savior. Instead of only reading the passage as a demand to become righteous like God, Luther now experienced the word *righteousness* as a gift proceeding from God. It was pure grace that a person could only receive passively—that is, without any works, commitments, or actions. "At this point I felt that I had been completely born again and had entered paradise itself through wide open doors. There a completely different face of the entire Scripture appeared to me."

If you can read Latin and German, you can find all of Luther's works in the *Weimarer Ausgabe* ("Weimar Edition"). At 121 volumes and more than 80,000 pages, the critical edition of his writing was a major undertaking.

Publication began on Luther's birthday in 1883 and wasn't finished until 2009. Its presence sparked what has come to be known as the "Luther Renaissance," an expansion of studying Luther that went beyond the legends and hero worship of earlier centuries.

If English is your language, *Luther's Works* (American Edition) is the most complete version. The original set took about three decades to produce and ran to 55 volumes. Twenty-seven more volumes are set to appear in coming years.

For a fine collection of new English translations of Luther's most important works, consider *The Annotated Luther*, edited by Hans J. Hillerbrand, Kirsi I. Stjerna, and Timothy J. Wengert, 6 vols. (Minneapolis: Fortress, 2015–17).

---

1. "Preface to the Latin Writings," TAL 4:501.

Luther's task in drafting the Small Catechism was to bring the proclamation of law (as demand) and gospel (as unconditional promise), what he called "the sweetest of all words,"[2] to those into whose hands his *enchiridion*[3] was placed. It would need to be as visceral and grounded in daily life as his own experience. Because Luther set himself to a matter of ultimate consequence for real people, both the structure and language he used would bear the same message as the catechism's content.

Words That Work as Hard as Real People Do

When reading the Small Catechism, one should marvel at the brevity and clarity of the work. That didn't happen by accident. Luther and his fellow reformers in Wittenberg were the best kind of wordsmiths. They loved language. Luther was a prolific writer in both Latin and German, and his sermons showed a particular penchant for lucidity. When Luther was in hiding in Wartburg Castle beginning in May 1521, he wrote many letters and treatises, including a collection of sermon helps for the Christmas season. By the end of the year, his to-do list mostly completed (including letting his tonsure grow out and developing a hefty beard for his disguise as Jünker Jorg— "Knight George"), he set himself the task of translating the New Testament from the original Greek into good German. He finished in eleven weeks.[4]

Portrait of Luther as Jünker Jorg by Lucas Cranach the Elder, 1521.

What Luther produced wasn't simply an exact word-for-word move from one language to the other. Instead, Luther regarded the work of translation as giving the underlying sense of the text; translation for him was always interpretation. Choosing the right word allowed the language that came from Christ's mouth or from Paul's stylus to come alive. Years later he wrote an open letter on translating that shows what he was after:

> We do not have to inquire of the literal Latin, how we are to speak German. . . . Rather we must inquire about this of the mother in the home, the children on the street, the common man in the marketplace. We must be guided by their language, the way they speak, and do our translating accordingly. That way they will understand it and recognize that we are speaking German to them.[5]

For Luther, the main thing was to give scripture to God's people in the same way Jesus' body and blood were given: "for you." Language that didn't strike an authentic chord was useless.[6]

---

2. TAL 4:502. 3. The Greek word *enchiridion* refers to something placed in the hand—first as a designation for a small dagger and then for a pocketbook collecting the essential information on a topic. The catechisms produced in Wittenberg during Luther's lifetime all had this name on the title page. 4. Martin Brecht, *Martin Luther: Shaping and Defining the Reformation, 1521–1532* (Minneapolis: Fortress, 1990), 46ff. 5. "On Translating: An Open Letter," LW 35:189.

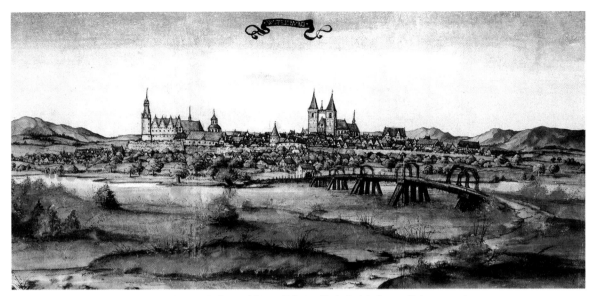
Drawing of Wittenberg in 1536 from the travel album of Count Palatine Ottheinrich. Pen and ink, watercolor.

When it came time to draft the Small Catechism, the same rule of thumb applied. Plenty of superb theological works have been published over the course of Christian history, but reading them isn't always easygoing. In contrast, Luther's language in the Small Catechism is down-to-earth and accessible. He could have spoken of God "at work in family life" or of "honesty in economics." But instead, he pulled in the details of daily life from the streets of Wittenberg and the farms in the surrounding countryside. In his explanations of the Commandments, he points to the value of a good name and reputation, to the harm of badly crafted goods and shady deals, and to specific ways we misuse God's name. In the Creed, he doesn't just say God created the world and sustains our lives. He confesses that "God made me" and provides a list of specifics God gives to accomplish the sustaining task: "shoes and clothing, food and drink, house and farm, spouse and children, fields, livestock, and all property."

The effect of the language is most vivid in its "by-heartedness." The faith described in the catechism never stays at the level of an intellectual idea or a theological proposition. There is no atonement theory here, but there *is* Christ who has "purchased and freed me from all sins, from death, and from the power of the devil, not with gold or silver but with his holy, precious blood and with his innocent suffering and death." Luther put the language of faith into the hearts of his people in a way that was cemented in everyday life. To be sure, Luther knew and confessed in the Nicene Creed that Christ was *homo-ousias* ("of one being") with the Father. But Luther translated the Creed's complexity into everyday language by writing that Christ is "true God . . . and also a true human being." And instead of thinking about God's gifts in general, the language of the catechism leads you to think about God's largesse when you encounter anything in Luther's list explaining daily bread. Indeed, when we notice any of these utterly ordinary things during

---

6. At the same time, Luther was also sensitive to the idiosyncrasies of the original language, sometimes preserving Hebraisms or Hellenisms to alert the German reader that something quite remarkable was happening in the text.

the day, the words jog our memory, reminding us of the God who provides everything needed for daily life.

For this reason, it is best when the language of the catechism becomes more than simply a recitation of right doctrine. With the language of Luther's original German, we get a text that is eminently memorizable.[7] And when it's memorized, the language can move from a mere explanation to a confession of faith. When the catechism sinks in, it puts words on your lips so you, too, might speak of God's countless deeds, from creation to the resurrection of the dead, to those who have never heard and to those who desperately need to hear again. The catechism leads to the same place Luther's understanding of justification by faith always led: to preaching, to proclamation, and to the pronouncement of mercy for Christ's sake. Indeed, the Small Catechism is less Luther's explanation of complicated doctrines than his own down-to-earth confession of faith to the simple people of his congregation.

Daily Bread	
Food	Upright children
Drink	Upright servants
Clothing	Faithful rulers
Shoes	Good government
House	Good weather
Farm	Peace
Fields	Health
Livestock	Decency
Money	Honor
Property	Good friends
Upright spouse	Faithful neighbors

Setting the Order

As he did with so many other types of writing consumed by the faithful in the pre-Reformation church, Luther took what had been passed on to him and turned it inside out and upside down. That's true of the structure of the Small Catechism. Plenty of earlier works taught the ABCs of Christian faith. Usually they started with something about the Apostles' Creed and the Lord's Prayer and only then brought up the Ten Commandments, or Decalogue. The thinking was that you first need to have faith and learn to worship, and then you get the guidelines for what to do with that faith.[8] In other words, first you give lip service to the Christian faith, reciting the proper prayers, and then you get a job description of what you must do to remain in God's good graces. But when you look for the Commandments in the Small Catechism, you find them right at the beginning. Luther uses the Commandments and his explanations to show how God moves in your life: how God reveals our sin at the deepest level (lack of fear and love of God) and how God unfolds us

A sixteenth-century physician.

---

7. That's one of the difficulties in translating the catechism into another language. Luther's language has depths of meaning that can't be completely rendered in English. And English versions will sometimes leave out alliterations and clever turns of phrase found in the original. The dilemma is whether to give people *exactly* what Luther said or to hand it on in such a way that it does the same thing in English as it did in German—though sacrificing faithfulness to the exact words. 8. Other late medieval catechisms were seen as preparation for the Sacrament of Penance (private confession to a priest) and thus began with the Creed (because even sinners could assent to the church's teaching), and then moved to the Ten Commandments and other lists of sins (in preparation for confession) before listing those prayers, including the Lord's Prayer, that the forgiven sinner, now in a state of grace, could say to continue to merit God's grace.

from our constant curving in on ourselves. About a decade before he published the Small Catechism, Luther wrote a short piece on the Commandments in which he described the three things Christians need to know: the law diagnoses our disease, the Creed says what medicine we need (God's grace), and the Lord's Prayer shows how to get the medicine and take the appropriate dose.[9]

In addition to this movement from diagnosis to prescription (grace) to filling the prescription, several scholars have noticed the chiastic structure of the first three parts, as the Commandments and first article of the Creed point to God as creator and sustainer of life; the Lord's Prayer links directly to the third article, thus leaving the second article of the creed at the catechism's heart.[10] In the catechism, the thing on which the meaning of everything else hinges is Luther's explanation of the second article of the Creed. In other words, the starting point for the whole project is the Lord Jesus. Without that section of the catechism, nothing else makes sense. With it we may delight in what Christ has done for us. When the proclamation of Christ in the second article of the Creed brings faith, then the catechism sends us both backward and forward. It turns us around—sends us back to the first article of the Creed and the Commandments—to see God as Creator in a new light and to reassess what the sinner in us regards as restrictive demands, seeing them instead as the Creator's way of protecting creatures like us and other humans in a broken world. And the catechism propels you forward toward the third article and the Lord's Prayer, where we discover how God's word works to create and sustain faith and where we beg for those very things in our lives. The Lord's Prayer becomes more than just some words to memorize so you can pray them at the end of every church meeting. Instead, it describes the shape of the true needs of the Christian life and God's generosity.

With his structure in the three main parts of the catechism, Luther sets you up for the additional pieces on the sacraments, confession, daily prayer, and the Household Chart. The explanation to the third article of the Creed says that the Holy Spirit calls, gathers, enlightens, and keeps the whole Christian church in the gospel promise. The additional parts of the catechism round out the traditional Lutheran understanding of the church as marked by gospel and sacrament and our understanding of the office of ministry in that church. The Augsburg Confession, the basic statement of the Lutheran witness to the gospel, read before the Holy Roman emperor Charles V in 1530 and still the single most important confession for Lutherans worldwide, points to the office of preaching (that is, proclaiming the gospel in word and sacrament). God uses these means to give the Holy Spirit "who produces faith, where and when he wills, in those who hear the gospel." Luther's explanations of the sacraments (baptism, the Lord's supper, and our return to baptism in confession and forgiveness) deliver what the Augsburg Confession teaches: "We have a gracious God, not through our merit but through Christ's merit, when we so believe."[11] Such things as daily prayers and scriptural passages about how you as a Christian might live a faithful life in your vocations are Luther's way of showing how good works grow out of faith.

---

9. Martin Luther, *Ein kurze Form der zehn Gebote, eine kurze Form des Glaubens, ein kurze Form des Vater Unsers* (1520), WA 7:204.   10. Albrecht Peters, *"Die Theologie der Katechismen Luthers anhand der Zuordunung ihrer Hauptstücke,"* in *Lutherjahrbuch* 43 (1976): 15–17. Charles P. Arand builds on it in his work on the catechisms: *That I May Be His Own* (St. Louis, MO: Concordia, 2000), 136ff.   11. Augsburg Confession, Article V (BC 40:3).

How the Catechism Frees

As a friar in the Augustinian monastery, Luther was well acquainted with a view of God's law as an unceasing string of demands laid out for the believer to fulfill. The view of the Christian life he was taught told him *Face quod in se est!* ("Do what is within you to do"). He took that demand seriously and learned it'll nearly kill you. Luther was present for all the appointed worship services; confessed his impure thoughts, words, and deeds; and was scrupulous about prayer. All the striving just left him open to more demands. He came to wonder how God's supposed graciousness squared with divine commands that took more and more from you without letting you know if you had really done enough. Attempting to meet God's demands never gave Luther a feeling of peace. Instead, it simply opened him up to more turmoil and made it seem like God was just as much a tyrant as the devil was.

Woodcut of Luther as an Augustinian friar in his monastic habit, 1521.

While in the monastery, Luther often went to private confession, where he would recite all his sins to his confessor, Johann von Staupitz, the head of his order. Getting everything out in the open was crucial. The Augustinians were known as a rigorous order when it came to confessing sins, so it's no surprise that Luther wanted to lay it all out. But he went above and beyond the normal confessions. Sometimes Luther would finish with confession and think of some sin he'd forgotten and race back to confess that one too. To deal with Luther's "scruples" (as the handbooks for father confessors called them), von Staupitz reminded Luther of the article in the Creed, "I believe in the forgiveness of sins," and asked Luther if he, too, believed this. Finally, as we saw above, Luther, "by the mercy of God," came to experience God's righteousness not as God's judgment against the sinner but as a gracious covering of the sinner with Christ's mercy.

Portrait of Johann von Staupitz from an 1899 copy of a sixteenth-century original. Staupitz is widely regarded as being an early mentor who opened up Luther's thinking by repeatedly telling him to look to Christ's mercy.

Luther would later draw on that experience while in hiding at Wartburg Castle in 1521–22. Philip Melanchthon, his young colleague at the University of Wittenberg, wrote and asked how he could become a better Christian teacher. Luther responded to Philip with an odd word: the only way to get better at the Christian life was to first become a real sinner rather than a sham sinner. What Luther meant was that you could confess all kinds of things you did wrong or the many good things you neglected, but that would not go deep enough to the true condition that drives all sin; it would just tiptoe around the most important matter: your deep rejection of God and desire to be your own God. The only way to teach the gospel with such strength is to "sin boldly"—and further, to trust Christ even more boldly. In other words, the only way to become a better Christian is not to become more pious, religious, or moral. It's to know how thoroughly sin runs in you, which in turn increases your understanding of what Christ has done for you and how the Holy Spirit uses God's word to create deeper trust in him. The language, structure, and content of the catechism all work together splendidly to turn you upside down, emptying you of your pretensions of goodness and, in turn, creating someone new in you.

Whenever and wherever God addresses us with the "living Word" (even in the Small Catechism or, we hope, by extension in this book), God turns the rudder each day so that we sail in a new direction. This daily drowning of the old creature of sin and rising up of the new creature of faith arise from baptism into Christ. That we do this daily (and not just one time in life) is connected to another insight Luther had into God's work on us and in us. We cannot untangle the sinful knot of our lives. This means that we experience the Christian life not despairing but surely under attack. The German word for that turmoil and assault is *Anfechtung*, and it, too, is a mark of the Christian life, as Luther explains in the sixth petition of the Lord's Prayer. Already in the *Heidelberg Disputation* (1518), Luther argued that "one must utterly despair of oneself in order to be made fit to receive the grace of Christ."[12] That's because as long as you think you have something to hand over as evidence that you're worthy of God's graciousness, you will have no need for Christ. Despairing of yourself, the very work of the law on us performed by the Holy Spirit, is the first part of the arc from unfaith to faith that the Small Catechism describes and instills. But that despair is immediately followed by faith in Christ as Lord and Savior, so that the Christian is *at the same time* sinner and righteous.

The catechism gives our brains, hearts, and tongues a good workout in using the language of faith. But what God really uses Luther's work for is to help us gain mastery over those same organs. In his great commentary on Galatians, Luther declared the great joy the gospel gives.

> God is repelled by sorrow of spirit; he hates sorrowful teaching and sorrowful thoughts and words, and he takes pleasure in happiness. For he came to refresh us, not to sadden us.[13]

When the gospel is yours "by heart," that is, when the Holy Spirit speaks the gospel into your heart, that's when God will set your lips to singing the language of the catechism: God's work "is done out of pure, fatherly, and divine goodness and mercy, without any merit or worthiness of mine at all!" Christ "has redeemed me, a lost and condemned human being." "I believe that by my own understanding or strength I cannot believe in Jesus Christ my Lord or come to him."[14] Arriving empty-handed before God and hearing the gospel in response will draw out these words of true confession, of being a real sinner, and of the greatness of Christ's gift on the cross and in the empty tomb. And God will move you to live faithfully because you're being created anew. No longer will you simply fear God's judgment, but now God will be the object of your love.

---

12. TAL 1:83. 13. "Lectures on Galatians," LW 27:93. 14. Small Catechism, explanations to the first, second, and third articles of the Apostles' Creed.

1

The Story of the Small Catechism

Introduction

"It was the best of times; it was the worst of times." Martin Luther might have been thinking something along those lines when he looked back on the year 1529, the year he wrote the Small Catechism. Luther certainly lived in interesting times—thanks, in part, to Luther. It was a time of rediscovery of God's unconditional mercy and the old ways of human merit; it was an age of excitement about the gospel and complete ignorance of the basics of Christianity. And Martin Luther was in the middle of it all.

Thanks to Luther's writings and teachings, the Bible was being interpreted in a new way, inspiring many to faith in Jesus. More and more pastors were being trained by Luther and his colleagues at the University of Wittenberg and influenced by their writings. These pastors held pastoral calls to congregations throughout Germany and beyond. The reform of the church was happening, really happening! The best of times!

At the same time, Luther had been informed—and eventually found out for himself—that a large portion of Germany's churchgoers had very little idea of the essential teachings of Christianity. They knew almost nothing about the Lord's Prayer, the Apostles' Creed, and the Ten Commandments, not to mention the rest of the Bible. The everyday Christian didn't know squat. The worst of times!

In a way, the story of the Small Catechism is a tale of two situations. The first situation had to do with the need to get the reforming churches on the same page, doctrinally speaking. The second situation had to do with the need to distill the new teachings into an easy-to-learn format that everybody—even children—could manage and understand. As such, the story of the Small Catechism is a good story to share. But in order to tell the tale in its fullness, we have to start at the beginning.

"Christian Basics" and the Bible

The story of the Small Catechism doesn't begin with Luther and the Lutherans. Fittingly, the story begins with Jesus and the disciples.

Another portrait of Martin Luther by Lucas Cranach the Elder, 1529.

The word *disciple* comes from the Latin word *discipulus*. A *discipulus* is a student or a pupil. A *discipulus* can even be an apprentice. In the New Testament gospels, the followers of Jesus are called students. In the Greek language of the New Testament, the word for student is *matheyteys*, which becomes *discipulus* when translated into Latin. Today the word *disciple* has more of a sense of being a follower, but the original sense of the word also includes the idea of being a student or an apprentice. Jesus' original disciples—those women and men who were nearest to him during his years of ministry—didn't just follow him around, tracking his footsteps throughout the Judean countryside and on up to Jerusalem. No, those early followers—those *discipuli*—were primarily *learners*. Even more than accompanying Jesus on his path, they learned from Jesus while on the path.

At the end of the path, Jesus left his disciples—those early church leaders known as apostles—with some final instructions. "Go, make disciples," Jesus said to those who were already disciples. These instructions are known as the Great Commission; you will find the words at the very end of Matthew's gospel: "Go therefore and make disciples of all nations, baptizing them in the name of the Father and of the Son and of the Holy Spirit, and teaching them to obey everything that I have commanded you. And remember, I am with you always, to the end of the age."

The disciples gather on the mountain where Christ sends them out to spread the gospel. Fifteenth-century painting by Cristoforo de Predis.

Now when you read the Great Commission out loud, it may sound like church language. But how does it sound when you paraphrase it a bit and put Jesus' words into everyday English? "Go and make students of all people, soaking them in God's holy name and teaching them everything that I told you. And don't forget that I'll be there with you to the very end." You can see that the Lord's instructions to his disciples—students—

are fairly straightforward. How do you make new students? One, you bring them to the water. Two, you teach them everything that Jesus taught. Again, that's (1) water them and (2) teach them. Indeed, when you look at how the Jesus movement started, you can see that the wet-teach two-step was how they did it. For instance, on the Day of Pentecost—sometimes called the church's "birthday"—we are told that three thousand new students were baptized. We're then told that those new students "devoted themselves to the apostles' teaching and fellowship" (Acts 2:41-42). Bring them to the water and teach them. This isn't rocket science, people!

By all accounts, the Jesus movement spread from Jerusalem throughout the Roman Empire rather rapidly. Within twenty-five years of the giving of the Great Commission, churches were set up all around the Mediterranean world of the first century. You can credit the fact that Christianity "went viral" to the effort of those first students, those apostles and others, especially the one named Paul. But you can also credit the Holy Spirit, who inspired those apostles to speak and who inspired more and more newcomers to join the movement and become disciples—students!—of Jesus. But surely some of the credit goes to the sheer simplicity of the process: add water, then add instruction.

Let's first talk about the water. When the Jesus movement was getting under way, almost everyone was a newcomer. The practice was to welcome the newcomers with baptism. Baptism was not just water only, but according to Paul, baptism joined the newcomer to the death and resurrection of Jesus (Romans 6:3-5). In the New Testament, when a man or a woman wished to become a student (disciple!) of Jesus, they were not required to commit to a lengthy, drawn-out period of instruction prior to baptism. Instead, baptism was bestowed immediately. Take the story of the Ethiopian man (in Acts 8:26-39). After hearing the story of Jesus, the Ethiopian man asked, "What is to prevent me from being baptized?" Apparently the answer was "Nothing," because he was baptized right there on the spot.

Same with Lydia, a woman living in Philippi, Greece (Acts 16:13-15). One day she was down by the river, minding her own business, when she heard the apostle Paul preaching. Lydia listened and, boom, "the Lord opened her heart." She was baptized the same day. And not just her, but "her entire household." The same thing happened to a man from Philippi, a prison guard, who heard the gospel (along with his

The prophet Joel in Luther's German translation of the Bible from 1534. Joel is preaching in the foreground and Peter is preaching in the background, in the middle of a very German-looking city. (See Joel 2:28-32 and Acts 2:17-21.)

Philip and the Ethiopian eunuch from a new Latin translation of the Bible published in 1558.

The modern outdoor chapel at the site in eastern Macedonia where Lydia is thought to have been baptized by Paul.

household) and became a believer. As a result, he and his entire family were baptized without delay. (Read all of Acts 16 for the full account of the Philippi baptisms!) Of course, since they were being baptized as disciples (aka students), you can be sure that after the water came the teaching. So what were the new students taught? And how were they taught?

The evidence shows that before the gospels were written down, the teachings of Jesus and the teachings about Jesus were told and retold, and the Hebrew Scriptures were read and reread. Through the telling and retelling, those early students committed the teachings to memory. Yes, some of those teachings were eventually written down, and some of what was written down eventually made it into the New Testament. But even after the written-down teachings started circulating, most early *discipuli* received the words of the Lord by hearing them repeated over and over. There wasn't much to it. There were no animated films or PowerPoint slides— not even felt boards or filmstrips. Instead, instruction happened and faith came the old-fashioned way: through hearing and speaking.

The New Testament contains many examples of memorizable teachings that were part of the collective memory of the earliest Christians. The Beatitudes and the Lord's Prayer and the rest of Jesus' "Sermon on the Mount" (Matthew 5–7; Luke 6) have a "pithiness" that suggests that these teachings were to be recited and received and recalled by those early disciples. Similar pithy sayings and formulas are embedded elsewhere in the New Testament. Consider Paul's articles of resurrection: "For I handed on to you as of first importance what I in turn had received: that Christ died for our sins in accordance with the scriptures, and that he was buried, and that he was raised on the third day in accordance with the scriptures" (1 Corinthians 15:3-4). Or this early creed: "[Christ] was revealed in flesh, vindicated in spirit, seen by angels, proclaimed among Gentiles, believed in throughout the world, taken up in glory" (1 Timothy 3:16). Clearly, these formulas were recited over and over so that they would be remembered and passed on to later generations of disciples/students.

This method of teaching and learning would have been familiar to those early students, especially if they were Jewish. The Torah would have been learned the same way. In fact, the written Torah—the first five books of the Old Testament—included God's own teaching about how to teach and learn the Torah:

> Hear, O Israel: The LORD is our God, the LORD alone. You
> shall love the LORD your God with all your heart, and with
> all your soul, and with all your might. Keep these words that
> I am commanding you today in your heart. Recite them to
> your children and talk about them when you are at home and
> when you are away, when you lie down and when you rise.
> (Deuteronomy 6:4-7)

This passage of the Torah is known as the Shema (*sh'ma* is Hebrew for "hear!"). The Shema was central to Israel's religion and worship; even today Jewish people around the world recite it as part of their daily prayers. The Shema is also central to Jesus' understanding of the Torah. When a religious expert asked Jesus about the most important teaching of the Torah, Jesus correctly responded with the Shema. Jesus explained that if you know that loving God and loving your neighbor are the two most important teachings of the Torah, then "you are not far from the kingdom of God" (Mark 12:28-34).

The first two words of the *Shema Israel* on the menorah at the Israeli Knesset.

The title of the *Didache* from a manuscript discovered in 1873.

So what does the Shema have to do with the story of the Small Catechism? Perhaps you noticed the part of the Shema that says that the teachings of the Torah should be recited "to your children." Perhaps you also noticed that it says you should talk about the teachings "when you are at home and when you are away, when you lie down and when you rise"—in other words, all the time and everywhere. Finally, perhaps you noticed that the Shema's tradition of reciting and discussing the key teachings over and over, day in and day out, has a purpose. The purpose is to *keep* the words "in your heart," to internalize them, to make them stick, so to speak.

The same goes for being a disciple of Jesus. To be his student means to learn his words and his ways by heart. The apostle Paul (in Galatians 6:6) uses the Greek word *katechoumenos* to describe those who are taught the word in this way. If you have a sharp eye for not-so-subtle foreshadowing, then you probably noticed that the word *katechoumenos* looks like it is related to the word *catechism*. You would be correct. In fact, *katechoumenos* (pronounced kat-eh-KOOM-en-ahs) means "the ones who are being taught." In English we would call such people "catechumens." More on these catechumens in the next section! For now, however, we need to share one more tidbit that will help us understand the backstory of the Small Catechism.

The story of the Small Catechism wouldn't be complete without telling you about the ancient Christian writing called the *Didache* (pronounced DID-ah-kay). The title is a Greek word that means—what else?—"teaching" or "training." The *Didache* represents "the teachings of the Lord given to the Nations by the Twelve Apostles,"

In ancient Greek, the root verb *katecheo* (*katechizo*) is made up of two parts: *kata* (again) and *echeo*, to sound forth or echo. Originally, it denoted a particular form of instructing, still used in places where books are scarce, where the teacher says something and the pupils echo it back—as in America's one-room schoolhouses. By Paul's day, it was the term for instructing in the basics. Because of its widespread use among early Greek-speaking Christians, Latin-speaking Christians brought it into their own language without translation, *catechizo*, meaning basic religious instruction. Augustine, bishop of Hippo, provided the first instance of the noun *catechismus*, referring to basic religious instruction. Luther for the most part uses the term not for his Small Catechism but for this basic instruction.

as its opening words suggest.[1] This ancient document is a compilation of different teachings—many of which reflect the teachings of Jesus in the gospels and other teachings found in the New Testament. It is no coincidence that the *Didache* begins with a sort of Shema of its own: "The way of life is this: first, you must love the One who created you; second, you must love your neighbor in the same manner as yourself." From this beginning, the *Didache* continues with lists of teachings, many of them familiar from the Sermon on the Mount: turn the other cheek, bless those who curse you, pray for your enemies, and so on. Other teachings evoke the Ten Commandments: do not murder, do not commit adultery, do not steal, do not bear false witness. The *Didache* also has a section on prayer that includes the Lord's Prayer and other guidelines. In addition, the *Didache* includes sections concerning baptism and the Lord's supper, as well as sections on how to practice hospitality, how to identify false teachers, and how to wait for the return of Jesus.

The *Didache* is a unique document, especially when compared with other early Christian literature. It's not a gospel—a narrative with a beginning, middle, and end, like Matthew, Mark, Luke, and John. It's not a theological treatise like Paul's letter to the church in Rome. Nor is it a letter of pastoral conversation and concern like Paul's letters to the church in Corinth. Instead, the *Didache* is a brief manual of how to live as a follower of Jesus in community with other followers of Jesus. It reads like a handout filled with bullet-pointed items, some with explanations, just begging to be memorized, discussed, and put into practice. The section on baptism even teaches that before newcomers are baptized, they should learn the teachings of the *Didache*. The *Didache* may in fact be the oldest surviving Christian catechism!

So, to summarize this part of the story of the Small Catechism, it's clear that from the very beginning, being a follower of Jesus meant being a student (aka disciple). It's also clear that being a student of Jesus meant learning some basic pieces of information and understanding some essential principles. Finally, it's clear that in the early days of the church, being a student of Jesus meant learning those basics by heart. More than that, being a student also meant keeping those essential principles in your heart, even making them habits of your heart.

Our story has started. Our story now continues with a look at, oh, the next fourteen hundred years! We promise to keep it brief.

Teaching "Christian Basics" through the Centuries

Let's imagine that it's the year 280 and that you are a Christian living somewhere near the city of Alexandria, Egypt. Now let's imagine that it's a warm, sunny day in the city center, where you are looking at the wares being sold in the stalls of the main market. You begin to hear someone speaking loudly and with enthusiasm. You draw nearer to listen and find that it's a preacher talking about Jesus and his crucifixion and resurrection. You keep listening. You hear the preacher explain that Jesus is a king who rules his people with grace, mercy, and love—unlike the Roman emperor who rules with an iron fist. You hear the preacher declare that Jesus lives and by becoming a citizen of the "Jesus Empire," you too will have a new life now and in the life to

---

1. For everything you may ever want to know about this curious first-century writing, check out Thomas O'Loughlin, *The Didache: A Window on the Earliest Christians* (Grand Rapids: Baker, 2010). If all you want is a good translation of the *Didache*, we like the one that you will find archived here: http://web.archive.org/web/20101009033540/http://ivanlewis.com/Didache/didache.html.

come. Now let's say that as you listen, your heart is strangely warmed and you feel drawn to this crucified and risen king.

"Trust in Jesus," the preacher proclaims, "and be baptized, and a new and eternal life is yours!" *That sounds great*, you think to yourself, so you say to the preacher: "I believe! I want to be baptized!" The preacher says: "That's great! We'll put you on the list." You ask, "Excuse me, but what is to prevent me from being baptized right now?" The preacher explains, "Well, we have to teach you some stuff first." You think to yourself, *Okay, so there are a few things I have to learn before I get baptized*. So you tell the preacher, "Okay, I'm in. I'll take the classes. How long before I'm baptized?" The preacher says, "Three years."

So what happened? How did baptism go from something that (a) did not necessarily require any advance preparation to (b) something that might have meant learning a few basics, to (c) something that required up to three years of formal education? How did it turn from a gift given without prerequisites to a privilege you received only if you learned all the material, passed the tests, met the conditions, and showed yourself worthy? One reason might have involved a desire not to cheapen the experience by right away immersing new believers in water—or pouring the water onto them. (The early churches baptized in different ways.) Another reason might have had to do with the notion that many potential converts believed in unholy things and lived unholy lives. The thinking here would have been to let newcomers unlearn some of their unholy habits before being baptized. This was especially true in places where it was thought that baptism didn't cover major sins committed after baptism, when there was a long, public process to get back into the good graces of your church.

There is one more reason to consider. From about 64 to 313, Christians periodically found themselves under persecution. Some persecutions—those under Roman emperors such as Decius and Diocletian—resulted in the arrests and deaths of many disciples. Consequently, some disciples renounced their allegiance to Jesus by offering a small sacrifice to the "spirit" (Lat., *genius*) of the emperor. Groups of Christians who remained sometimes went underground. To test their resolve, new converts were subject to a probation period. Whatever the reason, a period of time let newcomers "incubate" in the new teachings and the new ways of life.

A three-year period of preparation for baptism was truly the exception. Most scholars believe that those applying for baptism (which took place at fixed times during the year, especially on the Vigil of Easter), would be instructed in the months leading up to their baptism, although most would have already been attending Sunday preaching. In the case of an emergency, baptisms could be administered much more quickly. Given the references to "households" in the accounts in Acts, it would seem that children, and perhaps infants, were also baptized in nearly every era of the church's existence.

A third-century wall painting of Jesus' baptism and a fisherman from the Roman catacombs.

Remember that at the beginning of this section you were asked to imagine that you lived in Alexandria, Egypt, around the year 280, that you were a newcomer to the Jesus movement, and that you were looking at the beginning of a lengthy process before undergoing baptism and being fully welcomed into the fold. Now imagine that you are going to become part of the catechumenate. The catechumenate is what they called the group of people being taught how to follow Jesus, the group of people being considered for baptism into the death and resurrection of Jesus.

At that time (280), in that place (Alexandria, Egypt), there was a document in use by churches in the area. This document came to be known as the *Apostolic Tradition of Hippolytus of Rome*. There seems to be some question about whether Hippolytus (170–235), a Christian priest (presbyter) in Rome, ever had anything to do with this document, but that's beside the point. What is known pretty much for sure is that during the second half of the third century or early fourth century, this *Apostolic Tradition* was in use as a manual (or "church order") for many Christian communities. The *Apostolic Tradition* covers all manner of concerns that were present to those early communities: for instance, how to assign responsibilities to the leaders (bishops,

The baptistery of the Cathedral of St. John in Ephesus (sixth century).

presbyters, and deacons), how to support those who had been persecuted for the faith, how to live devout lives, how to pray, and how to worship, especially at Easter. There is also a lot of material on how to admit newcomers to the catechumenate and how to baptize catechumens at the end of their time of learning.

So, you want to be a catechumen? Not so fast. You first must submit yourself to one of the appointed teachers to see if you meet the initial requirements. Are you a sculptor who makes idols? A gladiator? A military officer? An executioner? An astrologer? A fortune-teller? A pimp? A prostitute? If so, you first must cease and desist being those things before you can start learning the word. Once you pass the initial screening process, your time in the catechumenate can begin.

For up to three years you will be taught the word and learn the ways of being a follower of Jesus and being a part of the community that worships him. When the three years are up, do you get to pick a day to be baptized? Answer: No. First, your teachers will test you to see if you are indeed ready for baptism. Second, your day for baptism has already been selected. In fact, the day is the same for everybody. This is why the *Apostolic Tradition* has a lot to say about Easter. Because it is early on Easter Sunday that you will be baptized—you along with all your fellow catechumens who have been declared ready to be baptized. Indeed, the Saturday *before* Easter

Sunday is a big deal because it marks the end of your time in the catechumenate, the conclusion of three years of intense learning! Here is how the *Apostolic Tradition* describes it:

> The ones who are to be baptized shall fast on Friday. On Saturday, the bishop will assemble them and command them to kneel in prayer. Laying hands upon them, the bishop shall exorcise all evil spirits, making them flee away and never to return. Then the bishop will blow breath in their faces, seal their foreheads, ears, and noses [with the sign of the cross], and then raise them up. Next, they will spend that night in vigil, listening to reading and instruction. . . . At sunrise [on Easter morning] prayers will be said over the water. If there is plenty of water, let it stream through the baptismal basin or be poured into it from above. If water is scarce, then use whatever water you can find. The ones being baptized will remove their clothing. The young children will be baptized first. If they can answer for themselves, let them. If they cannot, let their parents or other relatives answer for them. Then baptize the men. Next, the women. Let them loosen their hair and put aside any jewelry that they were wearing. Don't let anyone take anything with them into the water.[2]

Baptisms at twenty-first-century Easter Vigils.

All of this was just the beginning of the baptismal rite. Prayers, scripture readings, and professions of faith would follow. Questions were posed and exhortations were made. Oil was used for anointing, the laying on of hands was used to bless and to bestow the Holy Spirit. And at the heart of it was the joining of the catechumen to the death and resurrection of Jesus, through the water, in

St. Augustine Baptizes the Catechumens by Girolama Genga, c. 1516.

---

2. *Apostolic Tradition*, sec. 21, author's translation, based on that of Burton Scott Easton in *Apostolic Tradition of Hippolytus*, ed. and trans. Burton Scott Easton (Cambridge: Cambridge University Press, 1934), 44–45.

the name of the Father and of the Son and of the Holy Spirit. The Lord's supper would be shared by the whole Christian assembly, the newly baptized partaking for the very first time. It was quite the day and quite the celebration, as you can imagine.

Well, now that you have envisioned yourself as a third-century catechumen, you may yet have some lingering questions. One of them might be: Were they really naked? Another question might be: What did catechumens actually learn during those three years? Still another question might be: What about the children, the ones who couldn't "answer for themselves"? Were there babies among them? Did they ever have to learn the stuff that their parents learned?

To the first question: Were they really naked? Yes. This is part of why, for the sake of modesty, they baptized the men separate from the women.

To the second question: What did catechumens learn? For three years, those catechumens were taught the essential rhythms of the Christian life. They were taught basic understandings of Jesus—by the year 200 it appears that in Rome a precursor of the Apostles' Creed was already in use. (Other regions developed very similar creeds professing faith in the triune God.) Teachers would go over the parts of the Creed line by line. Catechumens listened to sermons and were exhorted to live godly lives. They learned prayers and psalms and passages from the gospels. They memorized lists of rules and learned Christian discipline. The curriculum was not the same from place to place or from teacher to teacher. But there was a common method of teaching, of testing. The teacher would ask a question, and the catechumen would respond with the prescribed answer. This question-and-answer approach was called *catechesis*, and it is still called that today. The content of the teaching is called *catechism*.

To the third question: What about the children? When did they learn? What did they learn? What's the difference between becoming a *discipulus* of Jesus after baptism instead of before baptism? The answer to all of the questions taken together is: it's complicated. Another story from the ancient church may help. This is the story of St. Augustine, bishop of Hippo, after whom the city in Florida is named. His story is important to the story of the Small Catechism.

About a century or so after the *Apostolic Tradition* had started making the rounds in Egypt and elsewhere, Augustine, a bishop from the area of

St. Augustine taken to school by St. Monica; a painting by Niccolò di Pietro, 1413–15.

Hippo Regius (an ancient city on the North African coast), began to rethink the whole connection of water and teaching, of baptism and catechism. When Augustine was born, his mother, Monica, brought him into the local church and had him blessed and dedicated to God. Technically, the dedication rite made the infant Augustine a catechumen. That is, because he was born to a baptized member in good standing, Augustine was in a way "preapproved" to prepare for baptism at some future date. But Augustine was not baptized as a baby or young child. As an older child, he fell ill and apparently begged his mother to arrange for an emergency baptism. Monica set it all up, but when her son recovered, she called it off.

It appears that just because children who could not "answer for themselves" were *permitted* baptism in churches of the time, not all children of believers were baptized. At the time and in certain circles, it was common for parents to decline baptism for their children. Imagining that believing parents at that time did not want to make that choice for their children may be easy, but that perspective simply shows how we have been shaped by a culture that obsesses a bit about freedom of choice. No, in Augustine's day, it was common for parents to take a pass on baptism for their children because they wanted to give their children some space to get any wildness out of their system before taking baptismal vows of the Christian life.

"Let them carry on, let them do as they please, since they are not yet baptized" is how Augustine described the prevailing attitude. This attitude appears to have been quite common, since Augustine noted that the idea was "sounded into his ears from all sides." Later in his life, Augustine complained about the laxity of allowing young people to explore their wild sides. But as a young man, Augustine did indeed have a wild side: partying, drinking, brawling, and carousing, "daring to run wild among various and shadowy loves," as he put it.[3]

Eventually Augustine settled down—if "settled down" can include having a stormy, fifteen-year relationship with a lover, having a son with her, moving them both across the Mediterranean Sea to Milan, Italy, and adding on a few affairs when the long-term relationship began to end. You can read all about the particulars of Augustine's struggles with lust, romance, and marriage in his autobiography, which he titled *Confessions*. Somewhere near the time of the end of his relationship, Augustine found himself in deep spiritual travail. Sitting under a tree weeping, he became aware of a child's voice. The voice said, *Tolle, lege; tolle, lege*: "Pick it up, read it; pick it up, read it." The "it" was the Bible. Augustine opened it to Romans 13:13-14: "Let us live honorably as in the day, not in reveling and drunkenness, not in debauchery and licentiousness, not in quarrelling and jealousy. Instead, put on the Lord Jesus Christ, and make no provision of the flesh, to gratify its desires."[4] So Augustine, who had been attending Christian worship especially to hear the sermons of Milan's bishop, Ambrose (c. 340–397), put himself on the list for a time of rigorous teaching and training for baptism.

Baptismal preparation lasted the entire season of Lent. Since Augustine had been raised a Christian, he had been considered a hearer of the word all along. He was therefore not subject to the three-year "rule" that was applied to complete newcomers. So, as springtime approached, Augustine joined the other catechumens who had been declared competent to receive instruction. Twice per day, he and the others were catechized by the great Ambrose. A heavy emphasis was put on Christian discipline as well as on prayer. The catechumens would have already known the Lord's Prayer, but for the first time they received detailed teaching about its deepest meaning and application. Toward the end of their catechization, on Palm Sunday, Ambrose imparted

---

3. *Confessions* 1.18; 2.1. 4. *Confessions* 8.29.

the Apostles' Creed to the catechumens. By that time in its history, the Creed was often thought to have originated with the initial twelve apostles—each one contributing a phrase. Ambrose spoke the words of the Creed and, over and over, the catechumens repeated them, driving the words into memory. In those final days of preparation, Ambrose preached to them on the meaning of each line of the Creed. Ambrose forbade his students from putting the Creed's words on paper; the words were to be written and safeguarded deep within the heart. With the Creed of the Apostles firmly embedded, Augustine kept vigil for the momentous day.

Saints Augustine and Ambrose, by Filippo Lippi, c. 1437.

As the sun rose on Easter morning in 387, Augustine put aside his old clothes and was at last baptized, clothed with a white garment. In the same year he was baptized, Augustine (along with his son) returned to his home territory on the North African coast. There he became a pastor and a preacher and, eventually, the supervisor (bishop) of the churches in and around the city of Hippo Regius. As bishop, Augustine had charge of the catechumens, teaching them the ways of Jesus. Initially, it appears that he did not press for parents to baptize their children. Instead, Augustine's preference for infant baptism evolved through his responses to two controversies that embroiled him.

The first controversy involved the teachings of a bishop of Carthage named Donatus (d. 355) who held that rebaptism was required for believers who had been baptized by bishops who (in his followers' opinion) had fallen from the faith during an earlier persecution. The other controversy involved a monk named Pelagius who taught that there was no such thing as original sin—people were born innocent and sin was a choice. In part, Pelagius was reacting to Augustine's statement in his already popular *Confessions* that everything depended on God's grace, not the human will.[5] Augustine's response to these challenges led him to conclude that it was "the firm tradition of the universal church" to baptize infants and that "the Sacrament of regeneration is given first." If the baptized child continues in the Christian life, "conversion of the heart will follow."[6] Baptism's power lay in God's word and not in the faith of the baptizand or the baptizer. Regarding original sin, the Pelagians argued that babies were incapable of committing actual sins and therefore were unaffected by the sin of Adam and Eve. They learned to sin from their surroundings but were not captive to sin. Augustine responded by insisting that all people born to sinners are themselves already sinners in need of God's grace and that the human will is from birth afflicted with humanity's "root" or original sin: the love of self.

---

5. The famous line from *Confessions* 10.29 was the prayer: "Give what you command and command what you will."   6. *On Baptism*, bk. 4, chaps. 23 and 24.

Translation: Handbook [*Enchiridion*]: *The Small Catechism for Ordinary Pastors and Preachers*. Dr. Martin Luther. Wittenberg. [Printed by] Nicholas Schirlentz (1536).

Augustine is one of the most important teachers in the history and development of Christian tradition and thought. Along with the subjects of baptism and original sin, he wrote on just about every major subject: the Holy Trinity, predestination, the nature of grace, the connection of faith and works, and the relationship of church and state (including the just war theory). One of his writings, called *Enchiridion*, is a book of teaching centered on the Apostles' Creed, the Lord's Prayer, and the Law of God, organized around the virtues of faith, hope, and love. The word *enchiridion* means, in Greek, "in the hand." The word was originally used to denote a small sword used for self-defense but came to be more commonly used as the word for a handbook, an instruction manual. At more than thirty thousand words in its English translation, Augustine's *Enchiridion* is hardly a "small" catechism. It's more of a lengthy sermon about the essentials of Christian belief and life—a "larger" catechism, if you will. Also, it's mostly about faith, including Augustine's classic observation that "faith accomplishes what the law commands." The section on the Lord's Prayer is relatively short, however. And the section on the Law is based on Jesus' teaching to love God and neighbor, rather than on the Ten Commandments specifically. Still, you can detect in the *Enchiridion* the three parts of what would much later become the traditional catechism: the Creed, the Lord's Prayer, and the Ten Commandments. No wonder Luther's Small Catechism always included in its title the word *Enchiridion*.

And one more thing. Augustine developed a little community of celibate believers with rules governing their common life that eventually came into use by a medieval group of friars called *Augustinians*. More than one thousand years later, in 1505, a twenty-one-year-old Martin Luther became an Augustinian. And to get to Martin Luther's part in our story, we must touch on the intervening one thousand years of church history.

About one hundred years after Augustine died, Emperor Justinian I decreed that *everybody* in the Roman Empire was required to be baptized. As you can imagine, this changed everything. With all the unbaptized being baptized and all future generations being baptized as babies, many traditional aspects of the catechumenate disappeared. True, parents and sponsors, with the support of clergy, were supposed to teach their children the basics of the faith: the Creed, the Lord's Prayer, and (by the thirteenth century) the Ten Commandments. On the other hand, Christianity became so embedded into the culture of the Empire, that the baptized absorbed the faith as much as learned it. There was the liturgy of Mass, with the eucharist at the center, available daily and emphasized on Sundays. There were Bible readings and sermons based on a prescribed cycle of readings (called *the lectionary*). There was the church calendar of saints' days, of feasts and fasts. There were processions and parades and plays. There was confession of sin (mandatory after 1215 for those receiving the eucharist) and manuals that priests would use to identify sins and offer absolution. There were works of art depicting the life of Jesus and the exploits of the saints, and popular publications, including the *Golden Legend [of the Works of the Saints]*; Dante's descriptions of hell, purgatory, and heaven (*Inferno, Purgatorio,* and *Paradiso*); and the *Ars moriendi*—"the Art of Dying"—which taught people how to die well in the Lord.

Still, the catechism didn't disappear. About one hundred years before Luther appeared on the scene, renewed interest and effort in teaching the catechism arose. Beginning in the early 1400s, Jean Gerson developed catechetical resources for uneducated laypeople, including children and youth. A bit later, Dietrich Kolde's *The Christian's Mirror or Small Handbook for Christians* (first published in 1470) was a bestseller in Germany and the Netherlands. Kolde's work, and similar catechetical manuals written by others, provided section upon section focused on conduct: how to understand what the Christian faith required, how to obey the Commandments, how to confess your sins, how to pray, how to take holy communion, how to honor the saints, and on and on. But in the Late Middle Ages, with society and daily life so saturated with religion, it was difficult for the average person to know which actions and beliefs were most essential. It was hard to know what lay at the heart of the good news about Jesus. Getting to the heart of the matter, therefore, is where Luther's catechism would excel.

Luther's Small Catechism and the Reformation

We are now at the part of the story of the Small Catechism that actually tells how Martin Luther came to write the Small Catechism. We'll start by teaching you a bit of German. Repeat after me: "*liebe vihe und unvernunfftige sewe.*"[7] Very good. Let's say it again: *liebe vihe* (LEEB-uh FEE-uh). Good. *Und unvernunfftige sewe* (oont OON-fair-noonf-tig-uh SOY-uh). Well done! *Wunderbar!* You've just learned how to say "simple cattle and mindless [or irrational] pigs" in sixteenth-century German! As we tell the story of how and why Luther wrote the Small Catechism, knowing how to say "simple cattle and mindless pigs" in German is important because comparing everyday Christians to cattle and pigs is how Luther introduced the Small Catechism when he wrote it (in German) back in 1529.

To understand why Luther referred to his fellow Germans as simpleminded cattle and pigs, recall that he was primarily a teacher, an educator. Popular images of Luther (for instance, in films, in cartoons, or in internet memes) depict a man in monk's garb nailing a sheet of paper to the church door, protesting the sale of indulgences, and sticking it to his opponents. This cultural depiction somewhat obscures the fact that Luther was simply doing his job—never mind the question of whether Luther actually nailed up the theses or just sent them around.[8]

In 1512 Luther was awarded the degree of doctor of theology and called to serve on the faculty of the University of Wittenberg, Germany. As a doctor (teacher) of the Church Catholic, Luther was sworn to teach the truth about God, Christ, and the gospel as the scriptures bore witness. In 1513 Luther began giving lectures to students. His first lecture series was on the Psalms. It took him almost twenty-one months, and that was lecturing two to three hours per week. Next was Paul's Letter to the Romans, which took nine months. At the end of his career, Luther preached on the book of Genesis—for ten years! Luther confessed that these lectures were "surely more verbose" than he had wanted them to be.[9] Here was a teacher not usually concerned with brevity or getting to the point, which makes the conciseness of the Small Catechism even more remarkable.

Coat of arms of the City of Wittenberg, 1541.

As Luther grew into his role as university professor, he also grew into that part of his role that required him to preach to the townspeople. Indeed, he was not only a teacher in the classroom, he was a preacher in the local parish. Consequently, Luther was tasked with helping to edify and educate the laity. As his teachings began to be published, many of his writings were of an instructional nature aimed at the common believer. Consider, for example, *A Sermon on Marriage, A Meditation on Christ's Passion, A Sermon on Preparing to Die,* and *An Exposition on the Lord's Prayer for Simple Laypeople,* all of which were published in 1519.

---

7. WA 30/1:266, author's translation.   8. For more on the "did he or didn't he" discussion, see the editor's remarks in TAL 1:22–26.
9. WA 42:1, author's translation.

We can discern that Luther, based on certain late medieval models, was already thinking of his parishioners as a kind of catechumenate—a community of *discipuli* in need of some teaching.

Prior to 1529 and prior to the cattle-and-pigs crack, Luther and his colleagues were aware that catechetical resources were needed to instruct and guide everyday believers not only in Wittenberg but throughout German lands. Three years before the Small Catechism was published, Luther wrote about providing a catechism to accompany the publication of a German-language liturgy:

> First, the German service needs a down-to-earth, plain, simple, and good catechism. Catechism means the instruction in which the non-believers, who want to be Christians, are taught and guided in what they should believe, know, do, and leave undone, according to Christian faith. This is why candidates were called catechumens when they had been admitted for instruction and learned the Creed before their baptism. I cannot present this instruction or catechization any better or more plainly than as it has been done since the beginning of Christendom and retained until now, that is, in these three parts: the Ten Commandments, the Creed, and the Lord's Prayer. These three parts contain plainly and succinctly everything that a Christian needs to know. . . . This instruction must be given from the pulpit at stated times or daily as may be needed, and repeated or read aloud evenings and mornings in the homes for the children and servants in order to make them Christians. Nor should they only learn to say the words by rote. But they should be questioned point by point and respond with what each part means and how they understand it. If everything cannot be covered at once, then take up one point today and another tomorrow.[10]

The Ten Commandments were a kind of latecomer to the catechism. To be sure, Augustine once used the Ten Commandments as the framework for some catechetical sermons, but for many centuries such things as the Seven Virtues and Seven Vices, aka "Seven Deadly Sins," and other lists were the favored rubric for teaching about the requirements of Christian conduct. Another way to teach the commandments was to use Jesus' summary: "Love God above all else and your neighbor as yourself."

Luther's vision for a catechism to accompany the German Mass is telling in a number of ways. First, Luther listed the Ten Commandments first. In the traditional catechism, the law typically came last, so it is already clear here that Luther intended a new order for his catechism. In the medieval formula, the catechism was mainly used to guide people to make confession and to amend their lives. Therefore, for example, Kolde's catechisms began with instruction about how to believe before moving to the Commandments (in preparation for confession) and ending with words to pray. Luther's new order, however, began with the teaching of the law so that believers would (a) recognize what God requires of them and (b) recognize that they fall short of God's requirements, so that they also (c) recognize their need as sinners for a savior.

---

10. See TAL 3:142.

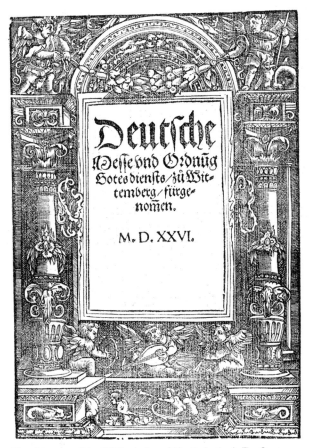

The title page of the 1526 printing of Martin Luther's *The German Mass and Order of Liturgy*.

Such recognition sets up God's grace revealed in creation, redemption, and being made holy, as described in the Apostles' Creed.

Second, Luther made clear that he expected that the catechism would be taught from the pulpit on a regular basis—even on a daily basis, if needed. Insofar as catechetical preaching was a hit-or-miss exercise in the Middle Ages, Luther intended that the evangelical churches would make catechetical preaching and instruction a priority. Third, Luther wanted the catechism taught and reinforced in the home. And finally, fourth, the method of that at-home instruction would be in the style of question-and-answer, both memorization ("by rote") and elaboration ("how they understand it").

In fact, in the very same introduction of the German Mass, Luther gave examples of what such question-and-answer instruction might look like. "In this manner they should be questioned":

What do you pray?
Answer: The Lord's Prayer.

What is it when you say: Our Father in Heaven?
Answer: That God is not an earthly, but a heavenly Father who would make us rich and blessed in heaven.

What is meant by: Hallowed be thy name?
Answer: That we should honor God's name and keep it from being profaned.

How do we profane or dishonor his name?
Answer: When we, who should be his children, live evil lives and teach and believe what is wrong.

And so on, [teaching them] what is meant by the kingdom of God, how it comes, what is meant by the will of God, by daily bread, etc., etc.

And also the Creed: What do you believe?
Answer: I believe in God the Father . . . to the end.

And so on from point to point, as time permits, one or two items at a time. For instance:

What does it mean to believe in God the Father Almighty?
Answer: It means to trust in God with all your heart and confidently to expect all grace, favor, help, and comfort from God, now and forever.

What does it mean to believe in Jesus Christ his Son?
Answer: It means to believe with the heart that we would all be eternally lost if Christ had not died for us, etc.[11]

Indeed, Luther advised, "You can get these questions in our *Little Prayer Book* where the three parts [of the catechism] are briefly explained, or make-up your own."[12]

While Luther encouraged church leaders to publish their own catechisms, he also referred them to the *Little Prayer Book*. Seven years before writing the Small Catechism, Luther wrote and published the *Little Prayer Book* as a kind of catechism! In the introduction to the German Mass, Luther indicates that readers will find examples of catechism questions in the *Little Prayer Book*. But there are no questions. Instead, the three parts of the catechism are organized and explained as series of statements suitable for personal devotions and prayer. Nevertheless, Luther believed that the items in the "brief" *Little Prayer Book* could easily be converted into catechism-style questions. And in at least one later catechism, published anonymously in Wittenberg near the end of 1525, the *Little Prayer Book* appears to have been consulted.

An exploration of the *Little Prayer Book* definitely helps teachers and students of the Small Catechism. The *Little Prayer Book*'s catechism features many profound explanations that do not have correlates in the later Small Catechism. Consider, for example, this part of the *Little Prayer Book*'s explanation to the second article of the Apostles' Creed:

---

11. TAL 3:143–44.   12. For the *Little Prayer Book*, see TAL 4:158–200.

I believe that for my sin and the sin of all believers Christ bore his suffering and cross and thereby transformed all suffering and every cross into a blessing—doing [the believer] no harm and even being salutary and most beneficial.[13]

Or this example from the *Little Prayer Book*'s explanation to the third petition of the Lord's Prayer:

Compared with your will, our will is never good but always evil. Your will is at all times the best, to be cherished and desired above all else. . . . Grant and teach us a deep patience when our will is prevented from happening or comes to nothing. Help when others contradict our will by what they say or do not say, do or leave undone, that we may not become angry or vexed, not curse, complain, protest, condemn, disparage, or contradict.[14]

Thus, the *Little Prayer Book* is something like a catechism in prayer form, so that the Small Catechism was not Luther's first try at writing about an overview of the basics of the Christian faith and life. Also, other Wittenberg-trained reformers had tried their hand at writing catechisms for congregational use prior to 1529. One of them was Johann Agricola, whose three catechisms from 1527 and 1528 did not so clearly follow the three-part format or, for that matter, Wittenberg's witness to the gospel. Agricola would eventually have a major falling out with Luther over the role of the law in the Christian life. Still, Agricola's catechism may have stimulated another Wittenberger, Philip Melanchthon, Luther's well-known colleague, to begin to write his own commentary, but he discontinued, perhaps because he knew Luther had finally begun writing his own.

All of this catechism-writing activity originated with Nicholas Hausmann, a pastor in the town of Zwickau, about 120 miles directly south of Wittenberg. In 1525 Hausmann wrote Luther with a request for a simple catechism. Apparently Hausmann did not think the *Little Prayer Book* was simple enough. Luther's first response to Hausmann was to write that he had put Agricola and another friend on the job, but when Agricola took a call to be the rector of the Latin school in Eisleben, the catechism project

Luther's *Little Prayer Book*

Perhaps the most important contribution of Luther's *Little Prayer Book* came in the foreword, where he explained the order of the catechism. "Three things people must know in order to be saved. First, they must know what to do and what to leave undone. Second, when they realize that, by their own strength, they cannot measure up to what they should do or leave undone, they need to know where to seek, find, and take the strength they require. Third, they must know how to seek and obtain that strength. It is just like sick people who first have to determine the nature of their sickness, and what to do or to leave undone. After that they have to know where to get the medicine which will help them do or leave undone what is right for a healthy person. Third, they have to desire to search for this medicine and to obtain it or have it brought to them. Thus the commandments teach humans to recognize their sickness, enabling them to see and perceive what to do or refrain from doing, consent to or refuse, and so recognize themselves to be sinful and wicked persons. The Creed will teach and show them where to find the medicine—grace—which will help them to become devout and keep the commandments. The Creed points them to God and God's mercy, given and made plain in Christ. Third, the Lord's Prayer teaches how they may seek, get, and bring to themselves all this, namely, by proper, humble, consolatory prayer. So it will be given to them, and through the fulfillment of God's commandments they will be blessed. In these three are the essentials of the entire Bible" (TAL 4:167).

---

13. TAL 4:181. 14. TAL 4:187.

was delayed. As time wore on, Luther indicated that he would take on the task himself. But here also Luther had to write Hausmann about further delays. In the meantime, the anonymously written, Wittenberg-published catechism mentioned above came forth. It was probably prepared by Stephen Roth who was studying in Wittenberg at the time but then returned to his hometown, Zwickau. Had Luther not written the Small Catechism, we might all be learning Roth's *Booklet for the Laity and Children* (1525). At the same time, it's probably safe to say that we probably would not be learning Agricola's catechism, with its title *One Hundred and Thirty Questions for the Young Children in the German Girl's School in Eisleben: On God's Word, Faith, Prayer, the Holy Spirit, Cross, and Love, as well as Instruction on Baptism and Christ's Body and Blood* (1528).[15]

Here is how Luther's Small Catechism went down. From 1527 to 1529, teams of officials toured some of the churches in the towns and villages of the German territory of Saxony. For these official "visitations," Melanchthon had drafted some Latin "Articles of Visitation" so that the "visitors" could guide the theology of the pastors in Saxony. These visitations were organized to gauge the quality of preaching and pastoral care and the financial situation of parishes, as well as to give an idea of whether and how the teaching emanating from Wittenberg had permeated the populace. Eventually even Luther himself left Wittenberg and interviewed pastors and parishioners about what they knew and what they did not know, but now using a German version of the Visitation Articles, on which he, Melanchthon, and others had collaborated: *Instruction by the Visitors for the Parish Pastors of Germany* (1528). Luther discovered for himself that the people were profoundly ill-versed in the basics of Christian belief. He was shocked—shocked!—at how bad things were among the common folk. Who did Luther blame for the widespread ignorance of the people? The pastors and bishops!

Title page of *Instruction by the Visitors*, with the seals of Luther (the rose) and Melanchthon (the serpent around the pole [see John 3:14]).

> It is not for trivial reasons that we constantly treat the catechism and exhort and implore others to do the same, for we see that unfortunately many preachers and pastors are very negligent in doing so and thus despise both their office and this teaching. Some do it out of their great learnedness, while others do so out of pure laziness and concern for their bellies. They approach the task as if they were pastors and preachers for their stomachs' sake and had nothing to do but live off the fat of the land.[16]

15. For an English translation of these texts, see Robert Kolb and James A. Nestingen, eds., *Sources and Contexts of The Book of Concord* (Minneapolis: Fortress, 2001), 1–30.   16. Large Catechism, preface, par. 1 (BC 379).

These words kick off the preface to Luther's "Large Catechism." Luther had preached on parts of the catechism three times during 1528. Based on this preaching, in late 1528 he began drafting his Large Catechism (which he titled *The German Catechism*), before starting work on the Small Catechism in early 1529. The Large Catechism is a solid overview of the essential teachings of the Christian faith for pastors. The original preface shows how deeply concerned Luther was about the low level of training. Luther accused some pastors and teachers of being "lazy bellies and presumptuous saints" and criticized them for acting as if they had nothing left to learn and nothing left to teach from the catechism. Luther suggested that preachers who despised the power and benefits of the catechism deserved to have their food withheld and deserved to be set upon by dogs and "be pelted with horse manure."[17] For Luther, it is especially pastors, teachers, and preachers who have been charged with doing something about the deplorable, wretched deprivation of the laity. In the Small Catechism's preface, he put it this way:

The title page of Martin Luther's 1529 Large Catechism.

> The deplorable, wretched deprivation that I recently encountered while I was a visitor has constrained and compelled me to prepare this catechism, or Christian instruction, in such a brief, plain, and simple version. Dear God, what misery I beheld! The ordinary person, especially in the villages, knows absolutely nothing about the Christian faith, and unfortunately many pastors are completely unskilled and incompetent teachers. Yet supposedly they all bear the name Christian, are baptized, and receive the holy sacrament, even though they do not know the Lord's Prayer, the Creed, or the Ten Commandments! As a result they live like simple cattle or irrational pigs and, despite the fact that the gospel has returned, have mastered the fine art of misusing all their freedom. . . . I beg all of you for God's sake to take up your office boldly, to have pity on your people who are entrusted to you, and to help us bring the catechism to the people, especially to the young.[18]

This is how Luther began the Small Catechism: with a loud wake-up call. This is vitally important material and vitally important work. At least Luther and his coworkers thought so. And generations of Lutheran pastors, teachers, and parishioners have thought so ever since.

---

17. Large Catechism, preface, par. 9, 13 (BC 381).   18. Small Catechism, preface, par. 1–3, 6 (BC 347–48). Read the entire preface on pages 207–10 of this book.

So What?

Already during Luther's lifetime, a pastor named Martin Bucer (1491–1551) of Strasbourg had the idea of reviving the old catechumenate. Bucer's idea was to pair catechism study with the rite of confirmation—a kind of catechumenate for the already baptized—and to focus this effort on adolescents and young adults. Whereas Luther's vision was for lifelong catechism of children and adults, the traditions that have formed around Bucer's vision are what have held sway in Lutheranism over the centuries. Bucer's approach continues to be an important part of Lutheran church life. To be sure, for centuries church leaders have complained about and worked on the problem of young people leaving the church after confirmation. Nevertheless, many denominations envy the centuries-old commitment of Lutherans to educate their young. Today the problem is perhaps more severe, as sociologists of religion note that more and more young people are walking away from the church and staying away.

Portrait of Martin Bucer, copper engraving by Jean-Jacques Boissard, 1599.

Over the centuries, millions upon millions of Small Catechisms have been distributed. Some of them have even been read and memorized! And among those who have read and memorized the Small Catechism, some have also internalized its content, that is, made the catechism into a habit of the heart. That remains our church's goal.

It is never too late to ask the question: What now? And to ask the other questions that derive from it: What is the future of catechism-based learning? What can modern pedagogies (teaching methods) teach us about best practices? Is it possible to renew the format and presentation of the catechism using the tools of the digital age? How may we translate the words of the Small Catechism into new, fresh language and idioms? How do the *discipuli*—the students!—of Jesus Christ remain faithful to the core of biblical teaching found in the Small Catechism? And most importantly, how can we stay true to Luther's witness to the gospel and his vision to embed the Christian catechism into all hearts and minds, so that, in the hospital we call the church, people may discover the sickness of sin, hear the good news about God's medicine of grace, and call on God for help in all of our need?

Martin Luther Institute, Tuscaloosa, Alabama. Confirmation class, 1936. ELCA Archives.

Our Savior's Lutheran Church, Omaha, Nebraska. Confirmation class, May 21, 1950. ELCA Archives.

Confirmation class at St. Luke's Lutheran Church, Park Ridge, Illinois, 2016, spelling out "Yes, Jesus loves me" in American Sign Language.

2

The Ten Commandments

The Commandments in the Bible

We know the Commandments from the family story of the Israelites' wilderness wanderings. God had worked overtime to free them from bondage in Egypt. To be enslaved was no light matter and meant more than just being forced to make bricks for Pharaoh's building projects. It meant having your body taken from you to be used as a tool for another's advancement and being subjected to an arbitrary system in which your life was not your own. But when God chose their ancestors Sarah and Abraham, they were given a new life based on God's word and election. To put the Israelites in slavery was to act counter to God's will, so God called Moses and used the various plagues to move Pharaoh to free this chosen tribe. To see to the preservation of their lives in the wilderness, God gave the Commandments to provide order, safety, and security. This is why, for the Israelites, the Ten Commandments begin with the words, "I am the LORD your God, who brought you out of the land of Egypt."

Most of all, God had established a relationship with the Israelites. The Commandments undergirded their relationship with their Creator and with their fellow creatures by providing both boundaries and blessings.

Numbering the Commandments
More than one numbering system is in use for the Ten Commandments.

The numbering question is already difficult when you look at the Commandments in Exodus 20. Try counting them and you will find way more than ten. But boiling everything down to ten works well when you have ten fingers.

Some numbering systems arrive at ten by keeping "no other gods" and "graven images" separate and combining the two about coveting. Luther followed the pattern set by St. Augustine and the Roman church's usage in part because he viewed them as reflecting the law for all nations. Thus, the command prohibiting "graven images" was simply a special case of the first commandment for the Israelites.

Moses and the burning bush. God the Father is handing Moses the two tablets with the Ten Commandments. Woodcut by Hans Sebald Beham. Printed by Hieronymous Andreae, Nuremberg, 1527.

The Ten Commandments by contemporary Chinese artist He Qi.

If we read further in the story (both in the Bible and in human history), we'll see that the Commandments didn't make the Israelites or us more moral or more pious. If the catechism gives us the basics so we can know God "by heart," it's clear from the story that the Commandments have never actually changed anyone's heart. At best, they have only ever told people how immoral, impious, and unfaithful they are.

St. Paul knew that our salvation never came from obeying God's law. In Galatians 3:6 he looked back to his Jewish ancestor Abraham for evidence. In Genesis 15 God made a raft of promises to the old patriarch (and presumably to his wife, Sarah): even though old and childless, they would have a child, God would give them a promised land, and they would wind up with descendants as numerous as the stars in the night sky. Paul remembered that Abraham had trusted God and that God reckoned his belief as righteousness. *Reckoning* is the same thing as doing basic accounting. It adds up assets and debits to find the bottom line. God didn't bring any of Abraham's deeds for good or ill into the reckoning. Instead, the only things that mattered were his faith and trust. By being righteous, Abraham was in good with God, and nothing else was required. From the very start of God's relationship with Abraham, with his descendants (including Jesus, the disciples, and Paul), and with Christians who were adopted into the family's promises, the law and Commandments were never part of the salvation equation. They weren't a checklist for our exit interview from this life or for a promotion to a higher heavenly calling after it.

Fear and Love: What the Commandments Are For

Although they were written in stone, for Luther the Commandments weren't written in stone. Instead of simply sitting there in Moses' arms as a set of rules to present to the Israelites, the Commandments are instead a vital and active thing. They go beyond merely judging you or giving you guidelines for successful living (although they do that too). By beginning each of his explanations with the words "We are to fear and love God, so that . . . ," Luther presented the Commandments as a description of how God moves us toward God's will. No longer were they about moving Christians from sinfulness to morality or piety. Now they were the essence of how God moves sinners from unfaith to faith.

Those who follow Luther's thinking often use the phrase *simul iustus et peccator* (simultaneously justified and sinful). It's a quick and easy way to talk about how Christians are always simultaneously saint and sinner. In his explanations of the Commandments, Luther holds together both sides of our identity. For Luther, progress in Christian living doesn't move forward or up. Instead, it goes deeper. Christian life means coming to understand more and more the presence of two people inside you. In *The Freedom of a Christian* (1520)[1] Luther talks about the two selves that live inside you: the old outer person of the flesh (the sinner) and the new inner person of the spirit (the saint). The old you must necessarily fear God and divine judgment. But as a new person of faith, you are so wedded to Christ that you trust and honor God. Until your dying day, your identity will always involve both these people. When you are finally laid to rest and there is no more power for the old sinner in you to try to wield, then all that will be left is the faith received according to the Holy Spirit's desire.

In between the words *fear* and *love* in Luther's explanations lies a life-changing—nay, life-giving—space where the Holy Spirit creates and sustains faith. That space holds all of eternity because that is where God's gospel promise in the Word, that is, in Jesus, takes up its claim on you. Luther said we are to

People often wonder why Luther said we are to *fear* God. In the summary explanation to the Commandments, he reminds us to "fear God's wrath," that is, God's righteous judgment. Thus, for Luther, God demands both respect (awe) for God's power as creator and dismay at our sin as creatures.

Ambigram tattoo: saint/sinner.

The Three Powers of Faith

In *The Freedom of a Christian*, Luther described three powers of faith, that is, the things the Spirit has the power to produce when faith is given.

First, because the gospel declares Christ to be the sole agent of your salvation, trusting the gospel frees you from the law. No one can ever demand that you do good works to please God.

Second, faith produces in you a desire to honor God. Where before, like Adam and Eve in the garden, the old sinner in you didn't trust God, now faith begins to see that when God makes a promise—as God does in Christ—God always follows through.

Third, faith functions like a pastor officiating at a marriage between you and Christ. When faith happens, you get everything that Christ your bridegroom brings to the relationship: grace, life, and salvation (and by extension Christ's own name and his place at the right hand of God). And what does Christ get out of the deal? Just your sin, death, and damnation. If that's so, then Christ becomes the most sinful person who ever lived (BC 496–502).

---

1. TAL 1:496ff.

fear and love God because God's Word is operative here. And it has two parts: commands and promises. God speaks in these two modes to deal with both yous. "Fear and love" parallel the outer and inner person in you. God's commands produce fear in the old sinner, and the gospel promise spoken in the midst of that fear creates the new person of faith.

The fulfillment of a command always depends on the action of the person being commanded. But because we're so captive to our own will (we call that condition Sin—capital S—rather than sins, which are all the bad things we do as a result of Sin), we stand judged by God and subject to God's wrath and condemnation. In today's church we often say that sinners will go to heaven. While it is commendable and comes from our desire to be good and kind to others and to emphasize God's mercy, it is not very biblical. Luther had a ready supply of vivid words to say about us sinners. On more than

Luther's language of "fear and love" was nothing new. St. Bernard of Clairvaux (c. 1090–1153) said the same thing: "Know yourself then, that you may fear God; know God that you may also love him. . . . Beware then, both of ignorance of yourself and ignorance of God since there is no salvation without the fear and the love of God. Everything else is indifferent" (Sermon 37 on the Canticle, no. 1).

Allegory of Law and Gospel by Lucas Cranach the Elder, 1529. This is a perfect illustration of the movement from fear to love. On the left, death, the devil, and the law (Moses holding the two tablets) drive the old Adam to hell, with Christ above coming in judgment. On the right, the new Adam is being covered with the crucified Christ's blood (i.e., righteousness) and blessed by the resurrected Christ, while John the Baptist points to the "Lamb of God who takes away the sin of the world." In the background the angel is appearing to the shepherds with "good news" (gospel).

one occasion he called himself a stinking pile of "Mist"—a mild translation of it would be "manure," but you can come up with a better translation. Unless you live in farming or ranching country, you may not have experienced a walk through the barnyard or past the pigsty. The scent of cow pies and hog flop isn't something to be distilled and delicately dabbed on your wrists. For Luther, the stench of Sin is too awful, and God won't have it stinking up the divine throne room.

When Luther said we should fear God, he was alluding to what it's like to stand before God. When Moses was allowed to look at God's backside, he came down the mountain so physically changed that his luminescence spooked the Israelites and he had to wear a veil over his head. Imagine what it would be like to come into the almighty, perfect, and eternal goodness of God at the judgment seat. It's not a pretty sight and not one you can easily don a veil to deal with. Luther said this seat is "for those who are still secure and proud and will neither acknowledge nor confess their sin."[2] In the Lord's Prayer we ask for God's will to be done, and the Commandments provide a clear window we can gaze through to see what that will look like. But more important is how the Commandments also function as a mirror. To paraphrase Hamlet, they tell us exactly how rotten things are in Denmark.

The law shows we don't have "understanding or strength"[3] to do God's will. We don't act rightly. We neglect our neighbors. We don't tend to God's word. We're blithe in our care for the creation. But what's worse, we don't *believe* rightly either, and that's what really gets us into trouble at God's judgment seat. We keep thinking that Newtonian physics functions well in our relationship with God. We assume that just because every action causes an equal and opposite reaction, our good works can cause God to bring a judgment of grace and mercy. But the Commandments force us to do what the Fourth Step in Alcoholics Anonymous calls "a fearless and searching moral inventory." They demand our honesty about our relationships with God and with our neighbors. The law judges us and brings down the hammer on both our claims of freedom before God (free will) and the possibility of our doing anything to gain a right relationship with God (i.e., salvation). Luther's declaration that we must completely despair of ourselves to obtain Christ's mercy arose from his own experience.

On February 18, 1546, Luther died in Eisleben, the same city he was born in over six decades earlier. The people with him were careful to record the entire process, noting his confession of faith and his dependence solely on Christ's mercy. After he died, among his things they found a scrap of paper on which he had written, "We are beggars. This is true." He had once written a piece about establishing a community chest in Wittenberg to deal with the nuisance of alms beggars in the city. He saw people on a regular basis who had absolutely nothing and whose only hope was to depend on the largesse of strangers. That was what lay behind Luther's last written words. In two pithy sentences, Luther had summed up the essence of our situation before God. We can come only with empty hands, hoping against hope for mercy, yet knowing full well that a judging God could never look kindly on our sin.

We have only to look to Christ's own words to see how deep this despair of our abilities must run. In the Beatitudes, the beginning of the Sermon on the Mount, Jesus presents life's disasters and losses as the place where God most dearly wants to be found. Then, as if he knows how little stock we'll place in that promise, he goes on to destroy the illusion that our successes can mean anything. Jesus pushes the demands of the law

---

2. "Sermon on the Sum of the Christian Life," LW 51:278.   3. Small Catechism, Creed, par. 6 (BC 355).

Martin Luther in Death by Lucas Cranach the Younger after Lukas Furtenagel.

to their furthest point: "You have heard that it was said. . . . But I say to you. . . ."[4] Each step of the way, Jesus makes it more and more difficult to imagine ever being able to live so perfectly that we could gain God's good pleasure. Eventually Jesus' listeners sink into despair and ask who could possibly do this. Jesus responds that no one can—except God. That's where Luther pulls us with the single word *fear*. Like blind Bartimaeus at the side of the road, we must cry out ever more loudly, "Jesus, Son of David, have mercy on me!"[5]

When the Commandments work on us, they "reveal individuals to themselves. Through the commands they know their inability to do good, and they despair of their own powers."[6] Now comes the promise of the

---

4. Matthew 5:21-48. For Luther's exposition, see LW 21.   5. Mark 10:47.   6. *The Freedom of a Christian*, TAL 1:494.

gospel that draws us out of fear and out of our life as old, empty-hearted sinners cast east of Eden and wondering how to get back home again. If the Commandments show us how little we can or want to do to heed God's will, God's promising word takes a different tack. Unlike demands, which require some action on your part for their fulfillment, promises make declarations that depend solely on the one making the promise. If someone promises you that a delicious box of donuts will be delivered to you on Monday, you aren't required to go to the local bakery, shell out some cash, and deliver them yourself. A promise is a true promise only if its promiser delivers the goods. The gospel is just this sort of true promise, because it is fulfilled, not as with the old covenant that human beings broke[7] with their faithless actions, but by God who takes on the entire burden apart from anything we could do. God makes this promise in the person of Jesus Christ, particularly in his sufferings and the cross.[8] There on a barren hill outside the holy city of Jerusalem, as far as you could move spiritually from the holiness of God's temple, God takes on all the work and leaves you to enjoy Christ's benefits. (You'll hear all about that in Luther's explanation of the second article of the Apostles' Creed in the next chapter.)

When the gospel is bestowed, the proclaimed promise of what God-in-the-flesh has done for you creates faith. Article V of the Augsburg Confession, the document the reformers presented to the Holy Roman emperor to summarize their teaching and preaching, puts it this way:

> To obtain such faith God instituted the office of preaching, giving the gospel and the sacraments. Through these, as through means, he gives the Holy Spirit who produces faith, where and when he wills, in those who hear the gospel. It teaches that we have a gracious God, not through our merit but through Christ's merit, when we so believe.[9]

If that's true, then the difference between fear and love in Luther's explanations of the Commandments is the difference between Christ not being preached and the gospel not being declared, on the one hand, and Christ being given and divine mercy being declared on the other. In the space between fear and love, the gospel must be proclaimed so that the promise can create faith in you. And now where you once feared God, you can instead love God and begin to live according to God's will. The Augsburg Confession (Article VI) calls this "the new obedience" where we "yield good fruit and . . . good works."[10]

How come faith is not a work we do? Many North American Christians confuse "deciding for Jesus" or "commitment to God" for faith, thus making faith into their own work. Such a definition is still law ("You must believe, or else!") and leaves persons trusting themselves and their decisions, not God. One helpful way to picture faith is as falling in love. God in Christ promises mercy (unmerited love) to us. Upon hearing that gracious word, we fall in love—not as a decision we undertake but as a work of the Holy Spirit in our hearts. Just as we don't imagine falling in love to be a decision we make (then it wouldn't be "falling"), so faith is a relationship into which we are swept up through the promises of the "Lover of our souls," Jesus Christ.

---

7. See Jeremiah 31:31ff. 8. Heidelberg Disputation, Thesis 20. 9. Augsburg Confession, V.1–3 (BC 40). 10. Augsburg Confession, VI.1 (BC 41).

God's Judgment Seat and Mercy Seat

What Luther presented in the two words *fear* and *love* in his explanations of the Commandments he did in a different way in his "Sermon on the Sum of the Christian Life" (1532). He talked about the difference between the judgment seat and mercy seat of God:[11]

> I say that, if we are ever to stand before God with a right and uncolored faith, we must come to the point where we learn clearly to distinguish and separate between ourselves, our life, and Christ the mercy seat. But he who will not do this, but immediately runs headlong to the judgment seat, will find it all right and get a good knock on the head. I have been there myself and was so burnt that I was glad I was able to come to the mercy seat. And now I am compelled to say: Even though I may have lived a good life before men, let everything I have done or failed to do remain there under the judgment seat as God sees fit, but, as for me, I know of no other comfort, help, or counsel for my salvation except that Christ is my mercy seat, who did no sin or evil and both died and rose again for me, and now sits at the right hand of the Father and takes me to himself under his shadow and protection, so that I need have no doubt that through him I am safe before God from all wrath and terror. Thus faith remains pure and unalloyed, because then it makes no pretensions and seeks no glory or comfort save in the Lord Christ alone.[12]

In his explanations of the Commandments, Luther held up God's law to rescue us from our stance before God's judgment seat and drive us to Jesus, God's mercy seat in the flesh. Only then, when we face our beggarliness, do we see clearly our own unrighteousness and God's mercy. We see our Creator as slow to anger and abounding in steadfast love. We see our neighbors no longer as competition or threat but as gift. We see the creation itself not as something to be exploited but as a gift to be cared for and used for good. And we see our good works not as evidence in proving our case for salvation to God but as an opportunity to serve others and discipline the old sinner in us. Luther never had a problem with Christians doing good works or striving to keep God's law and Commandments. What he had a problem with was our attempting to use our impotent efforts to keep the law as something we can bring before God's judgment seat to justify ourselves. Luther had had his fill of that in his attempts to live a blameless life. The catechism's look at the Commandments, though, reveals that when we are drawn out of our failures to turn to Christ, who presides at the mercy seat, in faith we can look at the Commandments and see them not just as boundaries but as blessings. In faith we experience the Holy Spirit transforming fear into love of God that is equal in depth to the awareness of our sin.

---

11. Romans 14:10; Exodus 25:17. In the Old Testament, the mercy seat was commanded by God along with the many other instructions for building the tabernacle in the wilderness. Technically, it was the golden lid placed on the ark of the covenant. Following Paul, Luther used the language to talk about what we will get in a judgment rendered by the revealed God in Christ Jesus.   12. LW 51:282.

The First Commandment

♥ You shall have no other gods.

What is this? or **What does this mean?**
We are to fear, love, and trust God above all things.

Worship of the golden calf (Exodus 32). In the printings of the Small Catechism during Luther's lifetime, each commandment, article of the Creed, petition of the Lord's Prayer, and sacrament was accompanied by a woodcut and (from 1536) references to the Bible story on which each picture was based.

In Jeremiah 31:33 God says, "I will be their God, and they shall be my people." Perhaps the simplest (and most difficult) thing to say about God is that God is an *electing* God: God *chooses* to be our God. That's 180 degrees from how it normally works with gods. Usually we're the ones to choose the god who seems most appropriate to us, the one that will serve our needs and produce our most desired outcome. Human history is rife with the names of other gods: Baal and Astarte; Zeus, Mercury, and Poseidon; Thor, Odin, and Fjörgyn; Shiva, Ganesh, and Kali, among many, many others. For Luther, your chosen god is that thing or being in which you place your ultimate trust.

When we think about what we most trust, it's easy to be pious and say, "Of course I trust God." But Luther wouldn't have stood for such a slick move. He took seriously the way we actually live. So, a better question is, "What do you most fear losing?" or "What in life do you love the most?" There we can see how variable our day-to-day pantheon of gods really is, for what we trust to bring in our desired future is constantly changing. If you think you trust God to secure your future, then wait until you lose something as inconsequential as your TV remote. It's worse when it's your car keys or your phone. At that moment, nothing else can possibly provide your desired future than the missing thing. And that thing becomes your immediate god, the idol you trust to make it through your days, or at least through that moment.

The traditional way to render Luther's question as "What does this mean?" may confuse readers into imagining that the parts of the catechism are obscure. But Luther's question, literally translated "What is this?" reminds us that Luther's "explanations" are actually more like a paraphrase of a clear text than an explanation of an obscure one. Thus, a better rendering might be "That is to say" or "In other words." By changing "You shall" to "We are to," Luther placed himself under the law with his readers instead of talking down to them.

It's not just spiritual beings in exalted places that can be gods. All kinds of other things can take the divine throne in our hearts. In the monastery, Luther's typical monastic vows like chastity and obedience could become idolatrous. And the life of a monk required him to intentionally purge himself of them. It's no different for us as we face our gods of control, status, or power. But the big idol Luther discovered he had clung to was himself—he had become his own god. We talk about what happened to our first parents in the Garden

Adam and Eve by Lucas Cranach the Elder, c. 1528.

The New Jerusalem by Lucas Cranach the Elder, 1522.

of Eden as the Fall. And we interpret the Fall as our move *away from* God and into disobedience, dissolution, and all kinds of nasty stuff that's best covered by fig leaves. But the serpent's temptation wasn't to eat forbidden fruit. The serpent's move was to draw Adam and Eve into unbelief and mistrust. Instead of becoming less godly by being in thrall to their fleshly desires, they put themselves in God's place. Suspecting that God was reserving some knowledge of good and evil that they ought to possess, they ate of the tree's fruit to establish their own rule and might, their own claim to create and sustain their own futures.

In this light, there is not a single person without a god, even the most fervent atheist.[13] So the question of whether God exists is beside the point. If we all have gods floating in and out of our days, it's more

> The serpent said, "You will not die; for God knows that when you eat of it your eyes will be opened, and you will be like God, knowing good and evil" (Genesis 3:4). The Hebrew phrase "knowing good and evil" could well be rendered "deciding what's right and what's wrong." Thus, the serpent's words tempt human beings into thinking they have control over God's judgment (no death), can think straight (eyes open), and can judge selfishly (decide good and evil)—all the things only God can do.

---

13. See Luther's Large Catechism, Ten Commandments, par. 2 (BC 386): "A 'god' is the term for that to which we are to look for all good and in which we are to find refuge in all need. Therefore, to have a god is nothing else than to trust and believe in that one with your whole heart. As I have often said, it is the trust and faith of the heart alone that make both God and an idol." Luther went on to discuss several of our most popular idols: wealth, "great learning, wisdom, power, prestige, family and honor" (par. 10, BC 387) and, finally, trusting our own works before God (par. 22, BC 388–89).

important to ask whether our god is a gracious one. Is your god of the moment truly able to provide for you the life and future you desire? The God of the first commandment declares that only this one can do it. The commandment kicks you out of the holy heavenly seat and pushes you away from spirituality and back to the flesh-and-bone stuff of human existence. God is the Creator. And you're not.

But if God will not allow you to function as your own earthly god, you're also not left hanging. By choosing to be God *for you*, with the same word that first brought the creation into being, God declares that all of what God has is now yours. With God's promise, you have now begun to live in the New Jerusalem, the city of God with its tree planted by the water.[14] The promise here is the same as was given in the Garden of Eden: get busy enjoying the gifts God has set before you. Open your eyes to the God who wears them all as a mask and see how gracious and merciful a God you have. You'll see exactly how the God of the first commandment chooses to reveal God's own self in the stuff of life when you encounter Luther's explanations of the Apostles' Creed in the next chapter. Luther couldn't separate the God of this commandment from the person of Jesus who in the Lord's supper declares that in his crucified flesh he himself is *for you*.

Blasphemy of Shelomith's son (Lev. 24:10-16).

The Second Commandment

♥ You shall not make wrongful use of the name of the Lord your God.

What is this? or *What does this mean?*
We are to fear and love God, so that we do not curse, swear, practice magic, lie, or deceive using God's name, but instead use that very name in every time of need to call on, pray to, praise, and give thanks to God.

"But instead" translates the German word *sondern*, a very powerful way of introducing the opposite. When interpreting scripture, Luther always made antitheses—in the case of the Ten Commandments, finding a positive side to prohibitions and (for the third and fourth commandments) adding a negative side to positive admonitions. Only with the first and sixth commandments did Luther state only the positive.

In the world of the ancient Israelites, a name had power. Old Testament names tell you something about the people who bear them. Jacob's name means "cheater." The prophet Hosea was told to name his children Lo-ruhamah and Lo-ammi, or "Not Pitied" and "Not My People," to reflect God's attitude toward the Israelites' faithlessness. Then there's Isaiah's kid Maher-shalal-hash-baz, whose name means "Quick! Go grab some

---

14. Revelation 21–22.

plunder!" Old Testament names tell you about a person's character, because names give you a person's essence. Luther himself changed his name for a time to reflect his new understanding of God's grace. It was common for people in the Humanist movement, who looked to the ancient Greeks and Romans as the source of the greatest human learning, to give themselves a Greek or Latin version of their name. Luther's colleague Philip Melanchthon's birth name was Schwarzerdt, or "black earth," but the name we know him by is the Greek form (*melan* [black] *chthon* [earth]), much more fitting for one of the best Greek scholars in Europe. The name Luther took on was Eleutherius. That is the Greek word for freedom, and it's a way even Luther's name could preach the gospel by reminding others of their freedom in Christ.[15] It's a kind of shorthand for what Paul wrote in Galatians: "For freedom Christ has set us free. Stand firm, therefore, and do not submit again to a yoke of slavery."[16]

Speaking from the burning bush, God reluctantly gave Moses the divine name, but it was something the old prophet needed to be careful handling. To speak God's name was blasphemy because, by being given the holy name, you had been given a piece of God's being. It's wrong to curl your tongue around God's name, and for doing it you could be subjected to a good stoning. But in his explanation of this commandment, Luther had no fear of speaking God's name.[17] Because God chooses to be your God in creating you, God opens the access door. God's name is holy, but not so holy that you can't use it. The problem is not speaking God's name, but instead what you're attempting to accomplish with it.

Luther heard God's name being bandied about in everyday Wittenberg life. The big blasphemers were easy to spot, but usually the misuse of God's name came in subtler ways. In the Large Catechism, he told about God's name being used to seal business deals or to commit perjury before a judge. He even pointed to how people might enter into a secret marriage by pledging their troth on God's name. Worst of all, though, was the matter of false preachers. These pastors claimed to know the truth about God and announced it in Jesus' name, but Luther could see that they had totally missed the point of the gospel and were really offering up spiritual job descriptions, demands for fervent mystical

The word *Humanism* was coined in the nineteenth century to describe an intellectual movement in fifteenth- and sixteenth-century Europe arising out of the Renaissance. "Umanistes" (a nickname given to teachers of the humanities by Italian students at the time) or "humanists" had a common interest in returning to the oldest sources in a field and in using classical (rather than medieval) Latin and, as it became better known, Greek.

Engraving of Philip Melanchthon by Albrecht Dürer in 1526, done during Melanchthon's visit to Nuremberg to dedicate the city's new Latin school. The inscription reads: "Dürer's skillful hand could make a sketch of a living Philip but could not depict his mind."

---

15. If you look at Luther's name on various documents he signed, you will discover that the spelling wasn't standardized. (It was Luther's translation of the Bible more than anything else that brought about spelling standards in German.) His father's name is spelled Luder. And you can find Luther using that or Ludher. Luther's first name was chosen because he was baptized the day after his birth in Eisleben on the feast day of St. Martin. 16. Galatians 5:1. 17. Nevertheless, in Luther's translation of Hebrew Scripture, out of respect he rendered the letters *YHWH* as "LORD" and the word *Adonai* as "Lord."

experiences, and feel-good bromides akin to those who speak a so-called prosperity gospel today.[18] In each instance, those taking God's name in vain aimed at something they thought was good, but in reality they had assumed sovereignty over God and used God's name as window dressing to make their worldly dealings holy.

Luther's explanation goes beyond restricting places where God's name should be off-limits. Next he declared what God's name is good for: prayer, praise, and thanksgiving. Where faith happens, a forgiven sinner has simply to reach out to God. God's name becomes the useful thing it's given to be: a handle to grab hold of God. It's only when the word changes you from the old outer person of the flesh to the new inner person of the Spirit that God's name will begin to rest easily on your lips. As he said in the Large Catechism:

> One must urge and encourage children again and again to honor God's name and to keep it constantly upon their lips in all circumstances and experiences, for the proper way to honor God's name is to look to it for all consolation and therefore to call upon it. Thus . . . first the heart honors God by faith and then the lips by confession.[19]

In Luther's German, prayer meant specifically "asking" (as did the original, nonreligious use of the English). Thus, he adds praise and thanksgiving as two other good uses of God's name.

The best way to become a person who regards God's name as sacred is to make a habit of commending yourself to God and asking for God's protection each day. That way, when illness, tragedy, or disaster arises, or when joyful events and treasured experiences occur, you will be quick to cry out to God for help or to give thanks.

In his years in the monastery, Luther's life was shaped by a regular pattern of prayer. You could hear standardized prayer from the Roman Breviary fall trippingly off monkish tongues day and night, at the various worship services throughout the day, and before and after meals. Thus, the habit of prayer virtually became part of Luther's own DNA, and God's name had become enmeshed with the reformer's very being.[20] He had come to know prayer as a direct line by which creatures can stay connected to their Creator. The commandment holds that connection as so vital that prayer becomes not just something you do but something you are. It protects the blessing of your relationship with God by making sure God's saving word and the words of your own heart remain tightly bound together.

---

18. Large Catechism, Ten Commandments, par. 53–54, BC 393.   19. Large Catechism, Ten Commandments, par. 70, BC 395.   20. Some may imagine that Luther would have abandoned all Roman rites and prayers, but he regarded this kind of praying so highly that he adapted them and included them in the Small Catechism.

The Third Commandment

♥ Remember the sabbath day, and keep it holy.

What is this? or **What does this mean?**
We are to fear and love God, so that we do not despise preaching
or God's word, but instead keep that word holy and gladly
hear and learn it.

Breaking and keeping the sabbath
(Num. 15:32-36). Sixteenth-
century people listening to a sermon
are contrasted with the man in the
background collecting wood.

The structure of the church's calendar was ever-present in Luther's day,
not just for monks and nuns but for every person around. We know the
main festivals, such as Palm Sunday, Easter, Pentecost, All Saints, and the
like, because we observe them too. But in sixteenth-century Germany,
nearly every day could be celebrated as a saint's feast day. In January, for
example, only a handful of dates *didn't* have festivals. Because human
sinners needed to collect as much grace as possible to counter their
many sins, the feast days served as a way for the church to deliver the
Mass and for people to balance their spiritual accounts. In the Augsburg
Confession, the reformers told the Holy Roman emperor and the
representatives of the church that they rejected such traditions when they
"serve to earn grace and make satisfaction for sin. For this reason, new
fasts, new ceremonies, new monastic orders, and the like were invented
daily." The church promoted these activities and implied that not
attending to the saintly bazaar of feast days, ceremonies, food restrictions,
and such would result in eternal condemnation.[21]

The result of all the requirements was what Luther called a "troubled
conscience." When Luther talked about the conscience, he didn't mean
an angel on one shoulder and a devil on the other who urge you in their
opposite directions. Instead, your conscience was your sense of yourself
relative to others before God. It was your standing before God, before your
fellow human beings, and before the world. By placing the requirements
of festivals, food, and confession on you, the church made your standing
depend on your own actions—especially on your religious activity. As if the
world hadn't already placed unending burdens on you with all the things
you needed to tend to in your work, family, relationships, art, advocacy,
and self-advancement, there was an entire spiritual realm of demands to
deal with as well.

Sixteenth-Century Saints' Days

Jan. 1:	New Year's Day
Jan. 2:	St. Basil, St. Gregory of Nazianzus
Jan. 3:	St. Genevieve
Jan. 5:	St. Simeon the Stylite
Jan. 7:	St. Raymond
Jan. 9:	St. Adrian of Canterbury
Jan. 10:	St. Paul the Hermit
Jan. 12:	St. Benedict
Jan. 13:	St. Hillary
Jan. 14:	St. Felix of Nola, St. Kentigern
Jan. 15:	St. Ita
Jan. 16:	St. Honoratus, Pope Marcellus
Jan. 17:	St. Antony
Jan. 18:	St. Priscus
Jan. 19:	St. Canutus
Jan. 20:	St. Fabian, St. Sebastian
Jan. 21:	St. Agnes
Jan. 22:	St. Vincent
Jan. 25:	Conversion of St. Paul
Jan. 26:	St. Paula
Jan. 28:	St. Thomas Aquinas

---

21. Augsburg Confession, XXVI.1–2 (BC 74).

It wasn't as though Luther himself didn't get up each morning and try to get things done. He was as pious as the next professional religious person. On top of the pattern of worship and prayer within the monastery, Luther's days were packed. In a 1516 letter, he told his friend Johannes Lang about his workaday life:

> Greetings. I nearly need two copyists or secretaries. All day long I do almost nothing else than write letters; therefore I am sometimes not aware of whether or not I constantly repeat myself, but you will see. I am a preacher at the monastery, I am a reader during mealtimes, I am asked daily to preach in the city church, I have to supervise the study of novices and friars, I am a vicar (and that means I am eleven times prior), I am caretaker of the fish pond at Leitzkau, I represent the people of Herzberg at the court in Torgau, I lecture on Paul, and I am assembling material for a commentary on the Psalms. As I have already mentioned, the greater part of my time is filled with the job of letter writing. I hardly have any uninterrupted time to say the Hourly Prayers and celebrate mass. Besides all this there are my own struggles with the flesh, the world, and the devil. See what a lazy man I am![22]

Luther's plate was full, but so was everyone else's. Late medieval life was not a life of ease. It required endless toil and backbreaking work within a deeply uncertain world and with death lurking around every bend. For him, the church loading so much pious pressure on people only made things worse.

Luther, of course, knew that the commandment to keep the sabbath day arose from the first creation story in Genesis 1 where God created everything and then rested on the seventh day. He understood how important physical rest is, especially for laborers. If you don't get a day off, the certain result will be physical and mental exhaustion. But in his explanation of the commandment, he went after a much deeper rest. He stripped away the religious ornamentation of feast days, festivals, and foods, and he zeroed in on the essence of worship: God's word. Although we do bring ourselves before God, much more important is what God does once you have been drawn there. And what you should find God giving you there is the ultimate rest of forgiveness. That rest comes only from the proclamation of the gospel. Christ's mercy not only provides release from your sins but also gives you the one who makes no demands on you whatsoever. To be bound by sin is always to be beholden to your own past and to shrink from what the future might hold. A sinful breach in any relationship, whether with a work colleague, a family member, or God, always shifts the trajectory of the relationship to a new downward spiral. But forgiveness breaks in from ahead of you and presents a new future. When someone you have wronged declares you forgiven, that one is saying, "I will determine the future of this relationship. It will not be determined by your troublesome past. You and I now exist in a new realm of peace."

So much more does it work that way with God. The gospel's declaration of forgiveness makes you new by inserting you into this new relationship. No longer is your ability to make good, make up, or make nice with God the criterion for your place in the kingdom of heaven. Now if there's striving to do, it can be for your neighbors who need your good works way more than your utterly self-sufficient God does. The sabbath day becomes holy because this announcement is present. And every other moment also becomes holy when this word is near.

---

22. LW 48:27–28.

The Fourth Commandment

❤ Honor your father and your mother.

What is this?* or *What does this mean?
We are to fear and love God, so that we neither despise nor anger our parents and others in authority, but instead honor, serve, obey, love, and respect them.

The drunkenness of Noah (Gen. 9:20-27).

Information about Luther's parents, Hans and Margarethe Luder, is scarce. We know Hans was involved in the copper mining industry near Mansfeld and Eisleben. Although Luther, thinking of his father's parents, could say he came from peasant stock, the Luders had some standing and financial means. Even so, Luther's decision to leave his legal studies at the University of Erfurt to become a monk came as a blow to his parents. His father was incensed at what he regarded as his son's rash decision (and the sixteenth-century equivalent of losing Social Security and pension in the form of your child's support in your old age), and the son himself thought the father couldn't see how important it was to serve God in a religious order. At issue was the fourth commandment and whether God's call to a religious life is greater than the command to honor one's parents. It took years, the destruction of Luther's religious striving, and the discovery of the gospel finally to repair the breach. When Luther came to understand the justifying faith provided by God in Christ, he made amends with his father and readily admitted the rightness of his father's anger all those years before.

To understand Luther's approach to this commandment, we first have to understand his sense of God's call within our daily lives. He used the words *Beruf* and *Stand* (calling and station or walk of life) to talk about our various vocations, the ways God uses us to work in the world. Just as we do, Luther lived within a web of relationships: he was a husband, father, professor, colleague, and citizen, a subject of both his prince and emperor, a loyal friend and regular preacher, a personal counselor and political adviser, not to mention household host to whatever evangelical vagabond he crossed paths with on a given day. None of us needs to go

Portraits of Luther's parents, Hans and Margarethe Luther, by Lucas Cranach the Elder, 1527.

Martin and Katie Luther's Children
Hans (b. 1526)
Elizabeth (b. 1527, d. 1528)
Magdalena (b. 1529, d. 1542)
Martin (b. 1531)
Paul (b. 1533)
Margarethe (b. 1534)

Luther Making Music in the Circle of His Family by Gustav Spangenberg, c. 1875.

questing after a vocation, because they are inherent in the structure of life. Neither are vocations unchanging, for our encounters with others constantly shift and change. That means your vocations can be as enduring as the lifelong vow of marriage or as swift and fleeting as meeting another vehicle at a four-way stop. Each of our vocations involves tasks and responsibilities, from changing diapers or comforting a colicky baby to honest labor and fairness in law making, from planting seeds in springtime fields to planting our loved ones' bodies in their final resting places. Our vocations are the place God's fingers move in the world, the way God creates and tends life.

The fourth commandment protects vocation at the start of life. It is from our parents that we first learn the most elemental vocational task: to love and trust others. Parents, by their example, show children the delight of life in the creation, the worthiness of service to others, and the presence of God when crosses are to be borne. There is good reason for Luther's explanation to call us to respect, obey, love, and serve our parents, for more than anyone else, it's mothers and fathers through whom God shapes us. To honor your parents is to honor God who installs us in our vocations. But this isn't the

Luther recognized a hierarchy in the Commandments, with the first three regarding our relationship with God (especially the first commandment) standing over the others. Similarly, the fourth commandment is "over" the fifth through eighth, since, for example, in Luther's explanation, the government can harm human life (through incarceration and other punishments), can declare a married couple divorced, can levy taxes and other financial penalties, and can speak judgment on criminals in a court of law.

same thing as doing whatever a parent demands. God's granting of their vocation requires parents to do the job called for by the office. In instances of neglect, abuse, and vindictive behavior, parents need not be obeyed, because at that point they have abdicated their vocations.[23]

The explanation's inclusion of other people in authority shows how Luther saw them as serving *in loco parentis*. That's a legal term found in countless statutes that says that people like teachers, day care providers, and government officials function "in the place of the parents." Your parents can't helicopter over everything you do, so God uses other people to take on the role of setting boundaries, providing direction, and even executing punishments. Just as it is for parents, the ultimate task is to protect and extend the life God creates, and to dishonor these authorities is also to dishonor God.

In 1525 southern Germany exploded with peasants lashing out in response to the ill treatment they received from the lords of the lands they farmed. After failing in a more moderate tract to get both sides to negotiate, Luther penned a fairly venomous treatise called "Against the Thieving, Murderous Hordes of Peasants," in which he was dismayed over their using his own writings as an excuse for civil revolt and granted that the lords should quell the rebellion with force if necessary. Some estimate that as many as 150,000 peasants died as a result. When critics rightly take Luther to task for the piece's harshness, they often miss the vocational framework for it. Luther's approach saw God's hand at work within the vocations in which both peasant and lord had been placed. He saw that the peasants themselves had honest complaints against the mistreatment handed them. But Luther regarded open rebellion as a breaking of the fourth commandment writ large. Neither side served in its vocation well, and those with less power suffered. Just as with parents, the vocations of authorities require much responsibility and care for those in their charge. Although Luther had admonished both peasant and prince in his more moderate tract, he never wrote an equally stern pamphlet criticizing the nobility's role in what came to be called the Peasants' War, while making it clear that all involved came under God's judgment for breaking this commandment. That's the fear part of the explanation. The love part, though, is that Luther knew that God is pleased with good order in the world and that the only truly effective measure for changing hearts was preaching, and that the only sword the church could wield was the word that brought faith.

Title page to Luther's treatise "Against the Thieving, Murderous Hordes of Peasants," 1525.

---

23. The word to children facing such a turn away from parental vocations must be "Go and tell," and God must then work through government and other authorities to serve where the parents haven't.

The Fifth Commandment

♥ You shall not murder.

What is this?* or *What does this mean?
We are to fear and love God, so that we neither endanger nor
harm the lives of our neighbors, but instead help and support
them in all of life's needs.

Cain slays Abel (Gen. 4:1-16).

After Luther delivered his refusal to recant any of his works before
the Holy Roman emperor and the arrayed representatives from the
Vatican at the imperial Diet[24] held in the city of Worms in 1521, he
left the city on the Rhein River to head back home to Wittenberg.
Although he had been promised safe passage to and from Worms
and crowds gathered to support him along the journey, that offered
meager consolation. Emperor Charles V issued what has come to
be known as the Edict of Worms. It condemned Luther's teaching,
ordered the burning of his books, and condemned the man himself. It
made Luther a wanted man—dead or alive—and declared anyone who

Portrait of Charles V, Holy Roman
emperor (1500–1558), by Bernard van
Orley, c. 1516.

Portrait of Frederick the Wise, elector of Saxony, by Lucas Cranach the Elder, painted
in 1533 from an earlier original.

---

24. A *diet* was a kind of parliament for the Holy Roman Empire. Representatives from the many principalities and bishoprics (large and small) and the
various free imperial cities gathered together to conduct the empire's business, including electing the emperor, raising and funding armies, and dealing
with controversies like the one sparked by that monk in Germany.

Edinburgh

NORTH SEA

DENMARK Copenhagen

IRELAND

Danzig

ENGLAND

Francis I and Charles V
both claim Artois
and Flanders

London

HOLY
ROMAN
EMPIRE

POLAND

Ghent

Cologne

ARTOIS

FLANDERS

Mainz

LUSATIA

Elbe R.

Oder R.

SILESIA

1530; Lutherans present
Charles V with
Augsburg Confession

BOHEMIA

MORAVIA

Seine R. Paris

Rhine R.

Danube R. Vienna

Duchy of Burgundy
claimed by
Francis and Charles

DUCHY
OF
BURGUNDY

COUNTY
OF
BURGUNDY

Augsburg

Vienna 1529

HUNGARY

Budapest

ATLANTIC
OCEAN

Nantes

CHAROLAIS

AUSTRIA

FRANCE

Trent

VENICE

Mohacs 1526

Milan

Venice

1516 Charles proclaimed
King Charles I of Spain

Toulouse

Avignon

Genoa

Francis I and
Charles V both
claim Milan

Florence PAPAL
STATES

Ottoman
Turks

ADRIATIC SEA

OTTOMAN
EMPIRE

NAVARRE

CORSICA

Rome

SPAIN

ARAGON

Barcelona

1519: Charles V crowned
Holy Roman Emperor
by the Pope

NAPLES

Naples

Madrid

SARDINIA

PORTUGAL

Tagus R. Toledo

Francis I and Charles V
both claim Naples

Lisbon

Balearic Is.

Seville

MEDITERRANEAN SEA

SICILY

Granada

Algiers

Tunis

Oran

Miles
0   100   200

0 100 200 300
Kilometers

	Inherited by Charles V
	Gained by Charles V
	Holy Roman Empire boundary

N.B. This does not include Charles V's overseas empire.

The Empire of Charles V. In the early 1500s, every little territory had its own ruler. Notice the wide swath of territory in which Luther was wanted—dead or alive—after the Edict of Worms.

assisted him to be an outlaw as well. Luther was in a precarious position save for one thing: because his prince, Frederick the Wise of Saxony, was one of seven official electors who chose the emperor and provided armies and funding,[25] the prince held some sovereignty in Saxony and could thus delay the imposition of the edict against Luther.

Wartburg Castle, Eisenach.

To provide protection to his monk, Frederick concocted a scheme in which Luther was "abducted" and taken in secret to a castle on a hill high above Eisenach: the Wartburg, one of the prince's holdings within his territory. When Frederick died in 1525, Luther preached at the funeral. Again in 1532, at the death of Elector John, Frederick's brother, Luther preached, reminding his grieving hearers that John's bodily death was nothing compared to John's real death that occurred in Augsburg in 1530, when he presented the Augsburg Confession before Emperor Charles V. Facing the most powerful man in Europe between Charlemagne and Napoleon, the prince confessed his faith, just as his older brother Frederick had defended and preserved Luther's life. Thus, Luther's two princes are fine examples of how his explanation of the fifth commandment works.

The commandment recognizes that God is the source of all life. It's a gift only God may end. People in the sixteenth century may have held life more dearly than we do today. In Luther's day death virtually roamed the streets and broke into people's homes. The British philosopher Thomas Hobbes, who lived a century after Luther, described life as "nasty, brutish, and short." In all likelihood, you wouldn't make it to adulthood due to childhood diseases. Up to a fifth of women died in childbirth or from its complications. But the plague was one of the biggest fears. The population of Europe dropped by a third, but in the cities the numbers were worse. Up to 60 percent of citizens died. Luther knew our last enemy well, and death was a regular topic in his preaching, teaching, and writing. He often wrote letters of consolation to people he knew who were grieving: colleagues at the university, the parents of one of his students, supporters across Germany. Death visited Luther's own home too. When his thirteen-year-old daughter Magdalena died, Luther suffered nearly incapacitating grief.

25. Frederick, a candidate for emperor, stepped aside in favor of Charles. The military crisis afoot was the advancing armies of the Turkish sultan Suleiman the Magnificent moving up the Balkan Peninsula toward Austria.

For human sinners death has always been inescapable, but in Luther's time no one could pretend to be immune. In Luther's explanation of the fifth commandment, he didn't rail against death but recognized how its presence makes life utterly precious. For Luther, life stems from God's will to create and is held in God's palm. Were God to turn away in anger, your life would end. But because God has chosen to be your God, your life doesn't belong to you—and certainly isn't something your neighbor could independently decide to end. The old sinner in us needs to fear the Lord, because we so readily assume the roles of judge, jury, and executioner. In our sinful need to preserve ourselves at all costs, we look to those around us and see either competition or threat. Whenever killing and murder happen, Sin's selfishness project always forms the foundation for the action.[26]

But where the gospel brings faith, you begin to love not only God but your neighbors as well. When your eyes are opened in faith, the threat and competition vanish and in their place stands the neighbor in need. Your neighbors become a gift, a place to exert your skills and talents in vocation, and most importantly a place for discipleship—where you can pour out your life for them as your Lord did for you. The move from fear to love of God in faith extends our care beyond the mere beginning and ending of life. It also calls us to nurture and cherish life as it exists and to keep from killing in any form: bullying, shaming, torture, and abuse—all places where one person seeks to bring another to accept the will to nothingness the tormentor imposes. By our fighting against such oppression, God keeps order in the world so that we may eat the bread, for which we pray in the Lord's Prayer, in peace.

The Sixth Commandment

♥ You shall not commit adultery.

What is this? or *What does this mean?*
We are to fear and love God, so that we lead pure and decent lives in word and deed, and each of us loves and honors his or her spouse.

Anyone who has ever seen a soap opera or a romantic comedy knows that sex on the screen means big money. It doesn't matter if it's opposites attracting or like finding like, we humans have an urge to merge. When God created

David and Bathsheba (2 Samuel 11).

---

26. Luther didn't look askance at all killing, though. Because of his sense of our vocations as the place God is working in the world, Luther saw God's hands behind government and its coercive power (see Romans 13:1-7 and Genesis 9:6). That meant that specific people had been given the task of carrying out God's judgment on murder, including the man who served as the local hangman.

human beings, God said it was *tov me-od*, literally, "way good." And the goodness includes our bodies, no parts of which are nasty or shameful. In 1 Corinthians 12 Paul talks about private parts as something we don't put on display because they need to be given honor. But long before the Puritan prurient mind-set pushed sex as perfidy, sex had already gotten a name for itself. Ancient Christians like Origen and Simeon Stylites saw their flesh and its urges as a problem and withdrew from the world to avoid temptations.[27] St. Augustine saw sin itself as being passed on from generation to generation through sexual activity. That view extended with the development of monastic movements. As part of taking up a life apart from the world, monks and nuns pledged sexual chastity. In Luther's day even sexual intercourse in marriage was considered sinful. Priests hearing confessions even had guidelines for asking about specific sexual positions that crossed the line from baby making to pleasure.

A sixth-century plate depicting St. Simeon Stylites on his column with a snake.

Although post-sexual revolution people may regard this attitude as unenlightened, the medieval thinkers knew something the sixth commandment also knows: fleshly urges are volatile. No sooner does God give sex as a gift than it gets twisted. It's used to manipulate and shame others, to validate our identity, and in our day to sell products in the televised marketplace. It's not God who deems sex dirty. It's human sin that sullies its reputation. In his explanation of the commandment, Luther recaptured the giftedness of sex. Nowhere did he say lovemaking is bad. Instead, he set it in a place of honor so it can do what God intends it to do: preserve the possibility of new life, enable us to delve into the deepest intimacy with the one who has vowed to stick with us for life, and allow us to see our bodies as "way good."

None of that was going to happen in a world where celibacy was considered a higher, more Christian form of life than marriage. When he was holed up in the Wartburg Castle after the Diet of Worms, not only did Luther translate the Bible, but he also kept thinking about the consequences of life under the gospel. Monks and nuns had begun to leave their monastic lives, including some who had been placed in monasteries as children. Luther published a pamphlet against monastic vows despite opposition from the Saxon court to keep it under wraps. But the issue couldn't be ignored. Not only did monastic vows do a disservice to people who had been taught that they could earn merit before God this way, but they also

---

27. For example, Simeon lived his life on a platform at the top of a pole as an act of faith.

Southern part of the ruins of Nimbschen convent in Grimma, Leipzig district, Saxony.

tempted people to break the sixth commandment. In taking up celibacy as monks, priests, and nuns, people were disavowing both the goodness God had declared in creation and the pattern God established with our first parents in the Garden.

When a group of nuns from the abbey in Nimbschen left under cover of night and showed up in Wittenberg seeking the reformer's help, celibacy became a concrete and personal issue for Luther.[28] It was no small matter to reinsert the eleven nuns back into the outside world. Some went home to live with their families. Luther and his fellow reformers found husbands or positions for the others. But one woman was a problem: Katharina von Bora.[29] She rejected one suitor, and another's family rejected her. She declared that she would only marry either Luther's colleague, Nikolaus von Amsdorf, or Luther himself (although Luther had been interested in another nun, Ave von Schönfeld). Luther agreed to the marriage, and they were wed on June 13, 1525. He hadn't intended to make such an act of political and

Portrait of Katharina von Bora by Lucas Cranach the Elder, 1528.

28. The Nimbschen nuns weren't the only runaways Luther knew. Elizabeth von Meseritz had been a nun in an abbey on the Baltic Sea near a church served by Johannes Bugenhagen. When Bugenhagen was called to Wittenberg to serve as pastor there, Elizabeth, who loved the evangelical preaching he had taken up after encountering Luther's writings, decided to go there for help. Bugenhagen's family took her in as a daughter, and she married a university student, Caspar Cruciger Sr., who became part of Luther's closest circle. And best of all, Elizabeth Cruciger became the first female hymnwriter published in a Lutheran hymnal. 29. She started at a convent school when she was five, entered the convent at nine, and took her vows as a nun at sixteen. She fled to Wittenberg when she was twenty-four and found work in the household of the great Reformation artist Lucas Cranach.

theological protest, but since he had advocated marriage for others, it would have been unseemly for him not to follow suit. He later reported what a surprise it had been to wake in the morning and find a pair of pigtails on the pillow next to him. Katie and Martin's marriage provided both foundation and fodder for the work of the Reformation until Luther's death just over two decades later.

It's the gift of this relationship that forms the context for Luther's language in his explanation of the sixth commandment. The sinner in you rightly fears God for your willy-nilly approach to sex, but the new faithful person in you understands how God protects the gift through the lifelong promises of marriage. While the church at the time regarded marriage as a sacrament, Luther saw it as part of the civil order—a way God structured life on earth to bring safety and security. Marriage provided an arena of safety where people could give themselves fully to their partner without fear or shame and in a way that worked to cement both their relationship and their family.

In the Large Catechism, Luther concluded his explanation of the sixth commandment this way: "This commandment requires all people not only to live chastely in deed, word, and thought in their particular situation (that is, especially in marriage as a walk of life), but also to love and cherish the spouse whom God has given them. Wherever marital chastity is to be maintained, above all it is essential that husband and wife live together in love and harmony, cherishing each other wholeheartedly and with perfect fidelity. This is one of the chief ways to make chastity attractive and desirable" (Ten Commandments, par. 219 [BC 415]).

The Seventh Commandment

♥ You shall not steal.

What is this? or **What does this mean?**
We are to fear and love God, so that we neither take our neighbors' money or property nor acquire them by using shoddy merchandise or crooked deals, but instead help them to improve and protect their property and income.

The theft by Achan (Joshua 7).

Luther's career didn't happen inside a pristine vacuum where all he ever had to concern himself with was the day's lecture, the next sermon, and the exploration of whatever theological question arose in his own mind. The reality was quite messy. Luther was absolutely a part of the world. In his childhood, he was connected through his father's work to the economics of the mining industry around Mansfeld and the burdens of high-interest loans. In Wittenberg the university was supported by the elector, who initially set up the All Saints' Foundation supported by income from a welter of church properties. And prior to 1518, some Wittenbergers were more than willing to pay for indulgences and other religious means of improving their standing before God. Luther was good friends with Lucas Cranach, the court artist to a string of Saxon princes, who had a sideline as the local apothecary, and served more than once as the *burgermeister*. And Georg Spalatin, the prince's counselor, surely discussed with Luther the political and economic consequences of his writings and actions.

Although economics was hardly the chief motivation for Luther's objections to indulgences expressed in the *Ninety-Five Theses*, several point out that one's money is better spent caring for one's own family or for the poor. What Luther did not know was that the archbishop, Albrecht of Brandenburg, had borrowed tens of thousands of ducats from the Fuggers, the banking family from Augsburg, to gain the position of Elector of Mainz (one of the people who elected the Holy Roman emperor). To pay off his debts, Albrecht gained permission from the pope to send Johann Tetzel into the territory on a campaign to sell indulgences, where half the proceeds went to help reconstruct St. Peter's Basilica in Rome but the other half secretly helped Albrecht pay off his debts. By purchasing a letter of this so-called Peter's indulgence, a person reduced or eliminated the amount of penalty owed for sin both here and in purgatory. Along with Albrecht's secret deal and this indulgence's stated purpose, there were also widespread suspicions that the money was not even going for its stated purpose at all, and charges against the indulgence preachers' extravagance were common. The catalyst that sparked the Reformation was both theological and economic.

Portrait of Cardinal Albrecht of Brandenburg by Lucas Cranach the Elder, 1526.

Trading for property is a basic part of human existence, even when barter rather than money serves as a society's financial structure. In Genesis 2–3, God gives

The sale of indulgences contrasted to King David's piety. Woodcut by Hans Holbein the Younger, c. 1529.

The need for acquisition doesn't stop when the hall closet, four bedrooms, and garage are full.

the garden to the first man and woman and requires them to care for it and use its fruits. Once in rebellion against God, humans continued using our opposable thumbs to grasp tools to work and grab whatever items could be pulled in to provide safety and security. The stuff around us and the means of getting it serve as a way of promoting and preserving life. The problem is that the need for acquisition doesn't stop when the hall closet, four bedrooms, and three-car garage are full. There's always more waiting to be had. For sinners, the business of getting and trading becomes a zero-sum game: the more someone else has, the less that's available for you.

Luther's explanation of the seventh commandment reveals his awareness of our life in two realms. In the heavenly realm where Christ is the only currency needed, there will be no trading or buying, because Christ is all in all. But in the realm of this world, we have to have stuff: shelter to protect us from the elements, clothes and shoes, the tools of our trade, cookware and utensils, and even something as intangible yet vital as an education. The commandment protects our goods and protects others from our desire to get their things in the easiest way possible, stealing. To steal is to take others' property without giving them a just and fair return on their goods. Luther gave a solid list of how we do it in his explanation. His economic objection to the sale of indulgences was that someone like the indulgence preacher Johann Tetzel sold something that purported to provide release from God's punishment but was a theological sham that provided the buyer nothing. It was no different from the practice of usury he regularly decried. Charging interest for lending someone money not only created an untrusting relationship between the parties, but also turned the lender into a parasite seeking something for nothing.

Luther's comments on the seventh commandment in the Large Catechism touch on this broader application: "In short, thievery is the most common craft and the largest guild on earth. If we look at the whole world in all its situations, it is nothing but a big, wide stable full of great thieves. This is why these people are also called armchair bandits [a nickname for usurers] and highway robbers. Far from being picklocks and sneak thieves who pilfer the cash box, they sit in their chairs and are known as great lords and honorable, upstanding citizens, while they rob and steal under the cloak of legality" (Ten Commandments, par. 228–29 [BC 417]).

Sign from Day 21 of Occupy Wall Street, October 6, 2011.

If the commandment's explanation forces the sinner's hand with its bottom line in the sand, it also shows how to engage our economy faithfully. Issues like wage levels, wealth disparity, the persistence of poverty, and the need for financial regulation all become objects of debate under the commandment. Although the means of accomplishing the goals are worth haggling over, what's never challenged is that where faith crops up among sinners, the Spirit will spur you to engage in an economy where empires cease, competition wanes, and you care for each other's means of making a living. It's just a glimpse of what's to come fully on the Last Day when your relationship with money will end and Christ's interest in you charges you with new life.

The Eighth Commandment

💚 You shall not bear false witness against your neighbor.

What is this? or ***What does this mean?***
We are to fear and love God, so that we do not tell lies about our neighbors, betray or slander them, or destroy their reputations. Instead we are to come to their defense, speak well of them, and interpret everything they do in the best possible light.

In Latin and Greek versions of Daniel, this story of Susanna and her false accusers was added and is part of the Apocrypha.

Originally the eighth commandment pointed to testimony given before a judge. Without honesty prevailing, it's hard to imagine any justice system working. But in his explanation, Luther, like earlier expositors, took the commandment from the courtroom to the consequences of our everyday wordsmithing. The old children's rhyme, "Sticks and stones may break my bones, but words will never hurt me," is a lie. It may be hard for us to see it in a world where the bickering and backstabbing of reality television and tawdry political discourse cheapen every word. In the Old Testament, words had power. They carried a life of their own. The nineteenth-century poet Emily Dickinson's poem #89 describes it well: "A word is dead / When it is said, / Some say. / I say it just / Begins to live / That day." When at the beginning God created the heavens and the earth by speaking it all into being, it was permanent. When Jacob and his mother connived to move Isaac to bestow his blessing on Jacob, rather than on Esau who had a right to it, his aged, blind father couldn't take back his words, claim a mulligan, and then bless the correct son. The word spoken was a word alive.[30]

---

30. See, for example, Isaiah 55:11 or Hebrews 4:11-12.

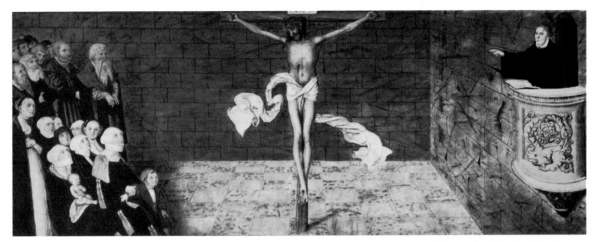

Martin Luther's Sermon (detail from a triptych) by Lucas Cranach the Elder, 1547. Altarpiece in the Church of St. Marien, Wittenberg.

Luther regarded language this powerfully. As he translated the New Testament in his solitary quarters at the Wartburg Castle and later translated the Old Testament with his colleagues back in Wittenberg, Luther took great craft and care with this task. Not only was it important to find the correct German equivalent for the Greek or Hebrew of the scriptures, it was just as vital to draft language that rested on its hearers so they would know it by heart—not just memorize it but internalize it. Human beings' identities are a mash-up of genetic determinism, your parents' child-rearing capabilities, and the world pressing in all around you. The role of language, which sorts, expresses, and assigns meaning, is central. When you let a word loose from your lips, it enters another's ear, where the sound waves travel upstairs as part of the lifelong process of shaping your brain. Luther knew that words *do* something.

Admittedly some words don't have a big influence on us. Whether it's a highway sign's words indicating a speed limit or the words on a fast-food menu, they're just there, and we pay little notice. So, too, with many of our daily interactions—and even with language we use to describe God. Hearing that God is omniscient, omnipresent, and omnipotent is a good thing if you're one of the church's public proclaimers tasked with orthodox preaching, but the words don't help much when you're shopping for breakfast cereal. And when you live in a culture that puts a barrage of words before you on your various devices, you begin to pay less attention to what's written or spoken, or you isolate yourself so you only have to hear the words that echo what's in the "skull-sized kingdom" of your own head.[31]

Luther's explanation knows of another kind of word. This is a word that does something when it's spoken. It delivers the exact thing it says. The best-known example of this kind of word is "I love you." A couple in the early stages of their relationship may be reluctant to speak these words, because they know that speaking them has such power. By declaring their love, they are giving the actual love, and when that happens a new bond is formed that won't be easy to disentangle from. These kinds of words can be fun, from "Come over here and kiss me quick" to "You are so hot!" You hear them and are changed. But negative words do the same

---

31. David Foster Wallace, *This Is Water* (New York: Little, Brown, 2009), 117.

thing. You could make a list of epithets slung at populations you regard as "other" than you. The goal in using them is to reverse what God has said. In the beginning God created out of nothing, but these words seek to bring the creation back to nothing.

Luther wasn't satisfied with keeping the discussion of words on an intellectual level. In the explanation, he brought it in close, to our daily interactions with others. The commandment seeks to become such a part of you that you become your own self-censor in all your conversations, always mindful not just of what your words mean but even more of *what they do*. Words can destroy reputations or build confidence. They can tear down a person's soul or lift it to new heights. As we will see when we come to his explanations of the Lord's Prayer, Luther will take us beyond these words and talk about *the* Word. This is the word that is the truth that Jesus says will set you free. His promise gives you leave to demand that words spoken by a preacher do exactly what the gospel has always done: make something out of nothing.

Luther remarked extensively in the Large Catechism on the harm that words do to our neighbors. "People are loath to offend anyone. Instead, they speak dishonestly with an eye to gaining favor, money, prospects, or friendship. Consequently, a poor man is inevitably oppressed, loses his case, and suffers punishment." Thus, Luther insisted that "all people should help their neighbors maintain their legal rights." Moreover, "wherever there are upright preachers and Christians, they must endure having the world call them heretics, apostates, even seditious and desperate scoundrels." Finally, the eighth commandment "forbids all sins of the tongue by which we may injure or offend our neighbor." For Luther, this included gossip and hearsay. In contrast, he wrote, "We should use our tongue to speak only the best about all people, to cover the sins and infirmities of our neighbors, to justify their actions, and to cloak and veil them with our own honor" (Ten Commandments, par. 258, 260, 262–63, 285 [BC 420–21, 424]).

The Ninth and Tenth Commandments

♥ You shall not covet your neighbor's house.

What is this? or *What does this mean?*
We are to fear and love God, so that we do not try to trick our neighbors out of their inheritance or property or try to get it for ourselves by claiming to have a legal right to it and the like, but instead be of help and service to them in keeping what is theirs.

Jacob cheating Laban (Gen. 30:25-43).

♥ You shall not covet your neighbor's wife, or male or female slave, or ox, or donkey, or anything that belongs to your neighbor.

What is this? or **What does this mean?**
We are to fear and love God, so that we do not entice, force, or steal away from our neighbors their spouses, household workers, or livestock, but instead urge them to stay and fulfill their responsibilities to our neighbors.

Joseph and Potiphar's wife (Genesis 39).

The last two commandments are the other side of the coin from the first commandment. In the first, God claims the divine throne and refuses to be shunted aside. In the following commandments, God gives seven words that, with their boundaries and blessings, tell you what your Creator has in store. In the last pair of commandments' explanations, Luther provided a glimpse into the insidious consequences of refusing to let God be God. Such sinfulness leads to a curved-in desire that always looks to self first. It demands freedom to take what it wants. It regards others as toys to be played with or tools to achieve your primacy in the world. When you grab what belongs to others, it's not just a matter of stealing. It's a declaration of divine right on your part. In Galatians, Paul has a mighty pointed list of what he calls "the works of the flesh" that are in keeping with the self-centeredness around which these commandments establish a boundary: "fornication, impurity, licentiousness, idolatry, sorcery, enmities, strife, jealousy, anger, quarrels, dissensions, factions, envy, drunkenness, carousing, and things like these."[32] In each of these works stands coveting's same rampant individualism, selfishness, and a diminishing of anything that stands in your way.

In the gospel moving us from fear to love, Luther knew that it all comes down to what happens with your will. In 1525 Luther engaged in a battle of printing presses with Erasmus of Rotterdam, one of Europe's greatest thinkers.[33] Erasmus had taken Luther to task for all his assertions about the gospel, and he argued in his treatise that the church has to exert itself so sinners crank up their will and freely choose to become better people. Luther didn't agree with Erasmus for a minute, but toward the end of his response he commended Erasmus. He said the great Humanist is the only one

Engraving of Erasmus of Rotterdam by Albrecht Dürer, 1526.

---

32. Galatians 5:19-21. For St. Paul's discussion of coveting and its disastrous effects, see also Romans 7:7-25.   33. Erasmus, *Diatribe on Free Will*; Luther, *The Bondage of the Will*, LW 33.

of all Luther's opponents who understood that the question of the will is central to every argument. As long as you're concerned with your will, you haven't yet understood this faith. The self-centered will inside you covets all you see, and God's only response can be commandments that hem you in and remove your choices. The commandments *must* show you the truth about your will's consistent, selfish choices that have nothing to do with God's will. But when the Holy Spirit opens your eyes to God's will to bring mercy in Christ Jesus and to put the law within your heart, then the blessing of the commandments grows. And the person of faith will join God gladly to control and discipline the old outer person by stemming the desire to play Jacob and grab hold of everyone else's heel.[34] You may even wind up for the first time honestly praying the words of the Lord's Prayer, "Your will be done."

Conclusion of the Commandments

♥ What then does God say about all these commandments?

God says the following: "I, the Lord your God, am a jealous God, punishing children for the iniquity of parents, to the third and the fourth generation of those who reject me, but showing steadfast love to the thousandth generation of those who love me and keep my commandments."

What is this? or **What does this mean?**
God threatens to punish all who break these commandments. Therefore we are to fear his wrath and not disobey these commandments. However, God promises grace and every good thing to all those who keep these commandments. Therefore we also are to love and trust him and gladly act according to his commands.

One way to understand God's wrath is to think of the inevitable consequences of sin. For example, if one smokes three packs of cigarettes a day or overeats terribly, there are often bitter (wrath-filled) consequences. Similarly, our own selfishness forces God to use "tough love," to borrow a term from Alcoholics Anonymous, to drive us to our knees in repentance—all so that the Holy Spirit may bring us as forgiven sinners to faith where we "love and trust God and gladly act according to his commands." This gladness arises only when our obedience is not forced from fear but arises spontaneously from love and trust.

The conclusion to the Commandments sounds so wrathful, almost a caricature of what so many think of as the vengeful God of the Old Testament. But there's more to the conclusion than that. Because we understand how God's two words work, we have to remember which side we stand on. God moves us from fear to love with law and gospel words. For Luther, God's aim is "to require true faith and confidence of

---

34. Genesis 25:26.

the heart, which fly straight to the one true God and cling to him alone."[35] That means God doesn't desire perpetual fear of him, but instead that we know him through Christ so we can love and trust him.

That won't happen if you see the Commandments as a religious stepping-stone to glory, righteousness, or heaven, because your heart and will won't have changed, and you'll be trapped in the nothingness and death that is sin. But the Commandments bring you back to Luther's last words, "We are beggars. This is true." They plant you right between the words *fear* and *love*, on the brink of new life. And now you're ripe to hear the promise laid out in the story of creation, salvation, and sanctification that Luther provided in his explanations of the Apostles' Creed. And when you can say, "This is most certainly true," you will know you have landed on the love side of the Commandments with the word in your heart.

---

35. Large Catechism, Ten Commandments, par. 4 (BC 386–87).

3

The Apostles' Creed

What Is a Creed?

A creed is a statement of belief. The word itself comes from the Latin *credo*, which means "I believe." But a creed is not only a statement of belief. When an opinionated uncle at the Thanksgiving table spouts off, "Well, I think . . . ," we have a statement of belief that is not a creed. A Christian creed is a summary of a whole set of beliefs, positions, inclinations, and orientations. In fact, it is very often a summary of the Bible. In the usual order of worship, the recitation of the Creed comes between the sermon and the prayers of intercession, just before the liturgy of the communion meal.

Summaries must necessarily include some things and leave out others. If someone asked you to tell the story of your life, for example, you would hit the highlights, omit the irrelevant or routine, and present a meaningful whole. If you said, "Well, I was born on day X, and then I cried for a while, then I ate for a bit, then I slept, then filled a diaper, then slept, then ate some more," that would be neither helpful nor meaningful to the person who asked the question. There is an art to including and excluding just the right elements.

An obituary is a summary of someone's life that follows a set pattern. A creed is not like that, because when creeds were developed, there was no existing form or pattern to follow. Early Christians simply needed a brief way to identify what it was they believed in and what was important to believe. A better example for what a creed is might be a demi-glace, a delicious sauce made by reducing stock further and further down, down,

The title page decoration for Luther and Philip Melanchthon's instructions to parish pastors on how to teach the faith. It includes their official seals (Luther's rose and the bronze serpent), depicts the Trinity at the top and the birth of Christ at the bottom—central in all Christian confessions of faith—and is flanked by a prophet and an apostle.

and down. It has an intense flavor that complements whatever it is served with, but it would make a terrible meal on its own. So too is the relationship of a creed to the Bible. By itself a creed is not a full meal, but with the meat and potatoes of scripture, it is nourishing and delicious. A summary of a poem can be helpful to explain to someone what the poem is about but is not the same as the whole poem.

In a Greek play, the gist of the story, or the synopsis of what the play is about, is called a *theoria* (literally, an overview). In that sense, a creed is kind of like a *theoria* of God. It's the gist of who and what God is all about. Some church denominations don't use creeds because they view creeds as contentious and divisive or unfriendly to newcomers. But this overlooks or misunderstands a creed's intended use. Creeds identify who God is and articulate the church's key teachings about God. They do not merely function as a test for belonging to a group or as something to be repeated mindlessly. Creeds are summaries that help keep the whole picture of the Bible in mind when we are looking carefully at a part of scripture. The view of the whole makes sense of the part, which then helps make further sense of the whole, and so on. For Luther, the chief function of the Creed is to summarize God's grace and mercy, describing all the things that God has done, is doing, and will do for us.

Luther's Small Catechism paraphrases the Apostles' Creed. There are other ecumenical creeds, the most widely used of which is the Nicene Creed, agreed to by Christians in the fourth century. The Apostles' Creed goes back to an ancient Roman baptismal creed and is the most widely known in the Western church. The text as we now have it is generally thought to go back to 404 CE (it is quoted in a text by Rufinus of Aquileia), but its predecessor forms are much older, going back to the end of the second century. It was probably used in oral instruction as a call-and-response way of summarizing what adult converts to the faith were learning about Christianity. Immediately before receiving baptism in the name of the triune God, the catechumen, the person being welcomed into the Christian faith, was asked, "Do you believe in God the Father?" They were then asked, "Do you believe in Jesus Christ?" and finally, ". . . in the Holy Spirit?" And the catechumen would respond, "I believe . . ." with each article of the Creed.

A seventeenth-century Russian icon of the articles of the (Nicene) Creed.

A Creed Timeline

30	Jesus' death and resurrection
50	earliest New Testament writings
110	latest New Testament writings
180	early version of Apostles' Creed circulated
325	early version of Nicene Creed written
381	Council of Constantinople lengthens Nicene Creed (resembling present-day version)
500	Athanasian Creed composed

The First Ecumenical Council of Nicaea as depicted in a fresco in St. Sophia Cathedral in Kiev.

Luther followed the medieval catechetical tradition by focusing on the Apostles' Creed, but he might have used the Nicene Creed. The first words of the Nicene Creed in Greek are different from the Apostles' Creed. Not "I believe" but "We believe." The reason for this "I"/"We" difference is historical. The Council of Nicaea was called in 325 to settle issues about the divinity of Christ. Hundreds of bishops and other leaders responded to Emperor Constantine's request to come to debate the relationship between the Son (or the Word) and the Father. The decision of the council was that the Son was "of one being" with the Father. The bishops came to agreement (except for a very few who dissented) and asked their people to add their voices to this statement. Therefore, "We believe. . . ." In 381 the Creed of Nicaea was expanded into the form we use today to address questions about the Holy Spirit's divinity.

So just as we saw the part-whole-part-whole dance between the Bible and the Creed, we have the I-we-I-we dance of belief. Both elements are important.

In 1524 Luther wrote a German paraphrase of the Nicene Creed (with music adapted from a medieval Latin *Credo*) for use in his *German Mass* (see *Evangelical Lutheran Worship*, #411). Unlike the Latin, which used the singular ("I believe"), Luther returned to the Greek plural: "We all believe in one true God."

When we confess "I believe," we testify to and claim the Christian faith as our own. When we confess "We believe," we avoid thinking that Christian faith is only about the individual and God. At times an individual believer may find it difficult to believe every word of the Creed. In those times we rely on the confession of others. Then confessing the Creed is like saying, "Okay, the church confesses this, and I pray with them so that God will see me through until such a time as I can really believe this." I believe, and we believe, and I believe.

The Creed has a trinitarian structure, and not only because it contains articles on the Father, the Son, and the Holy Spirit. When we say the Creed, we speak our faith *to* the Father, *with* the Son, and *in* the Holy Spirit. We dare to speak to God at all only because we join our voices with the voice of Jesus who prayed to the one he called his Father. And we do so in the Spirit who carries our voices to God who promises to hear.

An early printing of "We All Believe in One True God," Luther's German paraphrase of the Nicene Creed.

In Luther's day there were several different ways to divide up the Creed. Some used a sixfold division, and others, adhering to the legend that each of the apostles contributed one part, divided it into twelve. Luther, who dismissed that legend out of hand, chose instead to return to the most ancient division, reflected in the baptismal dialogue, dividing the Creed into three parts, confessing the Father, Son, and Holy Spirit.

The First Article: On Creation

♥ I believe in God, the Father almighty, creator of heaven and earth.

   What is this?* or *What does this mean?
   I believe that God has created me together with all that exists. God has given me and still preserves my body and soul: eyes, ears, and all limbs and senses; reason and all mental faculties.

   In addition, God daily and abundantly provides shoes and clothing, food and drink, house and farm, spouse and children, fields, livestock, and all property—along with all the necessities and nourishment for this body and life. God protects me against all danger and shields and preserves me from all evil. And all this is done out of pure, fatherly, and divine goodness and mercy, without any merit or worthiness of mine at all! For all of this I owe it to God to thank and praise, serve and obey him. This is most certainly true.

God depicted as a bearded man giving a blessing, surrounded by animals and encircled by clouds and the four winds.

In the first article of the Creed, we confess that God is creator. But immediately we cannot restrict God's creative act to a one-off action. God does not create and then walk away from creation, like a manufacturer who makes a product and then sells it. Creation and providence are two sides of the same coin. God provides for what God creates. God gives what is created a future. In fact, to give a thing a *future* is what it means to create a thing.

Think of a care package sent to a college student. It's full of candy bars, homemade cookies, and other sweets. But it also includes toothpaste! Because the sender loves the recipient, she wants him to be able to enjoy cookies for a long time to come, and so includes providential care (the toothpaste) along with her creative love (the cookies). Here's another example. If I want to start a charity, I not only create an organizational structure, bylaws, and a mission statement, but also set aside a sum of money or resources that will perpetually fund the charity. Of course, all earthly treasures will run out at some point, and even when we say that an institution will be around "forever," what we really mean is "a pretty long time." The same logic applies to God's creative act. The initial act of bringing into existence is always accompanied by the provision of structures and gifts that allow the thing to flourish, grow, and reach its potential.

Luther goes on to explain that in addition to creating *me*, God "daily and abundantly provides shoes and clothing, food and drink, house and farm, spouse and children, fields, livestock, and all property—along with all the necessities and nourishment for this body and life." It is a testament to Luther's earthy and this-worldly orientation that he thought to include such basic things as shoes and livestock in this article. Livestock are necessary for farmers' monetary well-being but would have been understood to benefit all people who need meat, eggs, leather, wool, and goose down for pillows.

Luther construed the creation as a kind of *relation*: "God has created me together with all that exists." A casual reading of that phrase might sound like, "God made me, and God made all the other stuff too." But this reading misses the point. God creates me *together* with all that exists. I exist only in relation to other creatures of God and in relation to God. I cannot be me without those other creatures, nor without God. I exist in and as a set of relationships with those things

In 1528 Luther preached on the parts of the catechism three separate times. His first two expositions of the Creed focused on the word *Father*, but by the third time he emphasized instead the word *Creator*, a viewpoint that also influenced the catechisms. He still addressed the Creed's use of the word *Father* but now as an adjective ("fatherly and divine goodness and mercy"). See also the comments on "Our Father" in the chapter on the Lord's Prayer, pages 106–108.

An inscription in Edinburgh, Scotland believed to date from 1544, "Blissit be God of al his gifts."

that are not me. Science confirms through observation what we know through faith; there are about as many atoms of things that *are not* me inside me as there are atoms of stuff that *are* me. If you add up all the cells of bacteria in your body, it is nearly the same as the number of cells of the body.[1] No one exists except as someone's daughter or son, mother or father, friend, acquaintance, coworker, or, most broadly, a creature of God.

Relational thinking imbued nearly all of Luther's thought. Nothing exists in and of itself, but only from a certain perspective, in a certain relation. Your existence is considered either *coram deo* (before God, or from God's point of view) or *coram mundo* or *coram hominibus* (before the world or before humans, that is, from a human point of view). We stand before God as creatures who owe everything to God. God, as creator, places us in this world, where we interact with and are a part of all creation. As we learn in the second and third articles, we also stand before God as *simul iustus et peccator*, saints and sinners at the same time. From God's point of view, we are beautiful and redeemed lovely things, even though when we view ourselves, we see only our sin. There is a righteousness outside of me (*extra nos*) that nonetheless works on me and brings me to life because Christ exists only for me (*pro me*).[2]

One of the ways God creates you in relationships and sustains you as a creation is through your physical body: "God has given me and still preserves my body and soul: eyes, ears, and all limbs and senses; reason and all mental faculties." All of these elements are ways that bodies reach outside of themselves to experience and offer themselves to other creatures. In Luther's thought, bodies are good. Sexuality is good, athleticism is good, eating tasty food and drinking luscious beer are good (all in moderation, naturally). His comments reveal no ascetic rigor forbidding the delights of the body because they hinder the soul's concentration on spiritual things.

Christ Healing the Deaf-Mute, from *Das Plenarium* by Hans Schäufelein. Hand-colored woodcut, 1517.

What about the bit about "eyes and ears" or "all mental faculties"? Does that mean that those who lack sight, hearing, or a sound mind are less human? No. Luther's point was always to marvel at and try to encompass all God's gifts of creation. To be sure, he thought (in tension with some contemporary disability studies) that those who are blind or deaf are deprived of something that God intends all to enjoy. But in contrast to much of the theology Luther would have received, he fought for dignity

---

1. A 160-pound person has about 40 trillion bacteria cells and 30 trillion human cells. Tina Hesman Saey, "Body's Bacteria Don't Outnumber Human Cells So Much After All," *Science News*, January 8, 2016, https://www.sciencenews.org/article/body%E2%80%99s-bacteria-don%E2%80%99t-outnumber-human-cells-so-much-after-all. 2. See the article "Relational Thinking" by Risto Saarinen in Derek Nelson and Paul Hinlicky, eds., *Oxford Research Encyclopedia of Martin Luther*, 3 vols. (New York: Oxford University Press, 2017), 3:245–58.

for the disabled. For instance, in a sermon on Mark 7:34, in which Jesus heals a deaf person and says, "Ephphatha," which means "Be opened!," Luther noted that the recovery of all lost senses would be experienced by the faithful in the resurrection.[3] Luther also removed many impediments to marriage that so frustrated those in the late Middle Ages who were blind or deaf. The church had increased the number of impediments, although exceptions could be purchased to overlook some of them. Luther's general perspective was to affirm the full humanity of those who seemed to lack reason, whose bodies seemed to lack sense, or whose life was made more difficult by the lack of one limb or another.

We turn now to the insight that God's creation includes provision for "all the necessities and nourishment for this body and life." Behind and within these ten little words lies an enormously influential and important theology of *vocation*. Think for a moment, as concretely as you can, what it takes for "the necessities and nourishment" of your body and life. What comes to mind? Food? Family? A job? Transportation to get to that job? How about a police force and sound government to make your community a safe place to live and work. A system of parks. What else?

Think of what it takes for there to be an economy, agriculture, parks, police, roads, hospitals, and all the other things that make life possible and delightful. Besides all the physical infrastructure, this takes *people*. God's creative Word spoken into the darkness of the void that there be light *commands* the support systems for life.[4] The concrete form that my response to God's creation takes is my *vocation*.[5] God commands safety for all people. Therefore, all are called to be good neighbors, and some are called to be police, first responders, building inspectors, seat-belt factory workers, or retirees. God commands health and well-being for all, and therefore some have vocations to work in nursing homes, as doctors, nurses, and technicians, and as researchers in the medical field. God commands that we not steal, which is another way of saying that all need enough "stuff" to live, and so there are businessmen and businesswomen, regional sales representatives, miners, farmers, truck drivers, and call center workers. As Luther wrote elsewhere, "If you are a manual laborer, you find that the Bible has been put into your workshop, into your hand, into your heart. It teaches and preaches how you should treat your neighbor. . . . Indeed, there is no shortage of preaching. You have

Many vocations are needed to make life possible, delightful, and safe.

---

3. See Oswald Bayer, *The Theology of Martin Luther: A Contemporary Interpretation*, trans. Thomas H. Trapp (Grand Rapids: Eerdmans, 2008), 113–14.
4. Genesis 1.   5. The best place to see this is still in Gustaf Wingren's *Luther on Vocation* (Philadelphia: Muhlenberg, 1954).

as many preachers as you have transactions, goods, tools, and other equipment in your house and home."[6]

In Luther's theological thinking, these *Stände* ("estates" or "walks of life") are where vocations happen—the household (including the economy, and therefore occupations), the church, and the temporal authority. Because the temporal authority had the responsibility, in Luther's view, to make good laws and even to wage defensive war to protect the weak and innocent, those appointed by their office to do that work acted justly. Luther counseled sternly against the abuse of the office. A lack of order tends to be bad for the vulnerable. An unregulated economy will be a boon for some but disastrous for the weak. For this reason, and for no other reason, God provides the estate of the temporal authority. Luther thus saw enormous responsibilities placed on the shoulders of the princes, where they themselves might have been tempted to see merely perks of an office.

In Luther's time the word *vocation* was reserved exclusively for ordained clergy and for cloistered monastics—monks and nuns. They were the ones called by God to live a holy life, for they engaged in continual prayer and self-abasement. In extreme forms of this theology, ordinary believers relied on the merits of those with vocations for their own reward in heaven. Luther found this unbiblical, and his rhetoric shocked some but delighted most. He thought that a mother nursing a child, a father changing a diaper, a baker at his oven, and a carpenter in his shop were all doing something as God-pleasing as a monk. "God, with all his angels and creatures, is smiling—not because that father is washing diapers, but because he is doing so in Christian faith."[7]

Seeing creation in terms of what God commands for it not only supports the idea that *everyone* has a vocation—not just religious professionals—but also gives us a theological ethic. Everyone has a role to play and a calling to answer in the grand and lovely creation God calls into being. All the others with whom I have dealings are therefore not simply my rivals competing with me for scarce resources. To know that God creates me along with all others compels me to see other

In his comments on the fourth commandment in the Large Catechism, Luther addressed the responsibilities of parents and governing authorities this way: "The real trouble is that no one perceives or pays attention to [their duties]. Everyone acts as if God gave us children for our pleasure and amusement, gave us servants merely to put them to work like cows or donkeys, and gave us subjects to treat as we please, as if it were no concern of ours what they learn or how they live. No one is willing to see that this is the command of the divine Majesty, who will solemnly call us to account and punish us for its neglect. Nor is it recognized how very necessary it is to devote serious attention to the young. For if we want capable and qualified people for both the civil and the spiritual realms, we really must spare no effort, time, and expense in teaching and educating our children to serve God and the world" (Ten Commandments, par. 170–72 [BC 409–10]).

Luther believed that a father changing a diaper was doing something as God-pleasing as a monk, because he was doing it in Christian faith.

6. *The Sermon on the Mount*, LW 21:237; WA 32:495, 19–21, 36–38.   7. "The Estate of Marriage" (1522), LW 45:40; TAL 5:69.

people in the same light in which I see and understand myself. These others are not enemies, as I might have been tempted to think. Instead, God has created them, too, with all these gifts and care. God needs me to be there for these other loved and redeemed ones whose lives are sometimes quite literally in my hands.

Lastly, Luther said that God offers and commands all this "without any merit or worthiness of mine at all!" That little word *merit* is likely to call to mind associations with scouts and badges. But the late medieval theology that Luther and (to some extent) his readers had absorbed was shot through with the language of merit. The church's saints had accrued merit like a bank accrues interest, and that merit could be used to offset or cancel the sin of us non-saints. This kind of thinking provided the foundation for the theology of indulgences, for instance.[8] But theologians were usually subtler than that. An important distinction contrasted *condign merit* with *congruent merit*. *Condign merit* means something like this: A worker does a fantastic job, and thus she deserves a raise. Because her employer is fair, and in rational observation of her good work, she is given a raise because she has merited it. No medieval theologian thought that God owed salvation to human beings in response to the good works we do, because no matter how good those works are, they don't deserve the "pay raise" of heaven. However, some (especially among Luther's teachers) thought that once a person was saved and in a state of grace, the works he or she did would earn them reward through condign merit.

However, congruent merit was thought by many theologians, including some of Luther's teachers, to apply to the Christian life. *Congruent merit* means something like this: God knows that our very best efforts are not "worth" enough to merit salvation. But God desires so deeply that we do show forth our desire for salvation that God decides to count our insufficient efforts as sufficient merit. Therefore, we are saved by our works, not because our works are truly good, but because God is pleased by the effort. An elementary school teacher who loves her students will award grades based on effort, not on whether the stories the students wrote were publishable masterpieces. It is because of the love of the observer of the works that the doer of the works is saved, and thus the merit conferred by God is sufficient to salvation.

Luther said that the whole discussion of "merit" has *no place whatsoever* in the matter of creation. Instead, God's dealings with the world are all about grace. God freely gives benefits to and freely welcomes back to fellowship with God those who have violated the Commandments in God's good creation.[9]

Luther concluded the first article with an "ought." As he reminded Erasmus in their debate over free choice, an "ought" never implies a "can." We ought to thank, praise, serve, and obey, but we do not. In the Large Catechism he even said, "Here much could be said if we were to describe how few people believe this article. We all pass over it. . . . Therefore, if we believed it, this article should humble and terrify all of us. For we sin daily with eyes, ears, hands, body and soul, money and property, and with all that we have" (Creed, 20, 22 [BC 433]). Like the Ten Commandments, the first article of the Creed also reveals our sin. The second article first reveals God's merciful heart in Christ.

---

8. For a refresher on indulgences, see pages 68–69 in chapter 2.   9. Luther placed the "I believe" at the beginning of his explanations of each article and paraphrased the "Amen" by ending each article with "This is most certainly true."

The Second Article: On Redemption

♥ I believe in Jesus Christ, God's only Son, our Lord, who was conceived by the Holy Spirit, born of the virgin Mary, suffered under Pontius Pilate, was crucified, died, and was buried; he descended to the dead.[10] On the third day he rose again; he ascended into heaven, he is seated at the right hand of the Father, and he will come to judge the living and the dead.

What is this?* or *What does this mean?
I believe that Jesus Christ, true God, begotten of the Father in eternity, and also a true human being, born of the virgin Mary, is my Lord. He has redeemed me, a lost and condemned human being. He has purchased and freed me from all sins, from death, and from the power of the devil, not with gold or silver but with his holy, precious blood and with his innocent suffering and death. He has done all this in order that I may belong to him, live under him in his kingdom, and serve him in eternal righteousness, innocence, and blessedness, just as he is risen from the dead and lives and rules eternally. This is most certainly true.

Christ crucified (Matthew 26–27). In the printings of the Small Catechism during Luther's lifetime, each commandment, article of the Creed, petition of the Lord's Prayer, and sacrament was accompanied by a woodcut and (from 1536) references to the Bible story on which each picture was based.

One of the hardest things to do in theology is not to talk about everything else when you're talking about Jesus Christ. But this second part of the Creed does just that—it connects Jesus Christ to Christian history, beliefs, and life. Who is Jesus and what does Jesus "mean"? The second article answers this question by affirming things about Jesus. What is hidden under the surface of those answers is a long tradition of also saying who Jesus is not.

First, there is the apparently uncontroversial claim that Jesus was born. But actually, this was debated in the early church! By asserting that Jesus was born, the Creed rejects a heresy called *Docetism*. This is the view, prevalent in some circles in Christianity's first three centuries, that Jesus was not *actually* human, but that he simply *seemed* human (the Greek word *dokeo* means "seem"). Docetists thought that Jesus was most truly a spirit, and that he "wore" a human nature the way we might wear clothes. We wouldn't have recognized or understood a disembodied spirit, and so to communicate with us, Jesus put on a garment of humanity. Some docetic Christians thought that the Savior entered a human body but remained somehow quite distinct from that body. Others thought Simon of Cyrene

An early North Netherlandish painting of Christ carrying the cross aided by Simon of Cyrene, c. 1470.

---

10. Or, "he descended into hell," another translation of this text in widespread use.

not only carried Jesus' cross (Matthew 27:32; Mark 15:21; Luke 23:26) but also died on it in Jesus' place.[11] Another early Christian leader, Marcion (whom we'll meet again in just a moment), thought that Jesus simply appeared on earth as a grown man. He refuted much of the material in the gospels, such as Jesus' birth. So, the claim that Jesus was born is not so obvious as it might first appear.

The claim that Jesus is God's only Son refutes *Gnosticism*. This was a widespread, eclectic philosophy that imagined the spiritual soul ascending through a complex system of spirits, principles, and divine beings called *aeons*, which emanated from higher to lower beings. Gnostics tended to be dualists, placing a high value on spiritual knowledge (the Greek word *gnosis* means "knowledge") and a low value on bodies. Some even imagined that the "Creator of Earth" was an errant aeon who trapped souls in matter. To say that Christ is *begotten* of the Father who created heaven *and earth* meant that Gnostic emanation cannot explain Christian claims about Jesus.

Christians find a difference between *creating* and *begetting*. Everything that is "created" is made from a separate material; a coffee mug, for example, has nothing substantial in common with the potter who created it. On the other hand, "begotten" (as Luther used it here, borrowing language from the Nicene Creed) implies that the Son comes from the Father sort of like a child comes out of its parents' substance. Calling Christ "begotten" makes him divine and not a creature. Thus, calling the Son begotten made clear that the Son was "of the same substance" or "of one being" with the Father. In the debates at the Council of Nicaea, the bishops decided that there was never a time when the Son had not been being begotten from the Father, and so the begetting was eternal, not just at a specific moment in time. So, as you can see, there is a lot behind the Creed's claim—and Luther's explanation—that Jesus is the Son of God "begotten of the Father in eternity."

A particularly strange and jarringly specific claim the Creed makes is that Jesus "suffered under Pontius Pilate." Many figures in the Jesus story *aren't* named, so why mention Pilate? Why couldn't there be a clause in the Creed identifying Jesus as the one who "had a good talk with Nicodemus" or "was anointed by Mary of Bethany"? The very specificity of naming a minor Roman official may itself be the reason for the inclusion of Pontius Pilate's name. He was governor in Judea for about eight years, and so mentioning him hones in on the

---

11. "Second Treatise of the Great Seth," in Derek R. Nelson and William C. Placher, eds., *Readings in the History of Christian Theology*, vol. 1 (Louisville, KY: Westminster John Knox, 2015), 4–5.

Icon depicting the First Council of Nicaea.

Christ before Pilate. Hand-colored woodcut by Wilhelm Schreiber, c. 1490.

The Egyptian god Osiris was related to fertility and agriculture. In myth his body was burned and scattered in the Nile so that the cycle of planting and harvest could begin again.

historical particularity of Jesus. The death and resurrection of gods *as a story* was quite common in the ancient world. The Greek god Adonis, for example, and his Egyptian counterpart Osiris were the subjects of stories wherein they died and later came back to life. But no one took the stories literally. They were firmly in the "once upon a time" category. Early believers in Jesus Christ, perhaps wanting to distinguish their God who really did die and really was raised from the dead, highlighted that it was at *one particular moment in time* that Jesus suffered, died, was buried, and rose from the dead, namely, "under Pontius Pilate."

Finally, the claim that Jesus will come again to judge the living and the dead developed to repudiate *Marcionism*. Marcion advanced a theology that contrasted the bumbling fool God of ancient Israel with the loving God of Jesus Christ. Thus, he rejected the Hebrew Scriptures and even those parts of the New Testament that referred to them. Marcion's version of Christianity also included no Second Coming and no judgment.

Lucas Cranach painted himself into this scene. It shows a stream of blood falling from the side of the crucified Christ onto Cranach's head as he stands next to Martin Luther holding an open book. Now *that's* a personal Jesus! Weimar Altarpiece, 1555.

Luther certainly knew his Christology, and therefore (as all Christians did) confessed Jesus to be true God and truly human. Luther also knew that affirming certain claims about Jesus meant that—inevitably—you also had to say no to other claims. But some of Luther's thoughts about Christ were new and led in fascinating new directions. One of those directions was his emphasis on the *personal* nature of the confession of Christ. Luther freely confessed the objective facts about Jesus: that he was begotten, that the begetting is eternal, that he is truly God, and so forth. But all this matters because Jesus is *my Lord*. He chooses to exist in relation *to me*. Unlike much speculative theology of the scholastics in the Middle Ages, Luther did not reflect exclusively on what kind of "thing" God is, nor only on what kind of "person" Jesus Christ is. Luther's question was often "What is it *to have a God*?" or "Who is Jesus Christ *for me*?" The key is the relationship of trust. Faith in Christ means trust in his promises.

Metaphors

Good thinking often happens in metaphors. "Master metaphors" name a general way of relating two complex things in a way that helps us understand the things being compared. Think of the master metaphor "Time is money." This metaphor is related to expressions such as "Don't waste my time," "I've invested a lot of time in her," and "Is that worth your while?" How you think about time affects how you think about money, and vice versa.

Many metaphors are possible for describing the saving work of Jesus, or salvation. Salvation might be purification, in which case sin is like a stain. Or salvation might be a kind of healing, and sin then is disease or sickness. Try to find the metaphors Luther uses in his explanation to the second article of the Apostles' Creed when he describes Christ's work. "He has redeemed me, a lost and condemned human being. He has purchased and freed me from all sins, from death, and from the power of the devil, not with gold or silver but with his holy, precious blood and with his innocent suffering and death."

To redeem is to get out of captivity. A prisoner who is redeemed is let out of prison. A deposit on a bottle or a pawn is redeemed. But the person Luther was thinking of being redeemed was not only imprisoned but lost and condemned. *Lost* and *condemned* do not mean the same thing. To be purchased and to be freed do not mean exactly the same thing, either, and evoke quite different images and internal logics. The power keeping us captive is neither prison bars nor the confusion of being lost. The power keeping us captive is sin, death, and the devil. Sacrificial imagery, such as blood, suffering, and death, seems to appear in this explanation

This depiction of the medieval act of homage in France shows the liege lord placing his hands over the praying hands of the vassal.

Of the many pictures that Luther uses to describe Jesus' saving work, his comments in the catechisms revolve around the word *Lord* (Ger., *Herr*). In Luther's day there were all kinds of "lords"—not only the territorial or manorial lords but city councilmen (*Ratsherren*), heads of households (*Hausherren*), and even parish pastors (*Pfarrherren*). Living in a time before the development of absolutism, lords and subjects in Luther's day had reciprocal (though unequal) relationships with each other. The subject obeyed and belonged to the lord; the lord was required to defend the subject and, for example, pay the ransom were they kidnapped. In the Large Catechism he describes it this way: "What is it 'to become a lord'? It means that [Christ] has redeemed and released me from sin, from the devil, from death, and from all misfortune. Before this I had no lord or king, but was captive under the power of the devil. I was condemned to death and entangled in sin and blindness. . . . Those tyrants and jailers have now been routed and their place has been taken by Jesus Christ, the Lord of life, righteousness, and every good and blessing" (Creed, par. 27, 30 [BC 434]).

too, but in fact was for Luther the ransom price and reflects 1 Peter 1:18-19. How are we to make sense of all these metaphors? What is going on here? Luther's use of metaphor points to the need always to rethink and express anew the one, timeless story of Jesus Christ. The story of Christ and his meaning is always bigger than the container we use for it. The variety of different ways to think of Christ's saving work kindles the Christian imagination and expresses timeless truths in timely ways.

Exchange

Another helpful way to view Luther's understanding of salvation, Christ's saving work, is through what Luther called the *joyous exchange*. In this exchange, Christ takes on our sin, brokenness, utter lostness, and death and gives us his blessedness, joy, holiness, and life. Commenting on this theme in his 1535 commentary on Galatians, Luther wrote, "By this fortunate exchange with us he took upon himself our sinful person and granted us his innocent and victorious person. Clothed and dressed in this, we are freed from the curse of the Law, because Christ himself voluntarily became a curse for us."[12] In the mystery of faith, the benefits of grace are conferred on you, the believer, and your pains are taken by Christ. To participate over and over in this joyful exchange simply *is* the life of faith.[13] Luther called this "the possession of the sacred cross."

Luther talked about different "exchanges" that take place between Christ and believers. Imprisonment may be exchanged for freedom, brokenness for holiness, evil for blessedness, or sin for righteousness. All that sin does to us is transferred to Christ, who brings these burdens to the cross, where they are conquered and covered forever by his righteous suffering. Thus freed by faith in Christ, we are empowered to serve the neighbor freely as Christ served us, and we thereby belong to Christ. In this great and joyful exchange, as Luther said elsewhere, "We become Christs, with and without an apostrophe." That is, we become "christs," and we become "Christ's."[14]

The Joyous Exchange

Already in 1516, in a letter to a fellow Augustinian, Luther used the language of the exchange of Christ's righteousness for our sin (LW 48:12–13). Likewise, in *The Freedom of a Christian* of 1520 (TAL 1:499–501) and in its forerunner from 1519, *Two Kinds of Righteousness* (LW 31:297–99), Luther used this imagery and connected it to the marriage of Christ and the soul. Roman marriage law distinguished between property (what one owned) and possession (what one had full use of) and held that in marriage the property of the one spouse became the possession of the other and vice versa. This "joyous exchange" (a word used by Luther in the German version of *The Freedom of a Christian*) occurs through the wedding ring of faith where our sin becomes Christ's and Christ's righteousness ours.

A woodcut of "Law and Gospel" by Lucas Cranach the Elder with Christ's blood covering the now believing Adam.

---

12. LW 26:284.   13. See also sermons from this time period where the exchange theme is prominent in LW 51:285 and LW 51:316.

14. "*Christi sumus in nominativo et genitivo.*" LW 22:286.

Our access to Christ, and thus our exchange with him, is connected theologically to baptism. In the waters of baptism, the old, sinful person is drowned and the new person is raised to new (resurrected) life. At the last, the believer will "serve him in eternal righteousness, innocence, and blessedness." Luther typically understood freedom, even the perfect freedom of eternal life in heaven, as being related to service. Freedom does not mean the absence of external restraint, but instead means freely and in faith devoting yourself fully to the God who is fully directed toward you.

The Third Article: On Being Made Holy

The first Pentecost with tongues of fire coming from the disciples' mouths (see Acts 2; Rev. 11:5).

♥ I believe in the Holy Spirit, the holy catholic church, the communion of saints, the forgiveness of sins, the resurrection of the body, and the life everlasting.

What is this? **or** *What does this mean?*
I believe that by my own understanding or strength I cannot believe in Jesus Christ my Lord or come to him, but instead the Holy Spirit has called me through the gospel, enlightened me with his gifts, made me holy and kept me in the true faith, just as he calls, gathers, enlightens, and makes holy the whole Christian church on earth and keeps it with Jesus Christ in the one common, true faith. Daily in this Christian church the Holy Spirit abundantly forgives all sins—mine and those of all believers. On the last day the Holy Spirit will raise me and all the dead and will give to me and all believers in Christ eternal life. This is most certainly true.

Luther's words are rather shocking: "I believe that by my own understanding or strength I cannot believe in Jesus Christ my Lord or come to him." It may not be an overstatement to say that many of us, if we are honest with ourselves, believe exactly the opposite. To say that the Spirit does these things (calls, gathers, enlightens, makes holy) is to say that the human being is not the one acting but the one acted upon. In matters of faith we *undergo* rather than *do*. Because faith is a gift,[15] then faith comes to us; it is not generated by us. This is startling news to able-bodied, hardworking, self-reliant

---

15. Ephesians 2:8; 1 Corinthians 12:9.

North Americans who are used to being recognized for what we achieve. But every time faith becomes a work we do or a decision we make, we are back to merit. To be needy and to have to receive faith as a gift rather than earn it is a bitter pill, even if it is medicine we dearly need.

Notice how in Luther's explanation *inability* becomes an article of faith: "I believe that . . . I *cannot*." In other words, it is necessary to believe in and to confess your own limits. Knowing your limits is a good thing. A parent teaching a child to walk, ride a bike, or use a fork and knife knows how vital it is to be clear about what the child can and cannot do. Likewise, no matter how resistant we might be to the teaching that our limitations are real, serious, and good for us, it is important to confess that particular inability. Then it is not merely a matter of knowledge but of experience. I can by my own reason and might believe in "a" god, one of my devising and idolatrous worship. I can imagine and fall in love with a picture of Christ, or a stereotype of God, but not God. God the Holy Spirit creates faith through the gospel, forcing us to confess our inability to do so on our own.

Yet the very next phrase shows the result. When I confess my inability to believe on my own and thus am driven to call on God to give faith, Jesus becomes my Lord and I become more valuable than I ever could have imagined. How? Because "the Holy Spirit has called me through the gospel, enlightened me with his gifts, made me holy and kept me in the true faith." And what is more, this thing that I have experienced, which is momentous and powerful on its own, is multiplied in force by millions because the same thing has been experienced by the whole Christian church on earth.

Lots of verbs (action words) are associated with the Holy Spirit. The Holy Spirit *calls*, *enlightens*, *gathers*, and *makes holy* (or *sanctifies*). Elsewhere in Luther's writing you get the sense that the Holy Spirit is kind of the "verb of the word." Here is the word of God on the page. How is it going to leap off the page, reach my ear, and attach to my heart? The Holy Spirit is the action verb that does all of those actions. But perhaps the most important verb the Spirit has is *raise*. That is what the Spirit of God did

One way to understand the passive nature of faith that nevertheless involves the entire person is to use the image of falling in love. We say "falling" because love can never be reduced to a decision or to mere knowledge. Yet the person is "in love" and thus may do all kinds of things—not to earn the beloved's affection but precisely because one already lives in that affection. The means through which this love (that is, faith) occurs is the gospel.

A gravestone with the Latin inscription *Resurgam*, which means "I shall rise."

A woodcut of the Second Coming in Luther's collection of sermons on the gospels appointed for the church year.

for and to the Son of God on Easter. The Spirit of the one whom Jesus called his Father raised him from the dead.[16] Now the death of his body is a past fact, not a future possibility. Now death is only behind Jesus, and so his availability to us is truly eternal and his promises for us are true unconditionally. The Holy Spirit is in the resurrection business, and he will not stop with Jesus. Indeed, "On the last day the Holy Spirit will raise me and all the dead and will give to me and all believers in Christ eternal life."

Two comments must be made about how Luther approached this issue of God raising the dead to life. The first is how the connections of time and eternity make it difficult to say what "going to heaven when you die" means. The second is the merely fascinating question of how the concept of universal salvation plays out

---

16. See Romans 8:11: "If the Spirit of him who raised Jesus from the dead dwells in you, he who raised Christ from the dead will give life to your mortal bodies also through his Spirit that dwells in you."

in Luther's catechism. Let's take them in that order. First, when you die, what happens to you? Well, two answers, both of which are right. In one sense (the physical, earthbound sense), you die and you stay dead until God raises *you* and everyone else on the Last Day. But in another sense (from the perspective of eternity), when you die you remain in communion with God. Because your death means the (temporary) end of your body and soul, there's no "you" there to wait in the sense of "you are waiting for God to raise you." Like a sleeping person who wakes up, the waking up and the falling asleep are instantaneous to the unconscious sleeper.

This twin notion of the dead being and staying truly dead but also being "with God" can be shown in the way Luther dealt with an awful tragedy. In 1542 his daughter Magdalena, a healthy girl of thirteen, suddenly became ill. Both parents were especially fond of "Lenchen," perhaps because her birth had helped them cope with the earlier loss of infant Elizabeth. Father Luther consoled the dying girl, asking if she was willing to go to her Father in heaven. She calmly affirmed her faith, then died in Luther's arms.[17] Katie wept for days, and Luther was virtually undone. As he had done when his father died, Luther grabbed his psalter and ran to pray alone. When Magdalena was placed in her casket, Luther could hear the pounding of the hammer as the undertakers nailed the lid shut. Luther cried out, "Go ahead—close it! She will rise again at the last day!" Thus, we see that the dead really are dead—body and soul and whatever else they might have been—and remain so until the last day when God will raise them. Yet because of the simultaneity of time and eternity, it is also right to affirm a kind of presence and blessedness with God that the dead experience. Just after Magdalena died, Luther composed a poem for her epitaph:

Death of Magdalena by Lucas Cranach, 1542.

> I, Lena, Luther's beloved girl
> Sleep among the saints of the world
> And lie here at peace and rest,
> For now I am our God's own guest.
>
> A child of death I was, 'tis true
> From mortal seed my mother bore me through;
> Now I live and am rich with God.
> And so I thank Christ's death and blood.[18]

Let us go now to the merely fascinating question, the issue of universal salvation. What can be said of Luther's views on this matter from a short phrase in the catechism? Perhaps not much. He clearly followed the Creed in his paraphrase here and insists that all will be raised. But here at least, rather than

---

17. LW 54:430. 18. WA TR 5:196.

focusing on who will enter eternal life and who will be damned to eternal hell, Luther concentrated on what he knew best: that believers in Christ will be welcomed to eternal life. Rather than making eternal damnation into an article of faith, Luther stuck to the good news from scripture that those with faith in God are raised to blessedness in glory. As for the others, it is best to leave them in God's hands, who alone will judge. Whether God, in God's infinite wisdom, justice, and mercy, will deal with unfaith in a way that brings faith is God's business. We can only cast our hope on the God who raised Jesus from the dead.

Back to earth. What can we make of this phrase "Daily in this Christian church the Holy Spirit abundantly forgives all sins"? This is the return to baptism. We believe in one baptism for the forgiveness of sins. But every day after that baptism, we sin. So we must return continually to the work of the Spirit to forgive all sins and come back to fellowship with God. What is meant by "forgiveness of sins" is both timeless and time-bound. It is timeless because all *sin* means is "that which is against God." Evil actions are against God, despair is against God, ugliness and hatred are against God, and so on. Always has been, always will be, thus timeless. But "forgiveness of sins" is also time-bound. Luther and his colleagues understood sin to be almost entirely a moral issue. What does that mean?

In the sixteenth century, "forgiveness of sins" was often a convenient shorthand that stood in for all kinds of reconciliations, redemptions, and healings. Christians experienced such anxiety as *guilt*. That is, fear and regret led to a sense of moral wrongness. Our experience today is perhaps a bit different. We may experience anxiety as not only guilt but also *despair*. For example, consider the ways in which we sometimes move from ignorance of a societal problem (like our earth's fragility or the disasters of our criminal justice system) to despair and hopelessness. Problems seem so big and complex; our ability to make any real change seems so small; and we feel so complicit in the systems of evil we experience that the feeling of despair is close at hand. While this is not primarily a moral issue (that is, we may not always feel "guilty" about climate change or systemic racism), it is still against God, and therefore it is sin and in need of the work of the Spirit to bring hope and healing.

The church is therefore the primary (but not the only!) place where the Spirit's work is done. The church is not a museum for perfect people, but a hospital for those who are in need of healing. The Holy Spirit "calls, gathers, enlightens, and makes holy the whole Christian church on earth and keeps it with Jesus Christ in the one common, true faith." Those are present-tense verbs, and they are ongoing. The work is not done. As Luther wrote elsewhere:

> This life, therefore, is not righteousness but growth in righteousness, not health but healing, not being but becoming, not rest but exercise. We are not now what we shall be, but we are on the way. The process is not yet finished, but it is actively going on. This is not the end but it is the right road. At present, everything does not gleam and sparkle, but everything is being cleansed.[19]

Our experience of the church is never one of perfect health, because it is populated entirely by sick people. But by faith we sense that healing is all around us. One of Luther's very last sermons makes this point elegantly. "We are now under the Physician's care. The sin, it is true, is wholly forgiven, but it has not been

---

19. LW 32:24. *Defense and Explanation of All the Articles*. Translation altered.

wholly purged. . . . The Holy Spirit must cleanse the wounds daily. Therefore this life is a hospital; the sin has really been forgiven, but it has not yet been healed."[20]

One way to view the Creed (and the Trinity) is "backward," so to speak. Although through time one goes logically from creation to redemption in Christ to being made holy through the Holy Spirit, we experience God in reverse. Luther put it this way in the Large Catechism:

> In all three articles God himself has revealed and opened to us the most profound depths of his fatherly heart and his pure, unutterable love. For this very purpose he created us, so that he might redeem us and make us holy, and, moreover, having granted and bestowed upon us everything in heaven and on earth [in creation], he has also given us his Son and his Holy Spirit, through whom he brings us to himself. For . . . we could never come to recognize the Father's favor and grace were it not for the LORD Christ, who is a mirror of the Father's heart. Apart from him we see nothing but an angry and terrible judge. But neither could we know anything of Christ had it not been revealed by the Holy Spirit.[21]

Thus, the Holy Spirit reveals Christ who is the "mirror of the Father's heart."[22] This is Luther's experience-filled, comforting approach to the Creed, which distills for us the very heart of the Christian gospel and, thus, of God.

In the 1960s an American Lutheran, Jaroslav Vajda, wrote a popular hymn for holy communion (*Evangelical Lutheran Worship*, #460), "Now the Silence." Not only does it contain no active verbs (or punctuation), but it, too, confesses the Trinity in reverse: "Now the Spirit's visitation Now the Son's epiphany Now the Father's blessing Now Now Now"

---

20. LW 51:373. It is characteristic of the later Luther that this tenderness and insight are paired with brutal criticisms of the Wittenbergers to whom he is preaching.   21. Large Catechism, Creed, par. 64–65 (BC 439–40).   22. Large Catechism, Creed, par. 65 (BC 440).

4

The Lord's Prayer

Praying in Luther's Time

The Ten Commandments tell us how we are to live in relation to God and our fellow humans. The Apostles' Creed confesses God's actions in creating, redeeming, and making us holy. But, as Luther writes in the Large Catechism, "we are in such a situation that no one can keep the Ten Commandments perfectly, even though he or she has begun to believe."[1] Now we learn how to talk with this God—and we learn to know God as the God who hears prayer.

Luther placed the Lord's Prayer third in his catechism. After hearing the words that God speaks to us, words of command and promise, words that tell us how God wants us to live and what God does for us, we are now offered the opportunity to respond. We might even say we are encouraged to "talk back" to God. Our words come in response to God's words to us. The catechism reflects the idea that God is in conversation with us, speaking to us and wanting to hear from us. Have you ever thought of the Christian faith as a conversation? Have you ever considered that God urgently wants to hear from you, especially in your need? So urgently that God commands you to pray? Have you ever realized that God's desire for relationship with you

Medieval catechisms often used the ordering of Creed, Lord's Prayer, Ten Commandments. In this way of thinking, the Creed represented "mere faith" (a knowledge of facts) that was insufficient for salvation. Such faith needed to be formed by works of love into saving faith. The Lord's Prayer became a way for people to ask for help in this process. Luther rejected this whole approach. He believed that faith—not simply a knowledge of facts but rather trust in God's saving work in Jesus Christ—was sufficient for salvation.

---

1. Large Catechism, Lord's Prayer, par. 2 (BC 440).

is so great that God promises to hear you? Luther knew that what we believe about prayer tells us much about what kind of God we have and how we understand our relationship with God.

In Luther's writings on prayer, he repeatedly emphasized both God's command to pray and God's promise to hear prayer. This echoes his understanding of God's work generally in the world—a work comprising both God's good intentions for our lives on this earth and God's good promises of mercy now and in eternity. Not only do we hear God's command to pray and promise to hear, but God even gives us the words to use in praying. "God takes the initiative and puts into our mouths the very words and approach we are to use. In this way we see how deeply concerned he is about our needs, and we should never doubt that such prayer pleases him and will assuredly be heard."[2]

Luther encouraged regular prayer, and he saw the Lord's Prayer as the paradigmatic prayer. Writing to his barber in 1535, Luther urged, "It is a good thing to let prayer be the first business of the morning and the last at night."[3] While urging and encouraging prayer, Luther and his followers encountered many misconceptions about prayer. Barriers to prayer existed then just as they do now. Consider some of the problematic prayer practices and beliefs that Luther confronted, many of which we still share:

Jesus Teaching His Disciples to Pray from the 1549 Leipzig edition of the Small Catechism.

1. Medieval people thought they had first to become worthy before God would hear them. So they hesitated to approach God and prayed instead to saints as intermediaries. Luther emphasized that we pray relying on God's command to pray and promise to hear us. Worthiness is not an issue—in fact, in a sermon published in 1519 Luther commented, "We pray after all because we are unworthy to pray. The very fact that we are unworthy and that we dare to pray confidently, trusting only in the faithfulness of God, makes us worthy to pray and to have our prayer answered. . . . Your worthiness does not help you; and your unworthiness does not hinder you."[4]

The Lord's Prayer by contemporary Chinese artist He Qi.

2. Large Catechism, Lord's Prayer, par. 22 (BC 443). 3. "A Simple Way to Pray: How One Should Pray, for Peter, the Master Barber" (1535), TAL 4:257. 4. *A Sermon on Prayer and Procession during Rogation Days* (1519), TAL 4:153.

2. Medieval people were taught to pray to the saints and to the Virgin Mary. Because medieval people felt they were not good enough to approach the holy and righteous God, they thought it would be helpful to have a particularly laudable person advocate for them before God. Luther pointed out that "there is not a single word of God commanding us to call on either angels or saints to intercede for us, and we have no example of it in the Scriptures. . . . Thus the worship of saints shows itself to be nothing but human twaddle, man's own invention apart from the word of God and the Scriptures."[5] In contrast, God, the Father of our Lord Jesus Christ, has both commanded us to pray and promised to hear us.[6]

A miniature altarpiece depicting the Fifteen Mysteries and the Virgin of the Rosary by a Netherlandish painter, c. 1515–20. Depicted in the upper registers are fifteen mysteries associated with Mary's life: five joyful, five sorrowful, and five glorious. The scene at the base illustrates a miracle by which a man was saved from death when he prayed to Mary. Each Hail Mary he recited became a rose that the Christ child then wove into a garland.

---

5. *On Translating: An Open Letter* (1530). LW 35:198–99. 6. See also the Augsburg Confession (Latin), XXI.2 (BC 59): "Scripture does not teach calling on the saints or pleading for help from them. For it sets before us Christ alone as mediator, atoning sacrifice, high priest, and intercessor. He is to be called upon, and he has promised that our prayers will be heard. Furthermore, he strongly approves this worship most of all, namely, that he be called upon in all afflictions."

3. Medieval Christianity regarded prayer as a good work. It could, for example, be used as a work of satisfaction in the confession process. Luther rejected the view that prayer is our good work, done to impress God or somehow to "make up" for our sins. Instead, Luther understood prayer as real conversation and communication with God—a result of God's forgiveness and mercy, not a cause.

4. Medieval Christianity emphasized repetition of prayers. Since medieval Christians viewed prayer as a good work, repeating that good work was considered beneficial. Luther believed God hears us because God has promised to hear us—not because we keep repeating ourselves. Luther advocated persistent prayer but not mindless repetition. In the Large Catechism, Luther said we should "call upon God incessantly . . . drum into his ears our prayer,"[7] but at the same time rejected the "kind of babbling and bellowing that used to pass for prayer in the church."[8]

5. Medieval Christianity thought prayer was primarily a work for the clergy. Luther believed God had commanded—in the second commandment— all people to pray and had promised to hear all people. Further, medieval Christianity sought to make monastic prayer practices the pattern for laypeople. Such patterns included praying at certain times of the day and praying particular prayers (often to particular saints) at certain times of the year and on certain occasions.[9] Luther rejected this, believing that these patterns were of no use to laity and encouraged false ideas about prayer.

What are the obstacles to prayer today? What distracts or discourages us from praying? Why do we fail to call on God? Why do we seek help elsewhere?

Prayer was an important part of Luther's life. Luther recognized early in his work that prayer needed to be taught, for although the need to pray comes naturally, the *words* to pray do not always come naturally. Luther taught prayer in many ways and in many genres of literature—prayer book, catechism, biblical commentary, sermons, even in polemics. His writings on the subject extend from very early in his career as a reformer to the end of his life. During Lent 1517 (before the *Ninety-Five Theses*!), Luther preached a series of sermons on the Lord's Prayer.[10] His "Appeal for Prayer against the Turks"[11] dates from 1541, just five years before his death. Multiple editions of Luther's works on prayer show that they were widely used. Those sermons from 1517 appeared at least twenty-three times between 1518 and 1525 in places as diverse as Basel, Leipzig, Wittenberg, Augsburg, and Hamburg.

Polemics
As soon as Luther published his *Ninety-Five Theses* in 1517, he came under attack. As a result, many of his tracts were pointed responses to his opponents that defended his own positions and harshly rejected theirs.

---

7. Large Catechism, Lord's Prayer, par. 2 (BC 440).   8. Large Catechism, Lord's Prayer, par. 7 (BC 441).   9. See, for example, Dietrich Kolde's "A Fruitful Mirror or Small Handbook for Christians" (1480), in Denis Janz, *Three Reformation Catechisms: Catholic, Anabaptist, Lutheran* (Lewiston, NY: Edwin Mellen, 1982), 29–130. Chapter 26 sets out an expectation that laypeople will follow a monastic structure in their prayers.   10. *An Exposition of the Lord's Prayer for Simple Laymen*, LW 42:15–81.   11. LW 43:213–41.

His 1519 "A Sermon on Prayer and Procession during Rogation Days"[12] was reprinted thirteen times between 1519 and 1523 alone. Luther's *Betbüchlein* (Little Prayer Book) was printed seventeen times between 1522 and 1525 and at least forty-four times total by the end of the century.[13] Even his "Appeal for Prayer against the Turks" was reprinted ten times in 1541–42.[14] It's clear that if you want to consider Luther's impact in his time, you have to consider his writings on prayer because they were so popular and widespread.

In his lectures on 1 John (1527), Luther complained, "In the past . . . we did not know how to pray but knew only how to chatter and to read prayers. God pays no attention to this."[15] Luther was trying to create a new evangelical prayer practice, one that encouraged persistent, thoughtful, bold prayer in contrast to the mechanical recitation of prayers, done largely by a "praying" (monastic) class. In his commentary on Psalm 118 (1530), he warned: "You must never doubt that God is aware of your distress and hears your prayer. You must not pray haphazardly or simply shout into the wind. Then you would mock and tempt God. It would be better not to pray at all, than to pray like the priests and monks."[16] Instead of using prayer to gain God's favor, or repeating a prayer because you think the repetition itself pleases God, you can rest in the confidence that God has created a new relationship and encourages you to pray within that relationship. You may address God with boldness and confidence.[17]

Evening prayer.

During his 1527–28 visits to congregations in rural Saxony, Luther discovered that people who called themselves Christian and were baptized were generally unfamiliar with the Christian faith.[18] He mentioned specifically that they did not know the Lord's Prayer. Luther saw teaching this prayer as an important pastoral task and the knowledge of this prayer as one of the marks of a Christian. Do we still see it as a priority to teach, learn, and speak this prayer in our congregations and homes?

Luther considered the Lord's Prayer the very best of all prayers.[19] In *An Exposition of the Lord's Prayer for Simple Laymen* (1519), he wrote:

> Since our Lord is the author of this prayer, it is without a doubt the most sublime, the loftiest, and the most excellent. If he, the good and faithful Teacher, had known a better one, he would surely have taught us that too.[20]

Luther viewed church practices such as prayer (or even the sacraments) as fraught with two dangers. On the one hand, when prayer becomes rote we might imagine that it does good simply through mindless repetition (effective *ex opere operato*, by the mere performance of the act). On the other, prayer could be thought of as a virtuous act done by us to earn something (effective *ex opere operantis*, by the work of the one performing the act). Either way, the promise of God and faith in that promise are compromised and we end up trusting ourselves.

---

12. TAL 4:147–57. LW 42:83–93. The publication statistics come from *Verzeichnis der im deutschen Sprachbereich erschienenen Drucke des XVI. Jahrhunderts* (Munich: Bayerische Staatsbibliothek; Herzog August Bibliothek in Wolfenbüttel, Stuttgart: Hiersemann [1983–]) (hereafter: VD 16), L6325–39. 13. VD 16, L4081–124. 14. VD 16, L1934–43. 15. LW 30:324. 16. LW 14:61. 17. In "A Simple Way to Pray," Luther noted, "A good prayer should not be lengthy or drawn out, but frequent and ardent" (TAL 4:278). 18. See chapter 1 for a fuller description of what Luther encountered during his visits. 19. The Lord's Prayer was commonly included in medieval catechisms and prayer books. Luther sees it as the preeminent prayer, not simply one among many. 20. LW 42, 21.

In his *Little Prayer Book* (1522), he wrote:

> And I am convinced that when Christians rightly pray the Lord's Prayer at any time or use any portion of it as they may desire, their praying is more than adequate.[21] What is important for a good prayer is not many words, as Christ says in Matthew 6[:7], but rather a turning to God frequently and with heartfelt longing, and doing so without ceasing [1 Thess. 5:17].
>
> And herewith I urge everyone . . . to get accustomed to praying this plain, ordinary Christian prayer. The longer one devotes one's self to this kind of praying, the more sweet and joyous it becomes. To that end may this prayer's Master, our dear Lord Jesus Christ, help us.[22]

In his Large Catechism (1529) Luther commented: "There is no nobler prayer to be found on earth, for it has the powerful testimony that God loves to hear it."[23] For Luther, authentic communication, honest prayer, does not mean you have to be creative or extemporaneous. We can use the words Christ gave us.

A focus on the Lord's Prayer as the primary and paradigmatic prayer became typical of Luther's movement.[24] This contrasted sharply with medieval teaching, which typically included many prayers, such as the Hail Mary and prayers for the monastic hours. Rather than trying to force people's prayers to conform to monastic patterns, Luther focused on the prayer Jesus taught and its relationship to our everyday lives.

Luther also recommended the use of catechetical elements to structure prayers and shape content. He demonstrated this both in his *Little Prayer Book* (1522) and in his letter to his barber, "A Simple Way to Pray" (1535). In each he expanded the petitions[25] of the Lord's Prayer into lengthier prayers. But he also cautioned:

> You should also know that I do not want you to recite all these words in your prayer. That would make it nothing but mere chatter and idle prattle, read word for word out of a book as were the rosaries by the laity and the prayers of the clerics and monks. Rather do I want your heart to be stirred and guided concerning the thoughts that ought to be comprehended in the Lord's Prayer. These thoughts may be expressed, if your heart is rightly warmed and inclined toward prayer, in many different ways and with more words or fewer. . . . It may happen occasionally that I may wander among so many ideas in one petition that I forgo the other six. If such an abundance of good thoughts comes to us we ought to disregard the other petitions, make room for such thoughts, listen in silence, and under no circumstances obstruct them. The Holy Spirit himself preaches here, and one word of his sermon is far better than a thousand of our prayers. Many times I have learned more from one prayer than I might have learned from much reading and speculation.[26]

---

21. Luther here implicitly rejects the imposition of monastic prayer practices on the laity. Such attempts manifested themselves, for example, in attempts to encourage laypeople to pray in accordance with the canonical hours. See Kolde's catechism, "A Fruitful Mirror or Small Handbook for Christians," 88–90, where laypeople are given a prayer for each canonical hour. Nevertheless, Luther also saw the good in regular prayer and provided traditional forms of morning, evening, and mealtime prayers in the Small Catechism. See chapter 7. 22. *Little Prayer Book*, TAL 4:166. 23. Large Catechism, Lord's Prayer, par. 23 (BC 443). 24. Giorgio Caravale details the efforts of the Roman Catholic Church to control prayer, devotional, and liturgical materials in sixteenth- and seventeenth-century Italy. Vigilant defenders of Roman Catholic orthodoxy regarded the mere fact that a work focused on the Lord's Prayer as evidence that it was a vehicle of Lutheran content. Giorgio Caravale, *Forbidden Prayer: Church Censorship and Devotional Literature in Renaissance Italy*, trans. Peter Dawson (Burlington, VT: Ashgate, 2011). 25. In Luther's German, the word for petition was *Bitte*, translated simply as "request." 26. "A Simple Way to Pray" (1535), TAL 4:263–64.

In 1535 Luther wrote movingly of his own use of the Lord's Prayer but also criticized its misuse:

> To this day I suckle at the Lord's Prayer like a child, and as an old man eat and drink from it and never get my fill. It is the very best prayer, even better than the psalter, which is so very dear to me. It is surely evident that a real master composed and taught it. What a great shame that the prayer of such a master is prattled and chattered so irreverently all over the world! How many pray the Lord's Prayer several thousand times in the course of a year, and if they were to keep on doing so for a thousand years they would not have tasted nor prayed one letter or one stroke of a letter of it! In a word, the Lord's Prayer is the greatest martyr on earth (along with the name and word of God). Everybody tortures and abuses it; few take comfort and joy in its proper use.[27]

Luther and the Lord's Prayer

For what do we pray? Luther said we pray that God may "give, preserve, and increase in us faith and the fulfillment of the Ten Commandments and remove all that stands in our way and hinders us in this regard."[28] That is, we pray that everything described in the first two parts of the catechism may be true for us. God's good gifts in creation, redemption, and sanctification do not produce a desire to live any way we want but rather produce a desire to live according to God's will as expressed in the Ten Commandments, and to trust the God whose works we confess in the Creed.

Notice that Luther does *not* divide the Lord's Prayer into petitions that pertain to God and those that pertain to me. Rather, for Luther, *all* petitions unite God and me. No separation exists between God's work and the result for me!

Notice some things about all the petitions:

- Prayer springs from trust in God. We can talk with this God because we know this God from the first two parts—Commandments and Creed—and we have experienced this trustworthy God.

- Our attitude is to be **bold**. Luther says we are to "call upon God incessantly and to drum into his ears our prayer."[29] We can ask God bluntly and clearly for what we most desperately need—needs revealed through the Commandments and the Creed.

- We don't make abstract requests. In the petitions, we describe exactly what we want.

---

27. TAL 4:266–67.   28. Large Catechism, Lord's Prayer, par. 2 (BC 440–41).   29. Large Catechism, Lord's Prayer, par. 2 (BC 440).

- We expect that something will really happen. The first three petitions describe how we can recognize that God is responding to our requests.

- We pray concerning *all* our needs—bodily, spiritual, and material.

- Our lives and our relationship with God are constantly threatened by the forces of evil. Yet we pray in confidence that God will preserve us and this relationship.

Introduction

♥ Our Father in heaven.

What is this? or **What does this mean?**
With these words God wants to attract us, so that we come to believe he is truly our Father and we are truly his children, in order that we may ask him boldly and with complete confidence, just as loving children ask their loving father.

In one of his earliest expositions of the Lord's Prayer (LW 42:26), Luther reminded his hearers that Christ "does not want anyone to pray only for himself, but for all humankind. He does not teach us to say 'My Father' but 'Our Father.'"

This introductory explanation mirrors Luther's attitude toward prayer—praying the Lord's Prayer is not about rote recitation but rather children begging God for help.[30] Think about how God is described here—as one who wishes to entice, attract, and encourage you to pray. This God wants so desperately to be in conversation with you that God not only commands you to pray (second commandment), but also draws you to prayer by promising to be a loving Father.

Luther added this explanation to the introduction in 1531 (the Small Catechism was first published in 1529). The Swedish scholar Birgit Stolt has traced how Luther's view of God as Father changed because of his own life experience. While a younger Luther often saw God the Father as grim and/or awe-inspiring, "the Luther of later years had a far more endearing image of God the Father than the young theologian."[31] Luther had become a father and was amazed by the depth and intensity of his own love for his children.[32] By the early 1530s, Luther saw God the Father as "kind, loving, comforting, joygiving" and felt that he was talking with "a father not principally awe-inspiring but a source of trust and joy."[33]

Luther's catechisms vary in how they address God. In the Commandments, Luther most often simply used the word *God*. Even in the first article of the Creed, he concentrated on God as creator, using the word *father* as an adjective. First with the second article do we discover God as "Lord." Here, in a section added to the second edition of the Small Catechism, Luther now referred to God as Father. His own recent experience as a grieving father (his infant daughter Elizabeth died in 1528) may have helped him discover God's "fatherly" heart.

---

30. The German word for prayer, *Beten*, was always associated with asking rather than with praise and thanksgiving, which Luther viewed then as separate responses to God's grace.   31. Birgit Stolt, "Martin Luther on God as a Father," *Lutheran Quarterly* 8 (1994): 389.   32. Stolt describes Luther's profound grief at the loss of his young daughter Elizabeth at the age of eight months in 1528. In a letter to Nicholas Hausmann, he wrote, "Never before would I have believed that a father's heart could have such tender feelings for his children" (LW 49:203).   33. Stolt, "Martin Luther on God as a Father," 389, 392.

Luther's statement that we may ask God "boldly and with complete confidence, just as loving children ask their loving father" contrasted sharply with some medieval explanations of this introduction. One medieval catechist, Dietrich Kolde, advised his readers to ask in three ways; only the third sounds anything like Luther. "First, you should ask as a criminal who asks the judge not to sentence him to death. Second, you should ask as a poor man asking a rich lord for gifts and possessions. Third, you should ask as a dear child fondly asks his dear father."[34]

Luther emphasized that at all times, and especially in times of need, we should turn first to God for help. We should not seek help from others—not a saint, not the Virgin Mary, and not any other god. We pray to God the Father, not to anyone else. No one else has promised to hear us and has the capability of hearing us. It is also important to recognize that asking for God's help means recognizing that God may send other humans to give us that help.[35]

Luther sees the Christian faith in terms of relationship. Luther was well aware that some earthly fathers were not as they should be, but rather than reject father language, he used it to teach what God the heavenly Father really is like and what our relationship with our heavenly Father looks like. In that relationship, we may boldly ask and be completely confident that God will hear.

Luther never doubted we should address God as Father. This name tells us what we need to know about what kind of God we have. However, Luther also recognized that sometimes we do not see God as loving but rather as angry and distant. Luther addressed this situation in a sermon for Maundy Thursday, which used Christ's prayer in Gethsemane as a lesson on the form and content of prayer. Christ prayed, "My Father, if it is possible, so take this cup from me, but not my will, rather your will be done." This, declared Luther, is the proper form of prayer that we also should use in temptation and misery. We address God as Father. Even though we see only God's anger, we still understand him as our Father who

In his 1522 *Little Prayer Book*, Luther addressed the contrast between the heavenly Father and earthly fathers: "Moreover, since you are not a physical father here on earth but a spiritual Father in heaven, not like an earthly, mortal father who dies and is not always dependable and may not be able to help himself, show us what an immeasurably better Father you are and teach us to regard earthly fatherhood, fatherland, friends, possessions, body and blood as far less in value than you. Grant us, O Father, that we may be your heavenly children, and teach us to value only our spiritual and heavenly inheritance, lest an earthly father, fatherland, or earthly goods delude, catch, and hinder us and make us into merely children of this world. And grant that we might say with true conviction: O our heavenly Father, we are truly your heavenly children" (TAL 4:184).

Jesus revealing God as Father, from an illustration of one of Luther's sermons for Advent 1544.

---

34. Kolde, 87.   35. Luther, in "Whether One May Flee from a Deadly Plague" (1527), made clear that people should use medicines and take measures to keep the body in good health. Those who intentionally exposed themselves to the plague, failed to take appropriate measures to avoid such exposure, or failed to use medicines and intelligence to take care of the body were not exhibiting faith but rather were tempting God (TAL 4:403–4).

loves us and protects us. Just as Christ cries to his Father, so also should we. We are, through faith in Christ, also God's children and heirs. "For that reason we should not only use these words in our prayer but also trust with our hearts that he, as a father, is kindly inclined to us and will not let us, his children, suffer want."[36] To doubt this, to carry the thought in our hearts that God is not our Father and does not care for us, is to dishonor God and to take away God's proper name.

The First Petition

This figure, based on the third commandment, depicts sixteenth-century preaching. The churches did not yet have pews, so that people would gather around the pulpit, with older people bringing their own clap stools to sit on, while youngsters sat on the floor and others stood. In the printings of the Small Catechism during Luther's lifetime, each commandment, article of the Creed, petition of the Lord's Prayer, and sacrament was accompanied by a woodcut and (from 1536) references to the Bible story on which each picture was based.

♥ Hallowed be your name.

What is this? or ***What does this mean?***
It is true that God's name is holy in itself, but we ask in this prayer that it may also become holy in and among us.

How does this come about?
Whenever the word of God is taught clearly and purely and we, as God's children, also live holy lives according to it. To this end help us, dear Father in heaven! However, whoever teaches and lives otherwise than the word of God teaches, dishonors the name of God among us. Preserve us from this, heavenly Father!

This petition leads us back to two parts of the catechism you have already encountered. Look at what the second commandment says about how we use God's name (reread pages 53–55 if you need a refresher). Remember that Luther saw this as a positive command. We properly use God's name when we use it to be in communication with God, that is, "to call on, pray to, praise, and give thanks to God." Just as you call someone's name when you want to talk with her, so, too, you call God's name when you wish to talk with God.

Luther's explanation includes the phrases "dear Father in heaven" and "heavenly Father." These phrases, of course, link to the introduction, where we as loving children boldly and confidently address our loving Father. In his Large Catechism, Luther explains, "Because in this prayer we call God our Father, it is our duty in every way to behave as good children so that he may receive from us not shame but honor and praise."[37]

Notice the double structure of the questions and answers for the first four petitions. Luther's concern was not with abstractions about God but with how God works *on me*. Notice Luther's emphasis that all these things be done *to*, *in*, and *among* us.

---

36. *Martin Luthers Werke: Kritische Gesamtausgabe* (Weimar: Böhlau, 1883–1980), WA 52:740. The translation is the author's.   37. Large Catechism, Lord's Prayer, par. 39 (BC 445).

In his explanation to the first petition, Luther holds two things together that we often separate, namely, Christian teaching (or doctrine) and life. The clear and pure teaching of the word of God has a result: holy lives. Luther wanted us to understand that this petition is not about God's holiness for God's benefit, but about the need for the word of God to be active among us, taught clearly and purely, resulting in lives in accordance with that word.

Why do we need to pray? Why do we need to talk with God? Because something is wrong in our lives, in our communities, and in our world. Proper relationship with God, proper use of God's name, is necessary to deal with this. What is the desired result? That our teaching and our lives are godly and Christian. (Do not see "godly" and "Christian" as two different things—Luther often used two words to describe one concept.) Notice the warning against those who teach and live otherwise. Luther in the Large Catechism explained that we can indeed profane God's name in either words or deeds:

> In the first place, then, it is profaned when people preach, teach, and speak in the name of God anything that is false and deceptive, using his name to dress up their lies and make them acceptable; this is the worst desecration and dishonor of the divine name. . . . In the next place, it is also profaned by an openly evil life and wicked works, when those who are called Christians and God's people are adulterers, drunkards, gluttons, jealous persons, and slanderers. . . .

> Just as it is a shame and a disgrace to an earthly father to have a bad, unruly child who antagonizes him in word and deed, with the result that on his account the father ends up suffering scorn and reproach, so God is dishonored if we who are called by his name and enjoy his manifold blessings fail to teach, speak, and live as upright and heavenly children, with the result that he must hear us called not children of God but children of the devil.[38]

Although Luther held the office of public ministry in high regard, he did not assign one task (teaching) to clergy and the other (holy living) to laypeople. Rather, he wanted everyone to learn their catechisms so that they might know what the clear and pure teaching of the word of God was and might be able to discern what was true and what was not true in what they heard. Making sure that our teaching (doctrine) is correctly taught and understood is a task for all Christians.[39] Similarly, all Christians are called to holy living by that word, which frees them to live as God intends.

One place to pray especially this petition is as preparation for worship, when we may pray that the pastor's words come to us as speaking and explaining clearly God's word to us.

---

38. Large Catechism, Lord's Prayer, par. 41–44 (BC 445). 39. See Mary Jane Haemig, "Laypeople as Overseers of the Faith: A Reformation Proposal," *Trinity Seminary Review* 27 (2006): 21–27.

The Second Petition

💙 Your kingdom come.

What is this? or **What does this mean?**
In fact, God's kingdom comes on its own without our prayer, but we ask in this prayer that it may also come to us.

How does this come about?
Whenever our heavenly Father gives us his Holy Spirit, so that through the Holy Spirit's grace we believe God's holy word and live godly lives here in time and hereafter in eternity.

This woodcut of the first Pentecost was also used for the third article of the Creed (see p. 92).

The second petition, as Luther understands it, humbles us: *We are not the cause of God's kingdom arriving on earth*. We do not create, build, sustain, or fulfill that kingdom. Luther's view in this regard contrasted (and still contrasts) sharply with some other Christian groups who fervently believed they were building God's kingdom on earth.[40]

Luther's explanation further humbles us by acknowledging that we have to ask God that the kingdom "may also come to us." Implicit in this is a warning—God's kingdom is coming and we may miss out on it! That is why we need to pray and acknowledge that this kingdom comes whenever God gives us the Holy Spirit. Recall the work of the Holy Spirit as described in the third article of the Creed (page 92). Luther makes clear again that God's Spirit causes us to believe in God's holy word (prayed for in the first petition), which precedes living a godly life.

Luther does not shove the coming of God's kingdom off into the future. The kingdom comes here and now—not just in eternity. What about that word *kingdom*? What does it mean? *Kingdom* simply means "the reign of God." Lutherans have recognized that God rules in two ways. Dietrich Bonhoeffer described it this way:

> In the second through fourth petitions, Luther seemed to pray the Trinity in reverse: first for the Holy Spirit to give us faith, then for victory over evil (which Christ wrought through the cross), and finally for daily bread, defined according to the explanation of the first article of the Creed.

> In his Large Catechism, Luther paraphrased the second petition in this way: "Dear Father, we ask you first to give us your Word, so that the gospel may be properly preached throughout the world and then that it may also be received in faith and may work and dwell in us, so that your kingdom may pervade among us through the Word and the power of the Holy Spirit and the devil's kingdom may be destroyed so that he may have no right or power over us until finally his kingdom is utterly eradicated and sin, death, and hell wiped out, that we may live forever in perfect righteousness and blessedness" (par. 54 [BC 447]).

---

40. Dietrich Bonhoeffer spoke in Luther's terms when he commented, "No one can pray for the kingdom who imagines himself in bold utopias, in dreams and hopes of the kingdom, who lives his ideologies, who knows thousands of programs and prescriptions with which to heal the world. We should look at ourselves very carefully when we catch ourselves thinking such thoughts." "Thy Kingdom Come! The Prayer of the Church-Community for God's Kingdom on Earth" in *Dietrich Bonhoeffer Works* (Minneapolis: Fortress, 2009), 12:289.

The kingdom of God exists in our world exclusively in the duality of church and state. Both are necessarily linked to each other. . . . Every prayer for the coming of the kingdom to us that does not have in mind both church and state is either otherworldliness or secularism. It is, in any case, a lack of faith in the kingdom of God.

The kingdom of God takes form *in the church* insofar as the church gives witness to the miracle of God. The ministry of the church is to witness to Christ's resurrection from the dead, to the end of the law of death of this world under the curse, and to the power of God in the new creation.

The kingdom of God takes form *in the state* insofar as the state recognizes and maintains the order of preservation of life and insofar as it accepts responsibility for preserving this world from collapse and for exercising its authority here against the destruction of life. Not the creation of new life, but preservation of existing life is its ministry.[41]

Knowing that God's kingdom comes in two ways may both enrich and frighten us. Bonhoeffer noted:

Christ's kingdom is God's kingdom, but God's kingdom in the form ordained for us; not as a visible, powerful empire, as the "new" kingdom of the world, but as the kingdom of the other world that has entered completely into the discord and contradiction of this world. At the same time it appears as the powerless, defenseless gospel of the resurrection, of miracle, and as the state that possesses authority and power that preserves order. Only in the true relation and delimitation of the two is Christ's kingdom reality.[42]

How does thinking about the coming of Christ's kingdom today in these two ways affect your own ideas about what God's kingdom is? And how does it enrich your understanding of the request that it may "also come to us"?

This petition encourages us to ask for the big stuff! Luther noted that "we are not asking here for crumbs" but rather "for an eternal, priceless treasure and for everything that God himself possesses." God has commanded that we ask for all this. Luther persistently pointed out that God is able to give far more than we ask for or can even imagine. "But because he is God, he also claims the honor of giving far more abundantly and liberally than anyone can comprehend—like an eternal, inexhaustible fountain, which, the more it gushes forth and overflows, the more it continues to give."[43] God wants us to ask for great things. This generous God wants to give them to us.

Some parents become especially worried when their older children slip away from Christian worship. Praying these first two petitions specifically with them in mind may be especially comforting, as we place into God's hands both their hearing the word (first petition) and, by the Holy Spirit, their believing it (second petition).

---

41. Ibid., 12:293. See also the description of the two kingdoms in chapter 7, pages 179–180. 42. Ibid., 12:295.
43. Large Catechism, Lord's Prayer, par. 56 (BC 447).

The Third Petition

❤ Your will be done, on earth as in heaven.

What is this? or **What does this mean?**
In fact, God's good and gracious will comes about without our prayer, but we ask in this prayer that it may also come about in and among us.

How does this come about?
Whenever God breaks and hinders every evil scheme and will—as are present in the will of the devil, the world, and our flesh—that would not allow us to hallow God's name and would prevent the coming of his kingdom, and instead whenever God strengthens us and keeps us steadfast in his word and in faith until the end of our lives. This is God's gracious and good will.

Christ bearing the cross. This reference to Jesus' crucifixion reminds the viewer of both his prayer in Gethsemane and the victory over all contrary wills through his suffering and death.

The explanation to this petition parallels the explanations to the first two. The question is not *whether* God's name will be holy, God's kingdom will come, or God's will is done. The question is: Will we be part of those events? We are put in our places again: "In fact, God's good and gracious will comes about without our prayer." Instead of seeing ourselves as indispensable, we must admit that we are unnecessary, that God can quite well do what God wants to do and do it without us. At the same time, a promise is implicit in this explanation. We can be certain that God's will can "come about in and among us." We pray not that God's will be done in some abstract theoretical sense, but rather to, for, in, and among us.

Luther saw this petition as related to the first two—those two petitions "embrace all that pertains to God's glory and to our salvation." This third petition pertains to the reality that we must be kept, defended, and protected in the faith. Luther was convinced that we suffer "an astonishing number of attacks and assaults from all who venture to hinder and thwart the fulfillment of the first two petitions."[44] We must pray for our own sakes—we need the protection of prayer.

You might have a hard time understanding this petition. It might seem like our choice is between God's will and our own will—and often we are not sure we truly *want* God's will. This petition can then sound like a demand for self-denial. Luther saw it differently. For Luther, the

---

44. Large Catechism, Lord's Prayer, par. 60–61 (BC 448).

alternatives were clear: either the will of the devil or the will of God will be done. So the choice is clear: we ask that God's will be done. This petition is not really about self-denial but rather about the recognition that a cosmic battle is going on in our lives. In this battle, we are not neutral observers. Rather, the powers at war will capture us and place us on one side or the other. Whatever side we may want to be on, God's will for us is going to have the final say.

Luther believed that the powers of evil (death, sin, the devil) were strong and active, threatening our relationship with God and our very lives. This belief can seem foreign—even laughable—to contemporary North Americans. We tend to think that we control our own lives and often deny the existence of forces (death, sin, hell, the devil, and evil) that we cannot control and that can do us great harm. For Luther, this would only be proof that the powers of evil are deluding and misleading us. To pray that God's will be done is to pray against the powers of evil and for God's final victory.

One way to imagine our praying this petition is as a shout from the back of the arena to encourage our champion. In this respect, Luther's hymn "A Mighty Fortress," with its references to the defeat of the devil through Christ, the champion "who comes to fight," is a helpful commentary on this prayer.

The Fourth Petition

The story of the feeding of the five thousand in John 6 points to God's concern to feed hungry people and to Jesus' act of thanksgiving.

💙 Give us today our daily bread.

What is this? or What does this mean?
In fact, God gives daily bread without our prayer, even to all evil people,[45] but we ask in this prayer that God cause us to recognize what our daily bread is and to receive it with thanksgiving.

What then does "daily bread" mean?
Everything included in the necessities and nourishment for our bodies, such as food, drink, clothing, shoes, house, farm, fields, livestock, money, property, an upright spouse, upright children, upright members of the household, upright and faithful rulers, good government, good weather, peace, health, decency, honor, good friends, faithful neighbors, and the like.

This is the first explanation of a part of the catechism that offers, strictly speaking, the meaning of something, since the words "daily bread" may seem to include only food. Otherwise, the standard question "What is this?" (German: *Was ist das?*) invites paraphrase and means "In other words."

In the early church and the Middle Ages, "bread" was often associated with a request for the sacrament of the Lord's supper. A late medieval pastoral manual gave "bread" three meanings: "The first is the spiritual bread of

---

45. Sometimes, it is easy to imagine that God helps only good people. Here Luther reminds us that God's merciful care covers all of us. See Matthew 5:45.

austere penance. The second bread is the sacramental bread of the eucharist. The third is the material bread of temporal substance."[46] Over his career, Luther slowly reoriented the focus of this petition to our earthy, bodily needs.[47]

Consider carefully the list of everything included under "daily bread." How often do you pray for these things? Do you believe that God is concerned with these things? How often do you reflect on how necessary each of these is to your individual and communal lives? Notice how the list moves from bodily needs to family and social life and then spreads into societal needs like good government. "And the like" invites you to fill out the list. What would you add?

Choose one or two items from the list to reflect on. For example, what does "good government" or "good friends" mean? What does it mean when we ask God for these? How does your context—the environment in which you live, work, worship, and play—influence how you think about each item? For example, what does "peace" mean for you? What might a prayer for peace mean for someone else whose circumstances are quite different from yours? What does it mean to confess that all these good things are gifts from God, who gives them to all kinds of people?

You might ask: Why do I have to ask God for these things? Doesn't God know what I need already? And would my prayer really change God's mind, anyway? Luther wanted to encourage a relationship in which we do not hesitate to bring our needs to God and believe that our prayers are effective. However, Luther made an important distinction between bodily matters and other matters. In matters that are not bodily matters—that God keeps us in the word, saves us, forgives us, and gives us the Holy Spirit and eternal life—in these matters God's will is already known and certain. God wants all people to be saved and wants all people to recognize their sin and believe in forgiveness through Christ. So it is not necessary, when praying for these things, to wonder whether God will do them or not. We know and believe that God wants to do these things.

> Luther recognized the threat that the powers of evil posed to all the things that make our earthly life possible. The fourth petition, along with every petition of the Lord's Prayer, is directed against the devil, the power of evil. Luther acknowledged all that God does to preserve and enhance our earthly lives.

Luther thought, though, that we cannot have the same certainty as to what God's will is in bodily matters. We often wonder whether God wants us to experience sickness, poverty, and other trials and whether those situations serve God's honor and our salvation. For that reason, Luther encouraged his listeners to ask for God's help but leave to God's will whether God wants to help immediately. Prayer in this situation is not in vain, for even if God does not help immediately, God will strengthen the heart and give grace and patience so that one may endure it and finally overcome it, as the example of Christ in Gethsemane teaches. God did not take this cup away from Christ but sent him an angel to

---

46. Guido of Monte Rochen, *Handbook for Curates: A Late Medieval Manual on Pastoral Ministry*, trans. Anne T. Thayer (Washington, DC: Catholic University of America Press, 2011), 290.   47. For the details of this change, see Paul W. Robinson, "Luther's Explanation of Daily Bread in Light of Medieval Preaching," *Lutheran Quarterly* 13 no. 4 (Winter 1999): 435–47; and Albrecht Peters, *Commentary on Luther's Catechisms: Lord's Prayer*, trans. Daniel Thies (St. Louis, MO: Concordia, 2011), 124–30.

strengthen him. Luther assured his listeners, "So it will also happen with you, even if God would delay or deny his help."[48]

In the face of the generous God, humans are sometimes unwilling to trust that this God will be generous to them. Referring to Ephesians 3:20, Luther remarked, "God's title and true name is this, that he is a hearer of prayers. But we . . . are called those who do not know how to pray or what to pray for."[49] In the fourth petition Luther names very explicitly the bodily matters for which we pray.

The Fifth Petition

The parable of the unforgiving servant in Matthew 18:23-35, depicted here, underscores Luther's insistence that God's forgiveness precedes and exceeds our own.

♥ Forgive us our sins as we forgive those who sin against us.

What is this?* or *What does this mean?
We ask in this prayer that our heavenly Father would not regard our sins nor deny these petitions on their account, for we are worthy of nothing for which we ask, nor have we earned it. Instead we ask that God would give us all things by grace, for we daily sin much and indeed deserve only punishment. So, on the other hand, we, too, truly want to forgive heartily and to do good gladly to those who sin against us.

This petition addresses the reality of the human condition. We are both those who sin and those who are sinned against. Thus this petition judges and humbles us—but it also tells us something about God. How are we to live in the midst of the reality that we are both those who sin and those who are sinned against? What kind of God do we pray to in the Lord's Prayer?

Luther reoriented the concept of sin. Even today, as in Luther's day, many people think of sin primarily as individual acts or failures to act. We reduce sin to thoughts, words, and deeds contrary to God's commands or to omissions of those thoughts, words, and deeds that would have fulfilled God's commands. For Luther, sin was first and foremost lack of faith, that is, lack of trust in God's forgiving and reconciling work in Jesus Christ for you. The powers of evil do not

Luke's version of the Lord's Prayer (11:4) uses the words *sin* and *debt*, while Matthew's (6:12) uses the word *debt*. Early English versions used the word *trespass* (to cross over a boundary, hence, to sin). Outside its use in the church, the word *trespass* has retained in modern English only its literal meaning of crossing over onto someone else's property.

---

48. WA 52:742 (author's translation).   49. LW 3:158.

simply cause you to do the wrong thing (or fail to do the right thing); rather, they cause you to despair of ever experiencing God's goodness and faithfulness and enjoying your relationship with God.

The order of events in this petition is key. We ask first for God's forgiveness. We acknowledge that we are not worthy of forgiveness, and that we deserve punishment. Then, just as God forgives us, so we, too, forgive those who sin against us. Notice that Luther does not merely say we "forgive heartily" but rather we "do good gladly to those who sin against us." Just as our generous God gives us all things by grace, regardless of our sin, so we also give to others.

Luther's reformation sprang out of a key insight: that God forgives us freely, without any merit on our part. God's generosity, God's forgiveness, enables us to be generous with our forgiveness. God's forgiveness is both gift and example. This is parallel to what Luther thought of Jesus himself:

Luther underscored this movement from God's mercy for us to our mercy for others in the Large Catechism: "But if you forgive, you have the comfort and assurance that you are forgiven in heaven—not on account of your forgiving (for [God] does it altogether freely, out of pure grace, because he has promised it, as the gospel teaches) but instead because he has set this up for our strengthening and assurance as a sign along with the promise" (Lord's Prayer, par. 96 [BC 453]).

> The chief article and foundation of the gospel is that before you take Christ as an example, you accept and recognize him as a gift, as a present that God has given you and that is your own. This means that when you see or hear of Christ doing or suffering something, you do not doubt that Christ himself, with his deeds and suffering, belongs to you. . . . This is the great fire of the love of God for us, whereby the heart and conscience become happy, secure, and content. . . . Now when you have Christ as the foundation and chief blessing of your salvation, then the other part follows: that you take him as your example, giving yourself in service to your neighbor just as you see that Christ has given himself for you. . . . Therefore make note of this, that Christ as a gift nourishes your faith and makes you a Christian. But Christ as an example exercises your works. These do not make you a Christian. Actually they come forth from you because you have already been made a Christian.[50]

An oil painting titled *Crucifixion* by Lucas Cranach the Elder, painted in 1532.

Luther was also realistic. He knew that there are times when you are unable to forgive. He recognized that forgiveness is not our work—we cannot produce it by ourselves. This petition includes our cry to God to enable us to forgive those who have sinned against us.

---

50. *A Brief Instruction on What to Look For and Expect in the Gospels*, LW 35:119–20; TAL 2:30–31.

The Sixth Petition

♥ Save us from the time of trial.[51]

What is this? or **What does this mean?**
It is true that God tempts no one,[52] but we ask in this prayer that God would preserve and keep us, so that the devil, the world, and our flesh may not deceive us or mislead us into false belief, despair, and other great and shameful sins, and that, although we may be attacked by them, we may finally prevail and gain the victory.

We may have trouble praying this petition because it is not the language we learned as children! The traditional language, "lead us not into temptation," may still be difficult because it seems to challenge our image of God. Does God really lead us into temptation? Is God responsible for our temptation? What kind of God do we have, anyway? Certainly not a God who tempts us! And certainly a God who answers prayer! What, specifically, does this petition say that God can do for us? God is the one who can "preserve and keep us," and God is the one who can give us the final victory over the powers of evil.

Luther had an acute sense of the power of evil in the world. Luther used different words than we might to describe evil, such as *sin, death, the devil, the world,* and *our flesh*. Whatever language he used, Luther was trying to convey that these powers are very real and active. He knew that these powers could deceive or mislead us.

This petition offers a realistic assessment of what happens in our lives. We are often deceived and misled. And not just by little stuff, either, but by "false belief, despair, and other great and shameful sins." Who are the attackers? "The devil, the world, and our flesh"—or the cosmic powers of evil, the powers and forces we know in this world, and our own selves. Luther saw the attackers as similar to swords, constantly probing, threatening, and tantalizing us.

What are we to do in times of trial? Luther saw in the stories of the Old Testament many examples of faith and conversation with God. When

This depiction of Jesus' temptation by the devil (Matt. 4:1-11) demonstrates how Jesus' victory protects the sheep. See also John 10.

A well-known biography by Heiko Oberman, *Luther: Man between God and the Devil*, recounts Luther's life from the perspective of the struggle between good and evil. Oberman notes, "All of the Devil's attacks are directed at certainty of salvation, that fundamental article of faith. All temptations, whatever sort they may be, are aimed at awakening doubts in God's reliability. Not only Luther the fearful monk but Luther the professor and 'reformer,' too, felt singularly affected by these 'critical doubts.'. . . Luther spoke freely of the fear these objections evoked in him. . . . Whenever he felt the Devil breathing down his neck in this way, there was only one answer left: God alone is absolute certainty, even if the Church at times is lost in a cloud of unknowing."[53]

---

51. Or, in some versions, including those used in Luther's congregation, "Lead us not into temptation." 52. Only in the past century or so have New Testament scholars come to realize that the Greek phrase refers not so much to temptation as to trials, especially trials near the end of time. Thus, Luther has to exclude the implication that God tempts us before explaining what this petition means. 53. Trans. Eileen Walliser-Schwarzbart (New Haven, CT: Yale University Press, 1992), 177–78.

Luther discussed Abram's conversation with God in Genesis 15:1-6, he noted that although we do not know the exact nature of the trial with which Abram wrestled, we have the general idea that he "began to have doubts as to the protection and the kindness of God." Several times Luther described Abram as doubting the fulfillment of God's promise. Abram lamented his childlessness. His trial was "his fear that the promise would be diverted from his own offspring and seed to his servant." Luther said that Abram was so distressed that he humbled himself and submitted to the will of God, but he did this with "profound grief and sorrow," for he thought

When Luther referred to "flesh," he didn't mean just our skin or just our physical body. He meant the whole human person. He wasn't saying that our minds, rational powers, or emotions are good but our bodies are bad. By "our flesh" he meant our entire selves. Luther recognized our own responsibility in the temptations we experience.

Abraham receives the promise that he will be the father of many peoples. Plate 22 from Julius Schnorr von Carolsfeld, *Die Bibel in Bildern* [The Bible in Pictures] (Leipzig: Georg Wigand), 1860.

that God was forsaking him and had "changed his will." Luther described Abram as pouring out "his complaint and the thoughts of a very troubled heart." Luther did not criticize this despair or doubt, nor did he criticize Abram for taking his complaint to God; rather, Luther found this good and proper. Several times he said that in such trials we should "commend our cause to the Lord." Luther was confident that "eventually [God] comes and encourages the humble."[54] For Luther, Abram endured troubles just as all the saints—and even Christ himself—did. Affliction drives and teaches the Christian to pray. Luther noted when such prayer frequently happens:

> It is characteristic of sublime trials to occupy hearts when they are alone. For this reason there is frequent mention in Holy Scripture of praying at night and in solitude. Affliction is the teacher of such praying. Thus because Abraham was occupied with these sad thoughts, he was unable to sleep. Therefore he got up and prayed; but while he is praying and feeling such great agitation within himself, God appears to him and converses with him in a friendly manner.[55]

Luther did not expect life to be easy. He said that if we are trusting God and living as God intends, we should *expect* attacks from the evil powers. He even included suffering as one of the signs of the true church. Writing in 1539, he said:

> The holy Christian people . . . must endure every misfortune and persecution, all kinds of trials and evil from the devil, the world, and the flesh (as the Lord's Prayer indicates) by inward sadness, timidity, fear, outward poverty, contempt, illness, and weakness, in order to become like their head, Christ. . . . In summary, they must be called heretics, knaves, and devils, the most pernicious people on earth, to the point where those who hang, drown, murder, torture, banish, and plague them to death are rendering God a service. . . . And all of this is done not because they are adulterers, murderers, thieves, or rogues, but because they want to have none but Christ, and no other God. Wherever you see or hear this, you may know that the holy Christian church is there.[56]

Even when we do not suffer these things directly, because all Christians comprise the body of Christ, when one believer in our congregation or around the world suffers, we all bear that suffering. Thus, we pray this petition (like the others) for others as well as ourselves.

When Luther spoke of affliction, he used the German word *Anfechtung*, which literally means "to be fought upon" and, hence, attacked. In such attacks, God is our only hope for rescue.

54. LW 3:12–17.   55. LW 3:17–18.   56. *On the Councils and the Church* (1539). LW 41:164–65; TAL 3:430–31.

The Seventh Petition

💜 And deliver us from evil.[57]

> **What is this?** or **What does this mean?**
> We ask in this prayer, as in a summary, that our Father in heaven may deliver us from all kinds of evil—affecting body or soul, property or reputation—and at last, when our final hour comes, may grant us a blessed end and take us by grace from this valley of tears to himself in heaven.

The story of the Canaanite woman's pleading for her daughter's deliverance from a demon (Matt. 15:21-28) provided Luther with a wonderful illustration of this petition and of the woman's remarkable faith, which (as Luther states in a sermon) turns Christ's "No!" into a "Yes!" For even dogs get crumbs!

Luther describes our life on this earth as a "valley of tears." He is not trying to be pessimistic, just realistic. Living in the most affluent nation on earth may insulate us from life's realities. Luther, however, saw suffering in every human's life and believed we must pray in the midst of that suffering. How would you describe the evils that threaten your body, soul, property, and reputation?

Luther rejected the fatalistic view that instead of fleeing from evil you should just accept it as God's punishment. Writing in 1527 about whether a Christian should flee the plague, he commented sarcastically that "by such reasoning, when a house is on fire, no one should run outside or rush to help because such a fire is also a punishment from God. Those who fall into deep water dare not save themselves by swimming but instead must surrender to the water as divine punishment." After several more examples, Luther concluded:

> Ultimately such talk will lead to the point where we abbreviate the Lord's Prayer and no longer pray, "deliver us from evil, Amen," since we would have to stop praying to be saved from hell and stop seeking to escape it. It, too, is God's punishment as is every kind of evil. Where would all this end? From what has been said we derive this guidance: We must pray against every form of evil and guard against it to the best of our ability in order not to act contrary to God.[58]

Luther did not want us to sink into fatalism but rather to pray actively and guard ourselves against evil. Luther's famous hymn "A Mighty Fortress" not only attests to Luther's belief that the powers of evil

A plague doctor's hood was worn by whoever was desperate or brave enough to treat victims of the deadly epidemic. The plague was thought, like all disease, to be spread through "miasma," the unpleasant air of decay and evil, so the doctors stuffed the beaklike nose of their hood with pleasant-smelling spices and other substances that they believed would ward off the deadly vapors.

---

57. In the Large Catechism, Luther explains that in the Greek the term for *evil* could also be translated "the Evil One" (Lord's Prayer, par. 113 [BC 455]). All of the petitions are summarized in this one, as we pray that Jesus' defeat of the devil (Matt. 4:1-11) also would support us.   58. *Whether One May Flee from a Deadly Plague*, TAL 4:396.

threaten us, but also affirms his certainty that God will triumph over the power of evil:

> Though hordes of devils fill the land
> all threatening to devour us,
> we tremble not, unmoved we stand;
> they cannot overpower us.
> This world's prince may rage, in fierce war engage.
> He is doomed to fail; God's judgment must prevail!
> One little word subdues him.
>
> God's Word forever shall abide,
> no thanks to foes, who fear it;
> for God himself fights by our side
> with weapons of the Spirit.
> If they take our house, goods, fame, child, or spouse,
> wrench our life away, they cannot win the day.
> The kingdom's ours forever!

Luther's manuscript version of "A Mighty Fortress."

Conclusion

♥ [For the kingdom, the power, and the glory are yours, now and forever.][59] Amen.

What is this? or What does this mean?
That I should be certain that such petitions are acceptable to and heard by our Father in heaven, for he himself commanded us to pray like this and has promised to hear us. "Amen, amen" means "Yes, yes, it is going to come about just like this."

When you converse with a friend, how do you know that your words have truly been heard? What would give you such assurance? For Luther, the "Amen" gives us that assurance. It is not our attempt to have the last word, but rather a cry of faith, faith in our listening and generous God. We can say "Amen!" because we can be certain that our prayer has been heard and will be answered. The amen is not a marker of the end, but rather a word of encouragement in faith. Luther's emphasis on God's command to pray and promise to hear us

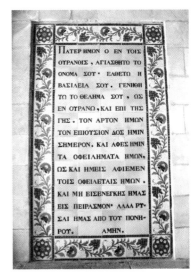

The Lord's Prayer in Greek, in the Church of the Pater Noster in Jerusalem.

---

59. Luther followed medieval practice and did not include this doxology. With the discovery and publication of much earlier versions of the Greek text, scholars discovered that the doxology was not part of the original Greek texts of Matthew or Luke. It likely entered into the text because it was a common response of faith by early Christians to God's rule, derived from 1 Chronicles 29:11-13.

comes through yet again. At the end of this prayer, we are to have no doubt that this God who promises to listen has indeed heard our requests.

Luther offered some friendly advice to his barber in 1535, reminding him not only that God would hear but that his fellow Christians stood united with him.

> Finally, mark this, that you must always speak the "Amen" firmly. Never doubt that God in his mercy will surely hear you and say "yes" to your prayers. Never think that you are kneeling or standing alone, rather think that the whole of Christendom, all devout Christians, are standing there beside you and you are standing among them in a common, united petition which God cannot disdain. Do not leave your prayer without having said or thought, "Very well, God has heard my prayer; this I know as a certainty and a truth." This is what Amen means.[60]

Repeatedly, Luther expressed his confidence that God hears our prayers. He saw in the stories of the Bible the evidence that God wants us to pray and will answer us. Writing in 1541 in his "Appeal for Prayer against the Turks," Luther reminded his readers that though they may not be the patriarchs of the Old Testament, nevertheless they can pray just as those figures did. "True enough, we are not a Joshua, who through prayer could command the sun to stand still [Josh. 10:12-13]. Nor are we a Moses, who through his fervent plea separated the waters of the Red Sea [Exod. 14:15-22]. Neither are we an Elijah, who by his prayer called down fire from heaven [2 Kings 1:9-12]. But we are at least the equal of those to whom God gave his word and whom the Holy Spirit has inspired to preach. Yes, we are no different from Moses, Joshua, and Elijah, and all the other saints because we have the same word and Spirit of God that they had. . . . They were human just as we are and were created by the same God. And God must answer our prayer . . . just as much as theirs, for we are members of his church" (LW 43:226–27).

---

60. "A Simple Way to Pray," TAL 4:263.

5

The Sacrament of Holy Baptism and Confession

Introduction

Luther appreciated the fact that since the baptism of Jesus himself, baptism has been one of the central practices for Christian identity. It continues to be, on the one hand, a unifying ritual for Christians and, on the other, a practice for which Christian communities and theologians have different rationales. Luther has been one of the most important teachers on baptism, not only on questions of infant baptism and the "necessity" of baptism but also on the centrality of baptism for the entire Christian life.

Baptized on St. Martin's Day, November 11, 1483, Martin Luther received his name from the saint of the day, St. Martin of Tours. As was common at the time, the calendar of saints and name days assisted parents in choosing names for their newborns, who typically were baptized as soon as possible. At a time when infant mortality was high and the church taught that baptism was necessary for salvation, parents took this important step to ensure the eternal safety of their children. Papal and imperial laws also demanded a swift baptism of citizens born under the umbrella of the Holy Roman Empire.[1] Add to this the lack

St. Martin of Tours by Simone Martini (1285–1344). Martin of Tours (315–397) was a patron saint of the poor, soldiers, winemakers, and conscientious objectors.

---

1. A map showing the border of the Holy Roman Empire appears on page 62.

of any kind of health care system or insurance coverage, and little protection for individuals, and the importance of baptism was huge—perhaps more than contemporary Christians can fully comprehend or appreciate.

Martin Luther never seriously questioned the centrality of baptism for entry into the Christian life and as the foundational rite of the Christian church. He did, however, need to reconsider the rationale for it and its proper practice in the "Reformations," that is, evangelical communities of faith. He had to address the option of adult baptism, or "believer's baptism," versus infant baptism, and in this deliberation he aligned with the preceding centuries' preference for infant baptism. As much as Luther the reformer broke with history when his reforming vision required it, he preferred to stay with the tradition, especially with practices that God had seemed to bless. Baptism was one of them. He saw no reason to implement changes for the sake of change. A proper education in baptism's benefits was rather what was needed.

In his Small Catechism, Luther offers a succinct theological rationale for baptism.[2] He names the Scriptures as the foundation for teaching his audience—whom he imagines to be every man, woman, and child of God. Embedded in his explanation of baptism is his vision for the foundations and the rhythms of a Christian life. He understands baptism as an intimate encounter with God. It begins a new life, a new reality for the baptized; and its impact continues in God's promise of wholeness despite the brokenness of our daily lives.

> Luther's confidence in the medicinal powers of baptism was notable: "Suppose there were a physician who had so much skill that people would not die, or even though they died would afterward live eternally. Just think how the world would snow and rain money upon such a person! . . . Now, here in baptism there is brought, free of charge, to every person's door just such a treasure and medicine that swallows up death and keeps all people alive" (Large Catechism, Baptism, par. 43 [BC 461–62]).

When explaining baptism, Luther always keeps in mind his fundamental notion of justification by grace through faith because of Christ alone. Understanding justification as a gift that grants both forgiveness and the indwelling of Christ, Luther describes a post-baptismal reality with two intertwined dimensions. One dimension is this visible, finite, sinful, and fallible life with its complex within-creation-relations where we struggle. The other dimension is the invisible, infinite, forgiving, and holy reality of Christ with the fundamentally sustaining, utterly completed-in-Christ relation to God. Baptism offers God's point of entry into our lives and the focal point from which to grasp this reality and orient one's life accordingly.

A 1536 woodcut, which shows the Holy Spirit over the baptismal party.

With his theology of baptism, Luther offers a God-centered, grace-bound spiritual orientation for following Christ in daily life where you can wear the promise and the effect of your baptism like a daily garment. At the same time, you are invited to cherish your baptism as the most precious jewel.[3] In Luther's vision, both baptism and the Christian life are humble and holy.

---

2. Luther's Large Catechism fleshes out the succinct theology of the Small Catechism. See *Large Catechism: A Study Edition* (Fortress, 2016), edited and language revised (based on BC 377–480), and introduced by Kirsi Stjerna.   3. "No greater jewel, therefore, can adorn our body and soul than baptism, for through it we become completely holy and blessed, which no other kind of life and no work on earth can acquire." Large Catechism, Baptism, par. 46 (BC 462).

On the Context

In the turmoil of the reforms that streamed from Luther's *Ninety-Five Theses* in 1517 and the calls for reform he broadcast in his four major reformation treatises in 1520, various groups began to separate from Rome. As Christians exposed to Luther's proclamation and publications and drawn to his interpretation of the Christian faith and renewed emphasis on the liberating power of the gospel chose to associate with the Wittenberg theologian and his peers, many practical questions arose.

For example, which rituals should the new faith communities continue to practice, and was baptism one of them? If so, how would baptism be understood in light of the Reformation's interpretation of the Scriptures and critical assessment of the existing rationales for Christian practices and doctrines? In addition to the ancient and medieval practice of infant baptism, other models emerged in the waves of the reforms: most significantly, the so-called Anabaptists stopped baptizing infants and instead embraced believer's baptism, with a significantly different theology—and results.

Not only did the issue have theological and ecclesial implications; it was also a legal matter. Since Emperor Justinian's (527–565) ruling *Corpus Juris Civilis* from the sixth century, infant baptism had been mandated by imperial law; failure to comply could lead to death. The background of this mandate was the decisive battle in the early church against rebaptizers, and particularly the schismatic group called Donatists, who wanted a pure, exclusive, true church and

After his *Ninety-Five Theses* in 1517, the four reformation treatises really set the program with Luther's criticism of the past and his vision for the future. Within just a few months, he wrote *Treatise on Good Works* (TAL 1:257–367), in which he says the Commandments define all the good works for the Christian life but good works proceed from faith; *To the Christian Nobility of the German Nation Concerning the Improvement of the Christian Estate* (TAL 1:368–465), which called the secular authorities to defend the gospel kept prisoner by the papal-led church; *The Babylonian Captivity of the Church* (TAL 3:9–129), which critiqued medieval Catholic sacramental theology and several practices and teachings that, in his view, kept people in unnecessary bondage; and *The Freedom of a Christian* (TAL 1:466–538), which inspired a theology of freedom in faith and responsible service to the other in love. These publications sealed Luther's fate with the Roman authorities even before he burned the papal bull and the canon law that effectively sealed his official excommunication in January 1521.

Anabaptist (Greek for rebaptizer) was originally a derogatory name for the Protestant individuals and groups that in the waves of the sixteenth-century reforms distanced themselves more radically from the institutional church and professed believer's baptism—even "rebaptism" (seen from a Lutheran perspective) in the cases of those already baptized as infants—for those joining their communities. Anabaptists were known for their lay leadership, for their refusal to take oaths, or to carry arms. These Christians were among the most persecuted in the sixteenth century. In 2010 the Lutheran World Federation publicly asked forgiveness from the Mennonite World Conference for sixteenth-century Lutheran Christians' violent acts against and condemnations of the ancestors of the Mennonite and Brethren Churches, among others, who are known for their pacifism.[4] Since the twentieth century, many from this tradition self-designate as Anabaptists.

The Donatists emerged from the trauma caused by the persecutions of the early centuries' Christians. They identified themselves as the pure, true church and demanded rebaptism from those joining. The validity and effectiveness of sacraments were tied in with the purity of the priest and the recipient. In the Middle Ages, theologians used some of Augustine's language to declare that the sacraments were viewed to be effective instruments of God's grace *ex opere operato*, that is, by the mere fact of being duly performed by an ordained priest. This decision, articulated at the Fourth Lateran Council (1215), was to protect the power of the sacraments "regardless" of any other factors. The reformers came to reject this language while in their own way they (and Luther in particular) held tightly to the anti-Donatist principle of the absolute validity of the sacraments regardless of the fact that they were administered by fallible human beings.

---

4. See *Healing Memories: Reconciling in Christ, Report of the Lutheran-Mennonite International Study Commission* (2010; https://www.mwc-cmm.org/sites/default/files/oea-lutheran-mennonites-web-en.pdf), and *Healing Memories: Implications of the Reconciliation between Lutherans and Mennonites* (2016; https://www.lutheranworld.org/content/resource-healing-memories-implications-reconciliation-between-lutherans-and-mennonites).

therefore rejected the validity of their opponents' baptisms. With the church father Augustine, and over several councils, Donatism and similar views were rejected. Rebaptism came to be seen not only as a theological error but also as a criminal act. The sacrament of baptism was thus not a light matter! There was significant pressure to "get this right." Lives, as well as the future of Lutheran faith communities, could be at stake.

Contemporary readers can gain perspective into the language about baptism by understanding the late medieval situation where not only matters of heresy and orthodoxy were at stake but also different religious factions potentially could cause political threats. Not all theological decisions were made fairly and for "pure" theological or biblical reasons—whatever such reasons might be. Politics have always been part of Christian deliberations in theology, as have various experiences that have shaped the teachings and practices often beyond the "official" decisions.

As he was gearing up to organize the teaching and religious life of the new evangelical communities, Luther received a reality check on exactly how much was needed to furnish people with sufficient means for their spiritual well-being. During these visitations to the surrounding areas, Luther saw with his own eyes how German-speaking Christians in rural areas were grossly illiterate in religious matters—in addition to lacking basic skills in reading and writing. This included the local priests who were not necessarily trained in theology and could have been illiterate themselves! One of the urgent remedies to this alarming situation was to educate the population, including boys and girls in the farmlands. Clergy education also became a priority, a reform to be implemented in both Protestant and Catholic contexts.

The burning of Anneken Hendriks, a Dutch Anabaptist, in 1571. She was charged with heresy by the Spanish Inquisition. Engraving by Jan Luiken (1649–1712).

Infant baptism with water being poured over the head.

Augustine, bishop of Hippo, was born in modern-day Algeria in 354. He was one of the most influential church fathers and was instrumental in shaping the language of Christian theology, particularly around sin, grace, and the human will. You can hear his voice behind mainstream Christian baptismal rationales. His articulation of original sin led to the teaching of the "necessity" of baptism in the face of inherited sin damning each newborn.

Luther's catechetical teaching on baptism was designed to address the realities he had encountered. The need to educate and to reestablish continuities as well as to disconnect with the medieval Catholic tradition on things that mattered—such as baptism—was behind the structure of his questions about baptism in the Small Catechism. Luther's question-answer model was set up to teach baptismal theology and the proper practice of this sacrament for the new evangelical groups.[5]

1: What is baptism?

♥ Baptism is not simply plain water. Instead, it is water used according to God's command and connected with God's word.

Anticipating questions from his readers and aware of the questions he had received from people around him, Luther starts with the bottom line: baptism is about God and God's action.

While rejecting views that in his mind reduced baptism to a mere symbol or a token of faith, Luther calls for a particular reverence toward the ritual. He makes it clear from the start that baptism is special; no plain water there, but God's water because of God's word. He wants to teach respect for the sacrament, its holiness, and its efficacy.

The baptismal water is holy water through which God works.[6] The focus is on God and what God does. This is in tune with the reformer's core theology emphasizing God's deeds and gifts for our well-being, in contrast to medieval teachers' emphasis on what we could do to please God. Here Luther is setting out a position over against the basic assumptions inherited from his time's theology.

With his question "What is baptism?" Luther gives the definition of a sacrament. Following Augustine's formula of "Word added to the [material] element," he defines a sacrament—a means of grace—as an action consisting of a physical substance and the Holy Word. Baptism is a sacrament because Jesus commanded it (the word) and because it uses the tangible substance of water (the matter). Luther is very clear on this, that the means of grace is not a magic word or tool but a holy, mysterious word made visible in the matter. The power of that word is not symbolic but *real* in conveying the grace promised.[7]

Prior to the publication of the catechisms in 1529, from 1527–29, Luther's prince, Elector John, set up official (but from their opponents' view, illegal) "visitations" of the churches in his territory. Teams consisted of two representatives of the court, a law professor, and a teacher of theology, in this case Martin Luther's colleague, Philip Melanchthon. For a brief time, Luther was also one of the visitors and saw for himself what the needs were for the new evangelical faith communities. The needs were serious and many, prompting him, finally, to publish the catechisms. In 1528 Luther and Melanchthon published a guide for parish pastors, *Instruction by the Visitors for the Parish Pastors of Saxony* (LW 40:263–320).

Augustine (354–430), bishop of Hippo (in North Africa), was the most prolific and influential Latin-speaking theologian of the ancient church. In sermons on the Gospel of John (the *Tractates*, no. 80), while commenting on John 15:3, he writes, "The word joins with the element and becomes a sacrament." Luther quotes this text in his exposition of baptism and the Lord's supper in the Large Catechism (Baptism, par. 18 [BC 458]) and Lord's Supper, par. 10 [BC 468]).

---

5. Catechisms were a major teaching tool and were for many people the primary or the only source of Christian doctrine. Aptly called the Lay Bible, the catechism offered the basics of Christian theology drawn from the Scriptures per Luther's interpretation. 6. "For the real significance of the water lies in God's Word or commandment and God's name, and this treasure is greater and nobler than heaven and earth" (Large Catechism, Baptism, par. 16 [BC 458]). 7. "*Accedat verbum ad elementum et fit sacramentum*, which means that 'when the word is added to the element or the natural substance, it becomes a sacrament,' that is, a holy, divine thing and sign" (Large Catechism, Baptism, par. 18 [BC 458]).

The Baptism of Christ by Piero della Francesca, c. 1450.

Detail of the *Seven Sacraments Altarpiece* by Rogier van der Weyden, c. 1445. This detail depicts baptism, confirmation, and penance.

With Augustine's definition and in light of the Scriptures, already in 1520, in the *Babylonian Captivity of the Church*, Luther explained why he reduced the number of sacraments from seven (as defined by medieval theology) to only two or three. Jesus explicitly commanded his disciples to do two things connected to external "means of grace," actions that contained special promises, which had their origin in Jesus' institution. In Luther's opinion, only baptism and the Lord's supper met these criteria.[8]

In the Middle Ages, the Christian community in the West entertained many more holy rituals as possible sacraments. Even the number seven, which was (and is) the practice in the Roman Catholic Church, is not a problem for Lutherans in itself.[9] Luther understands the good purposes for the other five he grew up with: confession (or penance), confirmation, extreme unction (last rites or anointing the sick), marriage, and ordination. In the final analysis, however, Luther considers the other five not to be sacraments, although they certainly could serve the spiritual well-being of Christians and the church. While good and helpful for the Christian life, these rituals were not explicitly commissioned by Christ and/or do not involve a specific material element as the tangible venue for grace. The latter is important to Luther, who underscores the real ways that God the creator, redeemer, and sustainer is present and works in human life.

To be sure, God can convey grace via any means God chooses, so that the medieval church recognized that God used a different set of "sacraments" in the Hebrew Scriptures. Sacraments are given for our benefit; God does not need any of them. The point of the sacraments is to make grace visible and tangible for the sake

---

8. Luther and his colleagues varied on whether to call confession and forgiveness a sacrament, which they viewed as a continuation of baptism and often called the Sacrament of Absolution (see p. 145).   9. After much debate, the Fourth Lateran Council of the medieval Catholic Church finally settled the number of sacraments at seven. This council considered that there could be up to thirty sacraments! Peter Lombard (1100–1160) was a key theologian in this decision-making process.

of our faith. For Lutherans then and now, baptism and the Lord's supper have been viewed as the holy means through which God chooses to work here and now in Christian communities where the word is proclaimed specifically. The Augsburg Confession defines the church by the external signs of word and sacraments.[10]

The Christian assembly is the framework for the practice and use of the sacraments. Without the faith community, these means of grace lack a central part of their proper application. Any conversation on the "necessity" of sacraments, such as baptism, makes sense only within this framework. Outside the experience of the Christian community that believes in the power of sacraments, the absolute demand for baptism changes. So a modern adjustment to Luther's emphasis on the vitality of the sacraments is this: they are not to be conceived as exclusive means of grace or conditions to holiness and life with God for all people and without exceptions. What God does outside of Christian sacramental communities is in God's hands. Thus, for Israel, the narratives of grace differed and in their diversity speak of the mystery and immensity of how the Divine establishes relations with human beings. In the spirit of Luther's teaching, we can focus on the grace narrative of our own tradition and take that opportunity particularly with the teaching of sacraments to experience God "for us," here and now.

What then is this word of God?

♥ Where our Lord Christ says in Matthew 28, "Go therefore and make disciples of all nations, baptizing them in the name of the Father and of the Son and of the Holy Spirit."

The foundation of baptism is in Jesus' words recorded in Matthew 28. It is Jesus' words that institute baptism. It is his command that "requires" his disciples, that is, Christians, to be baptized and to baptize.[11] Given Luther's emphasis on *sola scriptura* ("scripture alone") and the Scriptures as the norm for Christian belief, life, and teaching, this is not surprising. Not only is there the example of Christ himself receiving baptism but also his explicit words about baptizing others. Baptism is essentially tied to Jesus' action and words. It is one of the few very clear commissions that goes back to Jesus.

This woodcut depicting Jesus' baptism appeared in the 1545 Leipzig edition of Luther's Small Catechism.

---

10. See the Augsburg Confession, VII.2 (BC 42): "For this is enough for the true unity of the Christian church that there the gospel is preached harmoniously according to a pure understanding and the sacraments are administered in conformity with the divine Word." In articles IX–XIII, the Augsburg Confession includes as sacraments baptism, the Lord's supper, and absolution.   11. Luther's citation focuses only on baptism. The entire text of Matthew 28:18-20 reads: "All authority in heaven and on earth has been given to me. Go therefore and make disciples of all nations, baptizing them in the name of the Father and of the Son and of the Holy Spirit, and teaching them to obey everything that I have commanded you. And remember, I am with you always, to the end of the age."

Jesus baptized by John the Baptist. Jan van Eyck, 1425.

The Gospels of Matthew, Mark, and Luke all narrate Jesus' baptism by John the Baptist.[12] Combined, the evidence is compelling: this was an important event, well recorded and broadly witnessed, even if not consistently recorded, and combining the presence of Father, Son, and Holy Spirit. The last of the canonical gospels written, the Gospel of John, offers more of an interpretation of Jesus' baptism than a narrative of the event.[13] Importantly, they all attest to who Jesus was: the Son of God, the Messiah (Christ).

Although Luther refers to Jesus' baptism in his baptismal liturgy (in the so-called "Flood Prayer" still used by Lutherans today[14]), his primary interest here is not the reasons for Jesus' baptism but the call for Jesus' followers to imitate his action and to adhere to his mission. By performing baptism after Jesus' example, Christians also become heirs of God's kingdom with Jesus, as the catechism later spells out.

Luther points to the practical and explicit: the purpose of baptism flows from Jesus' command for his disciples to go and make disciples of all nations by baptizing and teaching them. In this light, Luther could not imagine a Christian community that didn't practice baptism. In this sense, it is a true command, a "must," for those who want to be disciples of Christ.

Note that Mathew's text says that baptism should be done in the name of the Father, Son, and Holy Spirit. This has been the

Some New Testament References to Baptism and Baptismal Theology
Matthew 3:11-12; 28:20
Mark 10:39
Luke 12:50
John 3:22-26
Acts 2:41; 8:12-13, 36-37; 9:18, 10:47-48; 16:15, 33; 18:8; 19:5
Romans 6:3-5; 8:9-11; 13:13-14
1 Corinthians 1:13-16; 3:23; 6:19
2 Corinthians 4:5-14; 5:17; 13:2-5
Galatians 2:19-20; 3:27
Ephesians 4:22-24
Philippians 1:21
Colossians 2:12; 3:9-10

Early Christian fresco of the baptism of Christ. Third century. Catacomb of San Callisto, Rome.

---

12. Matthew 3:13-17; Mark 1:9-11 (the oldest reference); Luke 3:21-22.   13. See John 1:26-36.   14. *Evangelical Lutheran Worship*, p. 230.

tradition for centuries up to today. Some scholars wonder if this trinitarian formula comes from Jesus or from the gospel writer who added it later. Why did Jesus not simply tell the disciples to baptize in *his* name? Perhaps these words really expressed how Jesus saw and spoke of himself—in unity with the triune God, the creator of life and the continuing presence of the Holy Spirit.

Early baptismal liturgies are an important source for tracking the initial development of Christian confessional language and communal statements. Based on baptismal records and the tracks of the confessional statements that led to the formation of the ecumenical creeds,[15] it is clear that creedal language and doctrinal formulations developed as part of the baptismal practice.

With roots in the Jewish ritual of purification, and perhaps with influences from mystery religions, baptism was from the beginning the central initiation rite into Christian communities. It involved a lengthy catechesis, studying the Creed and examination of it. At baptism the new Christian would receive the Lord's Prayer and be allowed to partake of the Lord's supper. Jesus' simple command to baptize and make disciples evolved with the parameters set for Christian faith communities and for the doctrinal language adopted within the empire. From fragmentary evidence, it can be seen how the simple confession of "Jesus is the Lord" grew into lengthier statements that identified three persons in the triune God in one deity and Jesus as part of that holy mystery of salvation.

This language arose from worship and expressed how early Christians experienced God, using language shaped especially by their leaders (bishops) and those who had suffered persecution for the faith. Much of their deliberation focused on the person of Christ (as divine and human) and his saving acts. The trinitarian language of the creeds evolved from the need to articulate who Christ was for humanity. The need to have a confession of faith articulated for baptismal use was a significant factor in the development of so-called orthodox Christian language.

In baptism Christians follow the example and command of Jesus. Because of who Christ is—God and human—in baptism Christians can expect to encounter the fullness of the Trinity

A contemporary *mikveh*. We know from archaeological evidence that Jewish communities practiced *mikveh*, immersion rituals of purification for those entering the temple precinct. This purification ritual was typically received at the base of the temple and was to be repeated. A gender-specific ritual of purification still practiced in accordance with the Jewish laws is the *mikveh* prescribed for women after menstruation and childbirth.

Since the conversion of the emperor Constantine (fourth century) and the subsequent emperors' making Christianity not only permissible but the legal, imperially accepted religion for the Holy Roman Empire, it was both politically and religiously important for Christians to stay united. From the initiative of the emperors, several ecumenical councils of bishops were held to find a unifying language on the essentials of Christian faith, confessed in baptism and guiding Christian living.

The emperors wanted a unified church, which was difficult as the gospel spread in the early centuries. The most important of these councils were the Council of Nicaea in 325, Constantinople in 381, Ephesus in 431, and Chalcedon in 451. The teachings of these councils still serve as the norm for orthodoxy, while the rejected views have not exactly died but have survived in the margins. Luther and his followers wholeheartedly accepted the decisions of these councils as derived from scripture and confessing God as triune, the second person of the Trinity as truly God ("of one being with the Father") and truly human, Christ as Savior, and the Holy Spirit as God.

---

15. The Apostles' and Nicene Creeds were baptismal creeds. These liturgical texts express belief in the triune God, in Christ's saving work, the mission of the church, one baptism, and the hope of resurrection and eternal life.

and the Trinity's saving action in Christ. Jesus' trinitarian statement in Matthew 28, even if it is a wording that may have evolved in its recorded versions, is significant. Theologically it implies what you can expect in baptism: for all of God to be fully present and to enter fully into your life as only God can. Baptism is thus the holiest of rituals because of the promised presence of the triune God. For the same reason, it is vital that Christians practice it correctly so as not to commit blasphemy.

Some contemporary Christians raise questions about the God-language used in Christian rituals and discourse. Given the male-centered contexts out of which Christian religious language arose, some ask whether the language of "Father" and "he" is indispensable in baptismal practices today. That is, would another expression of trinitarian language work as well, if not better, in naming the God present and active in the ritual? For Luther, this was not an issue. His concern was that the trinitarian formula continue in use, as a matter of orthodoxy and his experience of God as triune and in distinct relation to human beings. Within that trinitarian language, Luther's image of God was not gender-bound as the grammar conventions around pronouns might suggest. What mattered for him was that God in Christ had indeed become a real (hu)man. When speaking of the Holy Spirit or addressing God directly, Luther could use expressions drawn from women's experiences, such as motherhood. For Luther, in baptism the entire triune God is engaged with and unites with the person.[16] In contemporary discourse, to maintain the same emphasis requires nimbleness with the pronouns where their exclusive use suggests a more limited view of God than Luther experienced or intended.

2: What gifts or benefits does baptism grant?

♥ It brings about forgiveness of sins, redeems from death and the devil, and gives eternal salvation to all who believe it, as the words and promise of God declare.

What are these words and promise of God?

♥ Where our Lord Christ says in Mark 16, "The one who believes and is baptized will be saved; but the one who does not believe will be condemned."

This question of the gifts given in baptism gets to the heart of Luther's theological discovery and the resolution of a Christian's spiritual angst. Luther's main concern that led him on the reforming path was to assure people that God is gracious and forgives. From that experience he approaches everything else, including the power of the sacraments.

---

16. On the doctrine of the Trinity in contemporary discourse, see R. Kendall Soulen, *The Divine Name(s) and the Holy Trinity: Distinguishing the Voices* (Louisville, KY: Westminster John Knox, 2011); Catherine Mowry LaCugna, *God for Us: The Trinity and Christian Life* (San Francisco: HarperSanFrancisco, 1993); and Elizabeth A. Johnson, *She Who Is: The Mystery of God in Feminist Theological Discourse* (New York: Crossroad, 2002).

Luther knew what a bound and burdened conscience felt like. In a respected full-time religious calling as an Augustinian friar, he had tried to perfect his path and purge himself of sin—and had failed miserably. He felt no relief. Performing penitential acts, going to the sacrament of penance—obsessively perhaps—examining his conscience endlessly, and trying to please God only led Luther and his contemporaries into a corner, to a dark place where they hated God, whose righteousness seemed only to condemn. One of Luther's most famous descriptions of his situation comes from his preface to the first Latin edition of his works:

> Although I was living an irreproachable life as a monk, I felt that I was a sinner before God with an extremely distressed conscience. I could not have confidence that it could find peace through my performance of satisfactions. I did not love—I hated!—the righteous God who punishes sinners. Secretly, I expressed my anger with God, if not in the form of blasphemy, at least with intense grumbling. I said, "As if, indeed, it is not enough that miserable sinners, who are eternally ruined through original sin, are crushed by every kind of calamity by the law of the Decalogue,[17] without having God add affliction to our affliction by the gospel and also by the gospel threatening us with his righteousness and wrath!" I raged with a savage conscience that was in turmoil.[18]

Luther's rescue came from realizing "by the mercy of God" that human fulfillment of God's expectations had been unreasonable to begin with and that due to his human condition he was bound to fail. Recognizing that the vulnerable condition he knew in his core was not a condition unique to him, but was universal, changed everything. A whole new perspective arose from this experience—revelation that all human beings are born in sin and without any ability to rescue themselves or make themselves essentially better.

Luther was hardly inventing a radically new Christian theology. Rather, as an Augustinian friar, he was returning to the teachings of Augustine and to the teachings of Paul. Luther's reformation theology builds on Augustine's watershed conclusions about the human condition. Because we inherit original sin that curves us toward love of self and away from God, we are in need of a reconnection with God. The energy in this reconnection or restoration is one-sided: God does the restoration; God's grace is the reforming agent. Our own will has no decisions to make; we are utterly and completely on the receiving end of God's action.

Traditionally, we have used the language of "forgiveness" or "justification," being made right with God, to express this reconnection between God and us. Sin, which separates us from God, actually does not have the power to do that. God has altered our sinful path and prepared a new path to a life held in God. This "justification," being made right with God, is what Luther says absolutely happens in and is symbolized by baptism. He also uses the image of dying and rising to describe this change.

In his 1518 *Heidelberg Disputation*,[19] Luther writes about his life-changing realization that he could not make himself lovable to God, but that God must make him lovable first, and had already done so. This was completely opposite of how Luther had understood things before: that he was supposed to make himself lovable and worthy. This realization, this experience, that his own effort was excluded, had a profound impact on Luther. In his writings he consistently and quite zealously defends his understanding of being in absolute bondage to his willfulness with respect to salvation and his relationship with God. He would not budge

---

17. Ten Commandments. 18. TAL 4:501. 19. TAL 1:67–120.

on that point. Most famously and repetitively, he belabors the point in his seminal 1525 treatise, *The Bondage of the Will*.[20]

Luther's insistence on the bondage of the human will to sin and dependency on God's saving acts speaks of the existential freedom Luther discovered in the gospel. Upon realizing his own fallibility and recognizing his powerlessness in the face of the sin that potentially damns all of humankind, he came to see God and God's mercy in a new light. The immensity of God's grace first drove him to faith and then into service of others. In that moment of feeling absolute helplessness, he experienced freedom as God's grace working for him and in him without any "understanding or strength" on his part.[21]

Luther tried to articulate theologically in his various publications and sermons the freedom he experienced. In the Small Catechism, this freedom language is embedded in forgiveness language. Forgiveness, for Luther, means that we are free from all inherited guilt, from all personal guilt, and thus from damnation, that is, separation from God and the source of goodness. Forgiveness means that the evils, devils, and demons of the world do not have the power to destroy and kill hope, and they do not define human life. The baptized person is right with the Creator so that nothing in this world, not even death, can threaten him or her.

In other words, Luther was convinced that, due to our inherited guilt, forgiveness is necessary and is granted by God's action, and that action alters reality: we are carried into the reality of God where there is no death, no devil, no damnation. In contemporary language, we could understand the meaning of terms like *devil* and *damnation* to speak of universal experiences of grief, regret, suffering, institutional evils of injustice, and private hells of many kinds. Similarly, Luther's use of the words "eternal salvation" can be expanded beyond his late medieval view of salvation and hell as "places": eternal salvation could mean that the baptized person is free from death, the devil, damnation, and bondages of various kinds to live a godly life forever with God.

Luther's use of "all who believe it" in his explanation may sound like he is speaking of faith and believing as a condition for the wonders of baptism's effects. But this would contradict Luther's adamant insistence on the primacy of grace, of being loved first before loving back, of receiving grace before being "able" to believe. Yet, theologically speaking, saving faith for Luther is not about "believe and then" but rather about acceptance of "what is": that one is baptized in the faith that already is "given" and saves. Luther gives the

With the exclamation "But I am baptized!" Luther joins the centuries of Christians who have claimed their protection with these words. In the Large Catechism, Luther wrote, "Because the water and the Word together constitute one baptism, both body and soul shall be saved and live forever: the soul through the Word in which it believes, the body because it is united with the soul and apprehends baptism in the only way it can" (Baptism, par. 44, 46 [BC 462]).

---

20. LW 33:3–295. 21. See Luther's explanation of the third article of the Creed in chapter 3, p. 92.

small word *faith* an enormous meaning, a meaning independent from the believing individual's works or decisions. This is consistent with his teaching of grace *extra nos* (coming from "outside" us and independent of our efforts) and "salvation by grace alone." The faith-baptism connection thus takes the reader to the heart of Luther's grace-theology.[22]

3: How can water do such great things?

♥ Clearly the water does not do it, but the word of God, which is with and alongside the water, and faith, which trusts this word of God in the water. For without the word of God the water is plain water and not a baptism, but with the word of God it is a baptism, that is, a grace-filled water of life and a "bath of the new birth in the Holy Spirit," as St. Paul says to Titus in chapter 3, "through the water of rebirth and renewal by the Holy Spirit. This Spirit he poured out on us richly through Jesus Christ our Savior, so that, having been justified by his grace, we might become heirs according to the hope of eternal life. The saying is sure."[23]

"Baptism is a very different thing from all other water, not by virtue of the natural substance but because here something nobler is added, for God himself stakes his honor, his power, and his might on it. Therefore it is not simply a natural water, but a divine, heavenly, holy, and blessed water . . . all by virtue of the Word, which is a heavenly, holy Word that no one can sufficiently extol, for it contains and conveys all that is God's" (Large Catechism, Baptism, par. 17 [BC 458]).

In his catechism, Luther clearly wants to illustrate the spiritual significance of baptism as more than "just" a ritual done for the sake of membership or remembrance. Luther shifts the focus away from the person being baptized by pointing to God's word as the acting agent. At the same time, he makes baptism personal by describing its impact on the baptized person. Luther pairs word and faith as the actors, but he does not suggest that faith would be a work or requirement for baptism. Rather, he shows how the two function together for the benefit of the baptized in whose life a real change is about to occur while she or he is in the state of passivity as the recipient of this divine gift.

One way to look at the wording in the catechism is to consider the context in which Luther is writing. To be sure, at times the reformer is teaching his readers what Christians "have" to believe within a Christian church with its particular doctrines and practices, but he

Baptism is a grace-filled water of life.

---

22. For further discussion of faith, see above, p. 124.   23. Titus 3:5-8.

is also teaching Christian faith as it is practiced and confessed in a community of faith. The faith "required" already exists in the baptizing community, with or without the particular faith of the individual. Baptism as a means of grace administered in the church rests on the trust of the faith community that what God promises will happen in the baptism truly does take place. Without such a faith, one should not exercise or partake in baptism. Faith in this regard is vital.

Importantly, the baptized person's quality or quantity of faith is not measured. While faith in a broader sense is an essential factor in the meaning of and the rationale for the event, there is no individual person's "faith requirement" for baptism. Finally, it is not faith that makes the sacrament a true means of grace or that effects its promise; no, the word does that. Luther's theology is centered in God's word; faith is secondary, a result of God's gracious word.

Before and after Luther, this question of the relationship between faith and baptism has been one of the divisive matters among Christians: whether to consider faith a requirement for baptism and its effectiveness, or whether to practice baptism with the expectation that faith follows. Also the nature of this faith with baptism has evoked different questions: Is it a conceptual faith in terms of beliefs about "what is," or is faith something else, less about what one believes actively and more about a way of naming the connection with the new actual reality with God?

In the words of the catechism, faith implies a specific trust in the word that is actively working in the sacrament. The emphasis in this statement is not on faith, but on God's word. The word is present and active in the water and with the water. This present and active word reveals God's heart—also present and active in baptism—and, thus, in the context of sacraments, reveals that sacraments are from God, God's doing, from God to human beings. In this sense, faith with baptism implies trust in God's promise. It is not a matter of a right belief or comprehension or conviction. Here Luther underscores the passivity of justification and of being made right: it is not a matter of *doing* but just *believing* that it is so. The wording with faith suggests the completeness of what has already happened. This is because of the word that works.

In this section of the Small Catechism, Luther defines baptism over against two other theologies. On the one hand, people viewed baptism as a form of magic that, without human beings or faith, simply effects something through the application of the water "by the mere performance of the work" (Lat., *ex opere operato*). On the other hand, people viewed baptism as a human act of commitment to God and thus effective "out of the action of the recipient" (*ex opere operantis*). As with the Lord's supper (or even prayer), Luther emphasized instead the gracious word and promise of God and faith in that promise. Thus, baptism establishes a relationship between God and the individual within the believing Christian community.

The Latin version of the Augsburg Confession (XX.23–26 [BC 57] defines faith this way: "People are also reminded that the term 'faith' here does not signify only historical knowledge—the kind of faith that the ungodly and the devil have—but that it signifies faith which believes not only the history but also the effect of the history, namely, this article of the forgiveness of sins, that is, that we have grace, righteousness, and forgiveness of sins through Christ. Now all who know that they are reconciled to the Father through Christ truly know God, know that God cares for them, and call upon him. In short they are not without God. . . . Augustine also reminds his readers in this way about the word 'faith' and teaches that in the Scriptures the word 'faith' is to be understood not as knowledge, such as the ungodly have, but as trust that consoles and encourages terrified minds."

Iguazu Falls in Misiones, Argentina.

Philip Melanchthon performs a baptism. Cranach altarpiece in the City Church of Wittenberg. In Luther's time, and even before it, either children were immersed three times or water was poured over them three times. Melanchthon was not ordained and never actually performed a baptism; his presence on the Wittenberg altar shows his importance and demonstrates that in an emergency midwives or other laypersons could perform valid baptisms.

After stressing the working of the word, Luther moves on to unfold how exactly that word works: with the Holy Spirit. While a less emphasized dimension in Lutheran language, the work of the Holy Spirit is essential in understanding the real impact of God's word in human life. The word would not do what it promises without the actual, personal action of the Holy Spirit. The Spirit's work is shown most clearly in its result: rebirth. Quoting from Titus 3:5-9, Luther spells out the true impact of the sacrament: a life-changing Spirit-encounter. The rebirth promised in the sacraments happens not because of the person's faith but because of God's Spirit who is present and active in the water and word. The water that does this is "grace-filled" water, that is, water where God is present and active. The impact of the encounter with such water is rebirth, regardless of who the person is. Faith then simply believes this: that grace happens.

What can we conclude from Luther's teaching on baptism so far? Symbolically and concretely, whether one is immersed or showered with water, baptism performed with the faith of the community that seeks God's daily presence rests on trust that God comes to human beings in many ways, even and specifically through the most mundane yet precious element of water. The moment of individual baptism brings specificity to God's generous and constant grace-giving as the source of new life. Baptism marks each individual person's connection to the water source. It is a reminder, but it is more than that: through the word the water in baptism is God's water, godly water, and it has the capacity to mediate grace and transform lives. The water makes invisible grace visible to our human eyes.

4: What then is the significance of such a baptism with water?

♥ It signifies that the old person in us with all sins and evil desires is to be drowned and die through daily sorrow for sin and through repentance, and on the other hand that daily a new person is to come forth and rise up to live before God in righteousness and purity forever.[24]

The baptismal font in St. Peter and St. Paul's Church, Eisleben, Germany.

24. Similarly, the creedal language of Christ awaiting "his" own at the right hand of the Father suggests a place where heaven and eternity happen. In modern thinking, we can consider what that language indicates about human beings living with God who is the source of goodness and life. In contemporary terms, the language of salvation and eternal life and "right hand of the Father" might be understood as expressions of a life of justice and compassion, a life lived in holy relations where love rules and one feels no separation from the Divine, and where one does all in his or her power to share the divine love with others—that is, engages in the godly work of justice.

Where is this written?

♥ St. Paul says in Romans 6, "We have been buried with Christ by baptism into death, so that, just as Christ was raised from the dead by the glory of the Father, so we too might walk in newness of life."[25]

When explaining the meaning of baptism, Luther applies his doctrine of justification. First, because sin curves us selfishly in on ourselves and away from God, every single one of us needs to be reborn, receiving a new heart that loves God and our neighbor. Second, this rebirth is possible because of Christ's death, resurrection, and promise "for" us. This rebirth—even if it is mostly invisible in its fullness during this life—is generated "for real." Quoting Paul in his letter to the Romans, Luther names baptism as the moment when your old self actually dies with Christ and a new self rises with Christ. In this dying and rising you are transformed by God's grace-filled water and God's word. The change is simultaneously complete

Fourth-century gravestone depicting a girl's baptism.

In the Large Catechism, Luther reflects more deeply on this aspect of baptism. "These two parts, being dipped under the water and emerging from it, point to the power and effect of baptism, which is nothing else than the slaying of the old Adam and the resurrection of the new creature, both of which must continue in us our whole life long. Thus a Christian life is nothing else than a daily baptism, once begun and continuing ever after. For we must keep at it without ceasing, always purging whatever pertains to the old Adam, so that whatever belongs to the new creature may come forth" (Baptism, par. 65 [BC 465]).

Infant baptism by immersion.

Adult baptism by immersion in York, England.

25. Romans 6:1-4.

in God and yet partial in this life, so that it continues to occur "daily." Luther speaks here from his own experience.

The distinction between the old self and the new self follows Luther's logic regarding the different expectations for what happens in human life *coram Deo* (before God) and *coram hominibus* (before human beings): that is, in a person's relationship with God and other humans, their status has changed forever to that of a forgiven believer united with Christ in faith. In other relations, one continues a life of not perfection but fragility and all that characterizes human life and the difficulty of following in Christ's footsteps—which is the path one enters in baptism.

The words *simul iustus et peccator* (simultaneously saint and sinner) for Luther characterize the nature of this holy life lived in fragile human dependence on God, life lived here and now with all its limitations and sin but, at the same time, life already joined to God in Christ. These two realities, intertwined, hinge on the person and work of Christ, who has come to establish this reconnection between God and human beings.

For Luther, baptism promises not a rose garden but an unshakable foundation, namely the God of hope, who has come incredibly close to humanity in Christ and who continues to fuel faith through the Holy Spirit, offering new life daily and forever.

How Luther understands the impact of baptism and the continued force of sin reveals ultimately how he experiences God as one who seeks to be with us here, right now. This God desires to free us from our burdens and guilt. Life lived in this freedom is an active life. The new life of freedom calls for an intentional godly life arising from and oriented toward grace, not something to hold on to selfishly but to share. While we never stop falling short and our need for daily repentance continues, baptism always returns us to the starting point—grace.

When we return to our baptism, we give thanks that daily our old selves are drowned along with Christ in his death. At the same time, we give thanks for the new life to which we are raised daily, released from whatever binds us. With that dying and rising comes a call to the freedom of a godly life with Christ. Luther portrays

In Luther's day, many baptismal fonts were large enough for the immersion of infants (or the pouring of water over their naked bodies). Luther preferred such immersion not as a fixed law but because it showed what was actually going on in baptism: a drowning and rising. Already in 1520, in *The Babylonian Captivity of the Church* (TAL 4:71), Luther explained, "It is therefore indeed correct to say that baptism is a washing away of sins, but the expression is too mild and weak to bring out the full significance of baptism, which is rather a symbol of death and resurrection. For this reason, I would have those who are to be baptized completely immersed in the water, as the [Greek] word [*baptizo*] says and as the mystery indicates. Not because I deem this necessary, but because it would be well to give to a thing so perfect and complete a sign that is also complete and perfect." Both the original woodcut for this section of the Small Catechism and the depiction from the Wittenberg Altar demonstrate this. Thus, the legendary statement of Luther to remember one's baptism when washing one's face is incorrect on two fronts: first, it assumes regular face washing; second, it again deflects the sign of baptism from drowning to washing.

Christian life as receiving grace and new beginnings endlessly and regardless of one's sense of self-worth or lack of it, and as a call to gratitude for that grace and generosity in sharing it.[26]

When we look at the big picture, Luther's words on baptism can be understood as inclusive rather than exclusive. He wants others to share his experience. His starting point is his own personal experience of discovering in scripture the good news of a God who is for us. A whole new perspective on scripture opened up for him, one from which he never deviated, and one that defined the direction of his theology. It is thus most fitting for Luther to end his explanation of baptism with a reference to Paul's letter to the Romans.[27]

What his experience with Romans 1:17 entailed was a changed orientation toward the scriptures. Now when he read the Bible, he looked for Christ in every sentence. His discovery in Paul's writing meant he could no longer read the Bible without looking for Christ's face in it. In the same way, because it is God's word that works in baptism, Luther could hardly explain baptism from any other point than from the incarnate Word, Christ, the one who has promised to be present in baptism and with the baptized.

The question of infant baptism and its "necessity," a specific topic in the Large Catechism,[28] emerges from Luther's teaching. While the Small Catechism text does not specifically mention children and baptism as a special issue, it is clear from other sources that Luther saw no reason to discontinue the practice of his time and continued to endorse infant baptism. When asked about the matter, and especially when refuting the practice of rebaptizers, Luther is quite clear that the theology of grace is best practiced with infant baptism. In his *Concerning Rebaptism*,[29] published a year earlier in 1528, Luther flatly declares that history shows God has blessed the practice and there is no reason to stop it now! Theologically speaking, considering that the acting agent in baptism is the word, and the baptism is practiced within a faith community, infant baptism has all the ingredients needed. Luther argued that infants have just as much saving faith as grown-ups do: "We do know that our little children believe."[30]

For Lutherans in the sixteenth century, baptism was often done by pouring water over the infant or immersing the infant in the water, signifying drowning and rising.

---

26. This is the core message of *The Freedom of a Christian* (TAL 1:466–538).   27. Even if Luther preached or wrote on Romans relatively rarely, the importance of his earth-shaking experience with Paul's words is frequently noted in Luther scholarship.   28. See Large Catechism, Baptism, par. 47–63 (BC 462–64).   29. *Concerning Rebaptism* (1528), TAL 3:275–316.   30. Sermons on the Gospel of St. John 1-4 (1537), LW 22:174.

Where infant baptism became a most vexing issue in Luther's time was if a child died before baptism and parents worried for their child's fate, or when a new evangelical Christian wondered if a new baptism truly was needed to mark one's path in grace, or if an emergency baptism performed by a (secretly) Anabaptist midwife needed a repeat or a booster.

In all these cases, Luther is quite adamant that one should first of all not repeat one's baptism, regardless of the conditions under which the first (the one and only needed) ritual took place. Repeating one's baptism would be belittling Christ's "once and for all" work. Repeating baptism would shift the focus from what God has done *extra nos* (outside of us), somehow requiring human elements for the "right" baptism. Baptism done in the triune name is always valid, Luther concludes. It never needs to be repeated. This emphasis rests on his conviction of God working "for you" in the baptism and the sacrament carrying out its effect independently from the individual's active role.[31]

The matter of salvation and baptism can be addressed from this question then: Who needs it, and why? It is for the living who need it in this life. Since there is no human precondition for a relationship to God, baptism cannot be a precondition for salvation (whatever is meant by that) either. Instead, baptism is a transformative encounter with God, establishing a relation to the Divine in Christ that alters your foundation and orientation and from which you begin a new life.

Luther writes about these matters tenderly, not just as a learned theologian and a practicing preacher, but as a father. By 1526 he had witnessed the baptism of his firstborn, Hans. In 1528 he had buried his infant daughter Elizabeth, less than a year old. Between 1529 and 1534, he carried four more children to baptism: Magdalena, Martin, Paul, and Margaretha. Magdalena's death at thirteen in 1542 devastated her parents. In 1539 Katharina had a miscarriage. Luther thus knew firsthand the fears and feelings parents have for their children. He knew exactly what kind of comfort baptism brought.[32] He also knew that in life and in death one ultimately depended on God's grace, God's promise, God's word. A most poignant demonstration of Luther's flexibility in applying his theological convictions in personal encounters with real people, and certainly with the influence of his own experience as a parent, is the way he addresses grieving mothers of stillborn children: Luther consoled them by assuring them that their tears had been a sufficient baptism.

This kind of reflection from Luther is important in setting straight his intent, the breadth of his core beliefs, and his flexibility: God's grace saves, not baptism or anything else. Certainly God works our salvation and distributes grace through the means instituted by Christ. But God has even more options. Nothing is a requirement for grace, not even baptism. Baptism thus should never be made into a "must" or a law. It is best celebrated as a gift, as the beginning, as the centering point in one's journey as Christ's follower: dying to sin and rising daily to the new life of faith.

---

31. "To be baptized in God's name is to be baptized not by human beings but by God himself. Although it is performed by human hands, it is nevertheless truly God's own act" (Large Catechism, Baptism, par. 10 [BC 457]).   32. For more on this topic, see *Consolation for Women Whose Pregnancies Have Not Gone Well* (1542) in TAL 4:418–27.

How people are to be taught to confess

❤ **What is confession?**
Confession consists of two parts. One is that we confess
our sins. The other is that we receive the absolution, that is,
forgiveness, from the pastor as from God himself and by no
means doubt but firmly believe that our sins are thereby forgiven
before God in heaven.

Which sins is a person to confess?
Before God one is to acknowledge the guilt for all sins, even those
of which we are not aware, as we do in the Lord's Prayer. However,
before the pastor we are to confess only those sins of which we
have knowledge and which trouble us.

Which sins are these?
Here reflect on your place in life in light of the Ten
Commandments: whether you are father, mother, son, daughter,
master, mistress, servant; whether you have been disobedient,
unfaithful, lazy, whether you have harmed anyone by word or deed;
whether you have stolen, neglected, wasted, or injured anything.

While the version of the Small Catechism in *Evangelical Lutheran Worship*
ends here, Luther goes on to outline a simple form of private confession
and forgiveness (printed just below). A similar form, called "Individual
Confession and Forgiveness," may also be found in *Evangelical Lutheran
Worship* (pp. 243–44). We will examine Luther's order for confession
below because it reveals several important aspects of his thought.

❤ Please provide me with a brief form of confession! Answer: You are
to say to the confessor: "Honorable, dear sir, I ask you to listen to
my confession and declare to me forgiveness for God's sake."

Then say this:

"I, a poor sinner, confess before God that I am guilty of all my
sins. In particular, I confess in your presence that although I am
a manservant, maidservant, etc., I unfortunately serve my master
unfaithfully, for in this and that instance I did not do what they

A depiction of private confession
from the sixteenth century.

told me; I made them angry and caused them to curse; I neglected to do my duty and allowed harm to occur. I have also spoken and acted impudently. I have quarreled with my equals; I have grumbled about and sworn at my mistress, etc. I am sorry for all this and ask for grace. I want to do better."

A master or mistress may say the following: "In particular I confess to you that I have not faithfully cared for my child, the members of my household or my spouse to the glory of God. I have cursed, set a bad example with indecent words and deeds, done harm to my neighbors, spoken evil of them, overcharged them, and sold them inferior goods and short-changed them," and whatever else he or she has done against the commands of God and their walk of life, etc.

Woodcut of a pastor listening to confession, from a 1530 edition of Luther's Large Catechism.

However, if some individuals do not find themselves burdened by these or greater sins, they are not to worry, nor are they to search for or invent further sins and thereby turn confession into torture. Instead mention one or two that you are aware of in the following way: "In particular I confess that I cursed once, likewise that one time I was inconsiderate in my speech, one time I neglected this or that, etc." Let that be enough. If you are aware of no sins at all (which is really quite unlikely), then do not mention any in particular, but instead receive forgiveness on the basis of the general confession, which you make to God in the presence of the confessor.

Thereupon the confessor is to say: "God be gracious to you and strengthen your faith. Amen." Let the confessor say [further]: "Do you also believe that my forgiveness is God's forgiveness?"

[Answer:] "Yes, dear sir."

Thereupon he may say: "'Let it be done for you according to your faith.' [Matt. 8:13] And I by the command of our Lord Jesus Christ forgive you your sin in the name of the Father and of the Son and of the Holy Spirit. Amen. Go in peace." A confessor, by using additional passages of Scripture, will in fact be able to comfort and encourage to faith those whose consciences are heavily burdened or who are distressed and under attack. This is only to be an ordinary form of confession for simple people.

When it comes to the sacraments of the church, sixteenth-century Lutherans seem unable to count. Today most Lutherans would count two sacraments (baptism and the Lord's supper), but at the time of the Reformation, the reformers often added two others: confession and forgiveness (which they labeled the sacrament of absolution) and ordination.[33] When the Wittenberg reformers talk about the "sacrament of absolution," they almost always tie it to baptism, because the waters represent a daily drowning of the old creature of sin and a raising up of the new creature of faith. Indeed, Luther's fourth question on what water baptism signifies (see p. 138) is the proper introduction to confession and forgiveness.

Already in the very first of the *Ninety-Five Theses*, Luther revealed an aspect of biblical teaching often ignored or downplayed by Christians in his day and ours. "Our Lord and Master Jesus Christ, in saying 'Do penance'[34] [Matt. 4:17], wanted the entire life of the faithful to be one of penitence." The phrase "entire life" means that we do not graduate from being sinners into being saints but that believers remain at the same time righteous and sinner. This same approach to the Christian life affected Luther's view of baptism. It is never "one and done." That is, it can never become simply a memory of something that happened long in the past but is no longer effective once we sin again. Nor can it ever be simply reduced to a human rite to demonstrate our commitment to God. Instead, as Luther insists, baptism remains with us in *daily* contrition and repentance and in *daily* rising to new life.

When we think that baptism somehow recedes in our rearview mirror, we are constructing a "before-and-after" form of the Christian life. This leads either to judgmentalism, when we imagine that we are on a higher spiritual plane than our neighbors, or to despair, when we discover that we are still sinners despite God's grace and mercy. Instead, Luther discovered that we are "at the same time righteous and sinner" (*simul iustus et peccator*), so that the Christian life is less a journey to perfection and more a battle against evil, in which we can always trust that the victory always and only belongs to Christ Jesus raised from the dead.

In the first versions of the booklet form of the Small Catechism, published in 1529, explanations of confession and forgiveness were often omitted. Only with the fuller, second edition of 1531

The word *sacrament* as we use it today is not mentioned in the New Testament. Early in the Greek-speaking church, baptism and the Lord's supper often bore the label *mysterion* (mystery), translated into Latin as *sacramentum*. In the Middle Ages, the theologian Peter Lombard (d. 1160) discussed seven sacraments in his popular theology textbook, used into the sixteenth century: baptism, the Lord's supper, penance, confirmation, ordination, last rites, and marriage. Two different definitions of sacraments meant two different ways of counting them. Luther sometimes used the definition of Hugh of St. Victor (d. 1142): sacraments are promises that have [visible] signs attached to them. Philip Melanchthon (1497–1560) stressed that sacraments were divinely instituted by Christ as signs of God's grace. The latter definition allowed for a more expansive list that included absolution and ordination.

Although many Lutheran churches still use the general absolution (which Luther and the Wittenberg theologians staunchly defended as a legitimate way to proclaim the good news), few have availed themselves of private confession. This is a sad thing, since when sins oppress us, there is no better relief than the absolution spoken directly from one Christian to another. One of the few places where such confession continues is in Alcoholics Anonymous, where in their fifth step participants make a rigorous accounting of how their disease has adversely affected others and themselves. Moreover, the fact that AA teaches that an alcoholic remains an alcoholic even in sobriety mirrors Luther's view of the Christian as simultaneously saint and sinner. We are recovering addicts to sin.

---

33. See the Apology of the Augsburg Confession XIII.3 (BC 219).   34. The one Latin or German word, *poenitentia* or *Buße*, may be translated into English as "penance," "penitence," or "repentance." Here Luther was taking a standard proof text for going to the sacrament of penance and making it applicable to Christian repentance at all times.

did Luther include a brief form for this sacramental rite. His explanation shows what he considered at the very heart of the matter: "Confession consists of two parts. One is that we confess our sins. The other is that we receive the absolution, that is, forgiveness, from the pastor as from God himself and by no means doubt but firmly believe that our sins are thereby forgiven before God in heaven." These two parts are the daily "drowning and rising" of baptism. The first occurs when God's law works on us, revealing our human frailties and sins. Thus, in the order of confession that follows, Luther refers to using the Ten Commandments. The second occurs with the absolution, when the confessor says: "And I by the command of our LORD Jesus Christ forgive you your sin in the name of the Father and of the Son and of the Holy Spirit." But Luther also suggests that the confessor "by using additional passages of Scripture, will in fact be able to comfort and encourage to faith those whose consciences are heavily burdened or who are distressed and under attack."

Luther then includes several suggestions for how people in different walks of life may confess. Like any good pastor, Luther realizes that the sins that people commit relate directly to the arena in life where they serve. Now, because the medieval church insisted that people had to confess *all* sins they had committed since their last confession—a practice that crushed many sensitive souls—Luther is quick to add that confessants "are not to worry, nor are they to search for or invent further sins and thereby turn confession into torture." The emphasis for him was *not* on the confessing (so that even a general confession of being a sinner sufficed) but rather on the absolution. Perhaps one wise pastor said it best: "In the Christian life there is nothing absolute but the absolution."

In Luther's order, after a person has confessed, the confessor asks, "Do you believe that my forgiveness is God's forgiveness?" Some people, who may also object to some lines in the general absolution in recent worship resources ("As a called and ordained minister of the church of Christ, and by his authority, I therefore declare to you the entire forgiveness of all your sins"), may construe these words as a power grab by the pastor. Nothing could be further from the truth.

First, it is true that any Christian can forgive the sins of another in God's name (especially when a pastor is not available). Second, the pastor never forgives on his or her own authority but only by Christ's authority, as reflected in Luke 10:16 and John 20:21. Third, this makes the confessor transparent, so that the one burdened by sin or sorrow hears Christ speaking as directly to him or her as Christ spoke to the man in Mark 2:5. After all, pastors are also human and sinful and may at times find it hard to forgive a person (or a congregation) from their hearts. But their job consists of announcing *God's* forgiveness, life, and salvation—in baptism, absolution, and the supper.

A Baptismal Teaching Confessed

Lutheran teaching on baptism and sacraments in general was written down and presented in the Augsburg Confession in 1530.[35] Luther saw baptism (Article IX) and confession (Article

---

35. The Augsburg Confession was chiefly drafted for the decisive Diet of Augsburg in 1530 by Luther's colleague Philip Melanchthon. It was based on writings prepared collaboratively by both Melanchthon and Luther, and was designed as a confession of the catholic (universal) faith before the Holy Roman emperor, Charles V. Rejected by him in favor of a Catholicism in union with the Roman papacy, it was not recognized as an alternate confession in the Holy Roman Empire until 1555. Almost all member churches of the Lutheran World Federation accept it.

XI) as dual gifts, and the starting point for Christian life supported by the rituals and proclamation of the church. In the end, baptism only really has a meaning and function within the church community that it in turn creates. Outside of a confessing church community, the means of grace do not work miraculously. Neither can they be reduced to signs of individuals' commitment. These insights are important for contemporary readers of Luther to engage when imagining the potential of baptism for the future. Not fear of damnation nor pride in one's own commitment but God's love and faith's commitment to Jesus could be the new starting point for baptismal rationales, leaving the matter of salvation where it belongs: in God's hands.

Baptism is a jewel insofar as it points to the wonders with which God has gifted us. For contemporary Christians, baptism offers many connections with the past, vistas for the future, and reasons to converse with Luther, whose life experiences made him such an effective teacher on baptism. Not all of Luther's conclusions may work in contemporary dialogue, but his emphasis on God's unmerited mercy and transformative grace and human beings' equality as recipients of that endless love is timeless, relevant, and empowering. A topic, indeed, worthy of continued study. Luther himself admitted, "In baptism, therefore, every Christian has enough to study and practice all his or her life."[36]

---

36. Large Catechism, Baptism, par. 41 (BC 461).

6

The Sacrament of the Altar

Simple meal, complex meaning

A torn fragment of bread or a smooth, flat wafer placed in an outstretched hand. A sip of wine from a chalice or a tiny cup, reverently consumed. Simple, familiar words spoken: "The body of Christ, given for you." "The blood of Christ, shed for you." In these small acts and few words, Christians return each week to the heart of our faith and to the most ancient ritual of our religion. With the "Amen" we may say as we eat and drink these tiny bits of food, we join ourselves together with every other believer who shares in the same meal, not just in that moment across the world, but in an age-old continuity reaching back to Jesus himself.

What Martin Luther called "the Sacrament of the Altar" in his catechisms has always been at the very center of Christian worship. It is our oldest, most meaningful, most complex ritual, both in its deep roots in our history, in its theological meaning—complex in its concrete forms of practice. It goes by many names: eucharist, the Lord's supper, holy communion, Divine Liturgy, Mass, Holy Sacrament, even just "the breaking of the bread." Each of these names expresses in some way a different aspect of what this meal represents, and reflects one or more of the many meanings Christians find in it. The

Names for This Sacrament
The many names used for this sacrament reveal its layers of meaning. *Eucharist* (from the Greek for "thanksgiving") and *Lord's supper* are both derived from the actual words of scripture and widely used by many traditions. *Divine Liturgy* (most common among the Eastern Orthodox) focuses on the ritual action. *Mass* or *Holy* (sometimes *Blessed*) *Sacrament* (more common among Roman Catholics) emphasizes the ritual or its outcome. *Holy communion* (among Lutherans and Anglicans) puts stress on the reception of the sacrament. Some less liturgical Protestant groups simply call the ritual "the breaking of the bread," an elegant and biblical solution.

names *holy communion*, the *Lord's supper*, and *eucharist* are the ones most commonly used by Lutherans for this sacrament.

What is the Sacrament of the Altar?

♥ It is the true body and blood of our Lord Jesus Christ under the bread and wine, instituted by Christ himself for us Christians to eat and to drink.

The Lord's supper, depicted as celebrated by Lutherans in the sixteenth century. Note that a laywoman is receiving the cup, that the last supper is depicted above the altar (artwork Luther had suggested go there), and that the priest is wearing a chasuble with a cross pattern.

The core belief that gives this form of worship its power and holiness is what Luther articulates here: that Jesus Christ himself is in it. In a way that Christians have long struggled to describe and understand, we believe Jesus to be with us in this sacrament in a unique way, giving himself, his very body and blood, to us in the bread and wine, to be taken into our own bodies through this eating and drinking. Jesus offers himself to us, comes into our presence in a powerful and holy way, and asks us to eat and drink the bread and wine that bring his body and blood really and truly into us. How Jesus is "really there" has occasioned centuries of theological explanation and definition. Indeed, the fact of Christ's "being there" has its own doctrinal name: the real presence.

Luther's description is simple: Jesus gives us himself in an extraordinarily direct way (his true body and blood) through and with (Luther said "under," as in "under the form of") the ordinary daily objects of bread and wine, and he bids us eat and drink him through this bread and wine. But this is where it becomes anything but simple: How can Jesus have body and blood now when we are so far removed in time and space from his physical, historical life in Palestine? How can Jesus' body and blood be in (or under) bread and wine today? How can a risen and ascended Jesus be in two places at once? What does it mean for us to eat and drink Jesus in these elements? What kind of a "presence" is this, really? Theologians have over the centuries used every kind of logic and authority—and quite a bit of imagination—in reconciling these apparently contradictory claims and explaining what seems very much like a mystery or paradox. Martin Luther, too, made his own contribution to this history of interpretation. In sum, Luther

Before the publication of the Large and Small Catechisms in 1529, Luther had written frequently about the sacraments and the Lord's supper in particular. Luther's main concern is to break down the old barriers of custom and move the church away from superstition and an overemphasis on the miracle of transubstantiation (see the sidebar on p. 165) without giving up the teaching that Christ is really present in the bread and wine. Luther's primary motivation is pastoral: confirming Christ's promises and making the sacraments about strengthening believers, not simply about showing the power of God. He writes all these treatises in German, emphasizing the pastoral aspect of this teaching—the eucharist is for the people, not just a debate field for theologians.

Communion table of the Bay Ridge United Church, Brooklyn, New York.

Altar of St. Arsacius Catholic Church in Ilmmünster, Germany.

Main altar and pulpit (1608) and the modern communion table (20th century) of St. Mary's [Lutheran] Church (Marienkirche), Wolfenbüttel, Germany.

Altar of Den Norske Lutherske Mindekirken, Minneapolis, Minnesota (c. 1922).

is more interested in the fact *that* Christ is present (because he promises ["This *is* my body"]) than in *how* Christ is present (a problem Luther dismisses as a "mathematical" question).

What is indisputable is that this partaking in and sharing of Jesus' presence in bread and wine is an important command of Jesus, has been at the heart of Christian worship and practice from the earliest days of Christianity, and still is central to us today. Most Christians hold up this sacrament—together with baptism—as essential to the practice of their faith, and they carry out Jesus' command with seriousness and devotion, experiencing forgiveness and growing in love.

This sacred ritual eating and drinking is practiced in many ways by many kinds of Christians. Some share it casually around a table; others surround it with elaborate, impressive formal ritual. Some offer it freely to all comers; others invite only those who belong to the local expression of the church. Whether we can share this meal together with other Christians marks a basic divide between and among Christians: Orthodox, Roman Catholic, Lutheran, other Protestants. Each of these traditions has some eucharistic sharing within its own historic family of churches, but for the most part the Catholic and Orthodox do not allow members of the other branches of the Christian church to receive holy communion in their churches.

The widest variety of practice occurs among the Protestant churches, and among them some formal agreements of mutual recognition and eucharistic sharing exist. It is no accident that the deepest church-to-church relationships we Lutherans have with other denominations are called "full communion" agreements, since the sharing of holy communion is the most important unifying point within them. To recognize another church's sacramental worship and teaching as being as valid as our own is a powerful form of acceptance; when we are able to welcome one another to the table and there is full equality in our sharing, our Christian fellowship is close and strong.

How does a simple sharing of bread and wine carry with it such deep importance that it has become in some sense "contested ground" among Christians? Even among Lutheran churches, the question of what holy communion means and who is admitted is not always understood and practiced the same way. How did the sacrament of unity with Christ become a sacrament of division? Much of the ecumenical theological discussion among churches today wrestles with this issue, particularly between churches with closely related traditions and much common history, like that which Lutherans and Roman Catholics share. The urgency is greater in places where the population is religiously mixed and intermarriage between adherents of different traditions is common. Married couples and families who can't share this sacrament together feel the pain of this separation very strongly, and they live in the cracks of a broken Christian church.

The Lord's supper is so important and meaningful that Christians long to share it not only with their families and within their congregations but between them and their Christian neighbors. The eucharistic meal is a deep sign of our common need for God, the forgiveness we experience, and the reconciliation with God and neighbor for which we long. Many of us pray often for a greater unity among our churches and a stronger mutual welcome to the eucharistic table, and we greet even gradual progress toward this goal with joy.

Where is this written?

💗 The holy evangelists, Matthew, Mark, and Luke, and St. Paul write thus:

"In the night in which he was betrayed, our Lord Jesus took bread, and gave thanks; broke it, and gave it to his disciples, saying: Take and eat; this is my body, given for you. Do this for the remembrance of me. Again, after supper, he took the cup, gave thanks, and gave it for all to drink, saying: This cup is the new covenant in my blood, shed for you and for all people for the forgiveness of sin. Do this for the remembrance of me."

Our scriptural basis for this sacrament comes from the gospel description of Jesus' last supper, where a communal meal becomes the context for teaching, clarifies who Jesus is for his followers, and makes deep and significant promises for the future of Jesus' people. Each of these things would be important on its own—so to bring them together and have them all revolve around the simple action of Jesus in taking bread and giving it to them and taking the cup and giving it to them to drink—well, this is almost spiritual overload. So let's take a closer look at how this came about.

Let's start (as Luther did) with Paul, whose description of the last supper ritual in 1 Corinthians 11:23-26 is basic to our own eucharistic liturgies, and draws word for word from a practice he clearly already knew. This is the clearest witness to the fact that even in the very first years after Jesus, his followers were repeating his words and celebrating this special meal. Paul's words predate the writing of the gospels of Matthew, Mark, and Luke. Setting the versions side by side shows us immediately the remarkable consistency among the four accounts. Only Luke's version has a slight rearranging of the events (reflecting the different cups of wine shared at the Passover); the other three are remarkably similar. These words were already a part of the collective Christian memory before Paul wrote them down. The versions used in ancient Christian liturgies and today always reflect a mixture (or even a separate oral remembering) of these words.

1 Corinthians 11:23-26: For I received from the Lord what I also handed on to you, that the Lord Jesus on the night when he was betrayed took a loaf of bread, and when he had given thanks, he broke it and said, "This is my body that is for you. Do this in remembrance of me." In the same way he took the cup also, after supper, saying, "This cup is the new covenant in my blood. Do this, as often as you drink it, in remembrance of me. For as often as you eat this bread and drink the cup, you proclaim the Lord's death until he comes."

Matthew 26:26-29: While they were eating, Jesus took a loaf of bread, and after blessing it he broke it, gave it to the disciples, and said, "Take, eat; this is my body." Then he took a cup, and after giving thanks he gave it to them, saying, "Drink from it, all of you; for this is my blood of the covenant, which is poured out for many for the forgiveness of sins. I tell you, I will never again drink of this fruit of the vine until that day when I drink it new with you in my Father's kingdom."

Mark 14:22-25: While they were eating, he took a loaf of bread, and after blessing it he broke it, gave it to them, and said, "Take; this is my body." Then he took a cup, and after giving thanks he gave it to them, and all of them drank from it. He said to them, "This is my blood of the covenant, which is poured out for many. Truly I tell you, I will never again drink of the fruit of the vine until that day when I drink it new in the kingdom of God."

Luke 22:13-20: So they went and found everything as he had told them; and they prepared the Passover meal. When the hour came, he took his place at the table, and the apostles with him. He said to them, "I have eagerly desired to eat this Passover with you before I suffer; for I tell you, I will not eat it until it is fulfilled in the kingdom of God."

One way to understand Luther's conception of these promises is twofold. Christ is saying, "Here I am [real presence] for you [consoling gift of forgiveness for faith]." His approach in his catechisms begins with the real presence before focusing on faith. In this way, Luther distinguishes his view of the supper from those who deny Christ's presence and those who turn the supper into a quasi-magical offering to God apart from faith.

Then he took a cup, and after giving thanks he said, "Take this and divide it among yourselves; for I tell you that from now on I will not drink of the fruit of the vine until the kingdom of God comes." Then he took a loaf of bread, and when he had given thanks, he broke it and gave it to them, saying, "This is my body, which is given for you. Do this in remembrance of me." And he did the same with the cup after supper, saying, "This cup that is poured out for you is the new covenant in my blood."

That the story of the last supper in three of the gospels is so consistent speaks to how deeply and powerfully these words of blessing and sharing became embedded in the Christian memory early on. They "sound like Jesus" in a way only a few other sayings do. And they contain an element of command: "Do this, for the remembrance of me." Jesus expected this moment to be repeated, for the sake of memory *of him*; to make him (not us) the center of the celebration and to bring him squarely into the believers' hearts. This is not just a sentimental remembering of a long-past event but an entering into Jesus' story—recollection, praise, thanksgiving, and a confession of faith all at once!

Bread was to be taken, and a cup of wine; blessings spoken and thanks given—and the bread and wine thus shared would manifest Jesus' presence, bring forgiveness, and strengthen his followers in connection to Christ and to each other. In the moment of blessing and sharing, Jesus' followers enter again into the mystery of his death, resurrection, and ascension. It is not surprising that these simple instructions were ones that early Christians wanted to follow as often as they could, and that they so quickly became the central form of Christian worship.

The Last Supper by Leonardo da Vinci, 1495–98. This late fifteenth-century painting marks a shift in focus from Christ's institution of the supper to the moment when Jesus announces his betrayal.

The Last Supper by Marcos Zapata (c. 1710–73). In this depiction, located in Cuzco Cathedral, Peru, Christ and the disciples dine on guinea pig.

Detail of fish and shellfish in a fresco of the last supper by Zanino di Pietro, 1466. Church of St. George, San Polo di Piave, Italy.

The Last Supper by Lucas Cranach the Elder. Many of the disciples' faces show strong resemblance to Luther's friends and neighbors; Luther himself is visible as a bearded man offering a cup of wine to a young man (who is thought to bear the likeness of the artist's son, himself a painter). Judas is shown next to Jesus, who is feeding him a morsel. The painting was completed in 1547, the year after Luther's death. Its position above the altar of Wittenberg's principal church makes it a bold public statement of a Lutheran understanding of the Lord's supper. Its unusual composition (Jesus is not in the center; there is quite a lot of food on the table) helps underscore the painting's naturalism. That Luther is depicted as he looked in 1521 and is offering the cup to a sixteenth-century layman memorializes the first time laypersons received the cup in Wittenberg (but while Luther was in Wartburg Castle).

We can even visualize the scene these readings describe: most of us know at least one artist's rendering of the scene around the table. Leonardo da Vinci's *Last Supper* is probably the most familiar, but there are hundreds of depictions. Most of them show Jesus and the disciples as having a simple meal around a table in a home. Often the "homey" elements are emphasized in art: the disciples sit in various levels of relaxation as Jesus speaks to them; the leftovers of a real meal are on the table. Often the food on the table reflects the culture of the artist more closely than that of first-century Palestine. An eighteenth-century Peruvian depiction includes grilled guinea pig, and a medieval Italian version shows a main course of fish and shellfish with lemon wedges—though shellfish never would have been at Jesus' Jewish table!

Discerning the body of Christ

Even though the early practice of eucharistic worship was likely simple and domestic, it was not without some controversy from the start. Already in the earliest references in 1 Corinthians 11, Paul followed his description of the Lord's supper with a criticism of those who failed to understand its significance, and thus—in his view—brought God's judgment on themselves by partaking of it in the wrong way. Only a few years in, and there was already concern among Christians about "not doing it right" or not understanding the sacrament correctly. So what was at issue and why did it matter? Here's what Paul went on to write:

One of the oldest depictions of the last supper shows fish as the most prominent food. Detail of sixth-century mosaic, Sant'Apollinare Nuovo, Ravenna, Italy.

> Whoever, therefore, eats the bread or drinks the cup of the Lord in an unworthy manner will be answerable for the body and blood of the Lord. Examine yourselves, and only then eat of the bread and drink of the cup. For all who eat and drink without discerning the body, eat and drink judgment against themselves. For this reason many of you are weak and ill, and some have died. But if we judged ourselves, we would not be judged. But when we are judged by the Lord, we are disciplined so that we may not be condemned along with the world. (1 Corinthians 11:27-32)

What's worrying Paul? Two things, it seems: that some participants in these meals did not understand them as revealing Christ's presence in the assembly; and that some came to this meal as they would to any other—with a primary interest in eating their fill and ignoring their poorer brothers and sisters (also part of Christ's body). Paul left it up to individuals to consider their own level of comprehension and "moral preparedness." This need to protect the unaware or careless from the consequences of their unworthy reception of the bread and wine was Paul's basic concern, but he put responsibility on the shoulders (and the conscience) of the adult believers and did not describe how to resolve the issue except through a warning.

Here we see another strain of thinking on the sacrament emerge: the need to treat it with the respect and love such a powerful sign of Jesus' love and presence deserves. This aspect became dominant in the centuries that followed, as the eucharistic celebration moved from the house church worship of early Christianity into the corridors of power,

Who Is Worthy?
The later history of Christian eucharistic practices is littered with attempts to "fence the sacrament" and to exclude the "unworthy" in an unworthy manner. Some placed the bar at the level of a proper mental understanding of Christ's presence; others made moral demands so high that (for example, in some Lutheran communities in the United States) people who communed (outside of when they were confirmed and shortly before death) were deemed "uppity," spiritual snobs who were not truly "worthy." In contrast, Jesus invites especially sinners and doubters to his supper, in line with his invitation in Matthew 11:25-30.

and the last supper of the gospels became the eucharistic liturgy of a newly powerful Christian church. The victory of Constantine over his rivals for control of the Roman Empire at the beginning of the fourth century, and the new emperor's desire to promote Christianity over against the traditional religions still practiced in Rome, gave Christian worship a more public face and far grander settings. Great churches were built as gathering places for hundreds to hear the word and celebrate the sacraments.

It is hard to overestimate the impact of Christianity's gradual rise from a persecuted sect to a powerful state religion. Naturally, its central form of worship, the eucharist, would change somewhat as well. What had been a more-or-less intimate form of teaching and sharing in smaller groups became the public performance of a cosmic drama, although many aspects of traditional Christian liturgy were in place by the second century. The increasingly grand eucharistic celebration lifted up some aspects of the sacrament: intensifying it as a proclamation of God's great power and Jesus' breaking of all physical bonds to be present in the bread and wine. But it limited other aspects: in becoming a larger-scale event, it emphasized the presiding minister (who in any case had been the local bishop since the second century) and the action of blessing the bread and wine, and reduced the "common meal" to a long line of communicants.

Imagine a great medieval cathedral, with soaring arches and a long nave leading to an elevated chancel ringed with mighty columns and towering stained glass windows. The great stone altar that is the focal point of the whole structure is the place exclusively dedicated to the celebration of this sacrament of Christ's body and blood. Everything about this structure—a powerful "sermon in stone"—preaches that what happens at this altar is

A sixth-century mosaic (547) from San Vitale Cathedral in Ravenna, depicting the emperor Justinian and the bishop Maximian with their retinues.

Constantine's Basilicas

Emperor Constantine the Great (d. 337), in consolidating his control of the Roman Empire after 312, commissioned the construction of what became the largest Christian churches ever built: the basilicas of St. John Lateran and St. Peter's in Rome. These churches (and others of the time) used the basilica model of major Roman public building: a long rectangular nave and a rounded apse at the far end used as the focal point for preaching and the celebration of the sacrament.

For Constantine, these major buildings were both an expression of personal devotion and a sign of power. With towering apses and room for many priests in the altar area, the monumental architecture Constantine built brought Christian worship to a whole new level of public display. In 335 he built another major church over the supposed tomb of Jesus in Jerusalem, the Church of the Holy Sepulchre. With the Church of the Twelve Apostles in his new capital, Constantinople, the emperor was one of the most significant shapers of the church's new powerful identity.

the most important thing the church does: it makes Jesus Christ present in the midst of the people of God, that they might "commune" with him truly in a setting of appropriate majesty. How different this is than a simple sharing of bread and wine around a dinner table! But this is the sacramental world in which Martin Luther lived, and centuries of medieval Christian piety have left their mark on our own practice as well. In some ways, even today's more modest churches with pews and aisles and communion rails for kneeling have reproduced this cathedral pattern on a smaller scale, and draw the worshipers' attention forward and upward to the "holy of holies"—the altar on which the elements of bread and wine are laid and blessed, and from which they are distributed.

What was at work in this shift from a domestic sharing to a great public ritual? Certainly the steady growth of the church's wealth and power over centuries had a great impact on how grandly its ceremonies could be performed, but there was more to it than that. Along with changes in practice came changes in emphasis. As theologians tried to define and understand precisely how Jesus was "truly present" in the eucharist, they put their stamp on piety and practice as well.

In lifting up the simple elements of bread and wine as the very presence of Jesus in our midst, priests and theologians tried to show them the reverence appropriate for a great miracle by disconnecting them from ordinary food and everyday eating. The details of the ritual and even the form of the bread became the subject of intense discussion. Varieties of local practices brought comparison and disagreement and attempts at standardization. As the church divided over centuries between a Greek East and a Latin West, the eucharistic practices also diverged, though the fundamental meaning of the sacrament remained.

Amiens Cathedral, France, constructed in the thirteenth century in Gothic style.

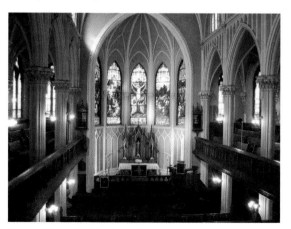

German Evangelical Lutheran Church of St. Paul, Manhattan.

Small matters of great significance

We modern folk are inheritors of many customs and traditions, the origins of which we may barely recognize. A simple disagreement between Eastern and Western Christians about whether the eucharistic bread should be leavened like normal bread (the Eastern Orthodox view) or unleavened like the bread of Passover (the Western Catholic view) led to firm patterns of variance. Many of our churches today still use flat, round, unleavened wafers, which we call "hosts" or communion bread. These developed in the West as a way to make holy communion simpler, more distinctive, and more beautiful—the smooth, round perfection of a wafer seemed preferable to the crumbly, uneven torn hunks of ordinary bread. And wafers kept better from one service to another, as the custom of reserving the leftover bread for later use developed over time.

Greek Orthodox communion table.

What kind of bread we use may seem trivial now but was very important once, since Lutherans were for centuries part of the Western, Roman church. It was important again specifically to Lutherans in the first centuries after the Reformation—because using wafers for communion was a way of distinguishing essentially conservative Lutherans from Calvinists and other, more radical Protestants who denied or questioned Christ's real presence. Those Christians wanted to renormalize the eucharist back into more of a communal meal, which they believed called for normal, everyday bread and not the special white wafers—among many other simplifications then opposed by Lutherans.

Roman Catholic Mass being celebrated in Nazareth.

Particularly in the Western, Roman church that was the spiritual home of Martin Luther, very complex ideas developed about how the sacramental bread and wine should be handled. These came through an intensification of the idea of Jesus being physically, materially present in the bread and wine—and particularly in the bread, as the more lasting, tangible element. Wine was by its nature harder to objectify, and tended to be entirely consumed during the ritual—eventually becoming reserved to the priest only; the unleavened bread of the eucharist could be kept for later use, and in its "keeping" took on a sacredness of its own apart from the actual worship service in which it had been blessed.

Wine served in individual cups and communion bread.

Elements in one ELCA congregation.

The simple existence of bread that had been blessed but not yet consumed developed in the course of the Middle Ages into a whole piety of the "reserved sacrament"—the physical presence of Christ in bread kept in a shrine in a church, itself worthy of worship. Elaborate tabernacles of stone or precious metals were built, just to protect the reserved wafers. The imagination and talent of goldsmiths went into creating chalices and patens (plates) for the eucharistic liturgies; and "monstrances"—beautiful jeweled devices with a central glass or crystal window—were invented solely for the purpose of protecting and displaying a consecrated wafer to be adored as Christ might himself be worshiped. The very sight of the consecrated host was thought to have spiritual power, and churches burned special candles to remind the faithful of the constant presence of Jesus with them in the blessed bread. In some ways, this use of the eucharistic bread as an object of visual devotion overtook for many its use as an actual food to be consumed.

In fact, the intensified idea of the sacredness of the bread and wine as bearers of Christ's reality had a gradual but real negative impact on their use as a holy meal. It was easier to gaze on a wafer displayed in a monstrance, or pray before a shrine containing the leftover bread, than it was to go to confession and do the penance expected of a person who was to receive communion. As a result, eucharistic worship became more about being present at the Mass than about partaking of the elements. In 1215 a decree by the Fourth Lateran Council made it a universal expectation of Western Christians that they commune at least once a year, in the Easter season. The remarkable thing about this decree is that this was considered a desired goal, an improvement on the current situation. Holy communion had become somehow "too special" and too intimidating for many ordinary Christians, so that in Luther's day most Christians communed *only* once a year.

Medieval Eucharistic Piety

The commonplace understanding in Christian teaching that the body and blood of Christ are present in the bread and wine of the eucharist gradually led to devotional practices that made the eucharist more than a meal to be received—a miracle to be honored. The view that a change occurs in the elements at the moment of their consecration—and that this change cannot be reversed—made it necessary to develop reverent ways to handle the bread and wine that remained after the eucharistic celebration was over.

Normally, the wine was consumed by those permitted to receive it (after 1215 only ordained priests), but the leftover bread was treated with great respect and continued to be understood as the physical body and blood of Christ, present in the midst of the people. Usually stored in a vessel of precious metal and locked in a secure tabernacle, the ongoing presence of Jesus was signaled by the burning of a single candle near the tabernacle toward which the faithful knelt upon entry into the church. Prayer in its presence became common, and by Luther's time, the consecrated host was used as a common object of devotion. On the Feast of Corpus Christi (established in 1264 by Pope Urban IV), the host was carried through the streets of towns in a monstrance and under a canopy, adored by those who came to watch.

It was commonly believed that seeing the host elevated by the priest at the moment of consecration was a kind of insurance against a sudden death that day; "going to Mass" became more about being present at the priestly miracle and viewing the elevation than about actually partaking.

The Fourth Lateran Council of 1215, called by Pope Innocent III (1161–1216) and lodged in the Lateran Palace in Rome, was one of the most important gatherings of bishops and other teachers of the church of the Middle Ages. Its decrees reinforced established church teaching and practice, and called for reform of abuses. It restated the established teaching of the church on the real presence of Christ in the sacrament, and for the first time used the term *transubstantiation* to describe the change in the elements from bread and wine to the body and blood of Christ. It accompanied this with a reassertion of the duty of the faithful Christian to take part in the sacrament at least once a year, at Easter and after confession—an acknowledgment that the reception of the eucharist was not as frequent as it should have been.

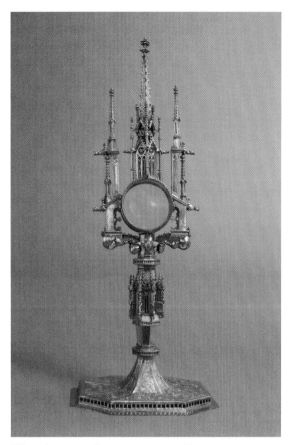

The Mass of St. Gregory by Simon Marmion, c. 1460–65. This painting depicts Pope Gregory the Great (540–604), who while celebrating the Mass is said to have had a vision of the dead Jesus in the tomb, surrounded by the implements of Jesus' passion.

Fifteenth-century German monstrance. Monstrances were invented to protect and display a consecrated wafer to be adored as Christ himself might be worshiped.

The central idea: the sacrament is a gift

It is easy to see an exaggerated sense of the holiness of the eucharistic bread and wine as the culprit in this shift away from the sacrament's reception to its adoration as an object. The lifting up of the eucharist as a sacred miracle, in which consecrated priests wearing rich vestments and splendid churches transformed mere bits of unleavened bread into the body and blood of Christ, had made the sacrament both more impressive and beautiful, but also more distant and forbidding. The trappings had obscured the central meaning and purpose of the eucharist as the food of unity with Christ and Christ's people and forgiveness from Christ. And the priesthood itself had become more about the special power conferred in ordination and needed to bless the bread and wine than about the service of God's people.

This was Luther's world: one in which a rich but confusing array of eucharistic customs had both objectified the elements as sacred and distanced them from ordinary people. In his rediscovery of the gospel truth that God's mercy and grace are a gift and not earned by ritual, piety, or good works, Luther undermined the use of pious practices as a way of pleasing God and earning credit with God toward the rewards of salvation. Luther's simple explanation of the sacrament in his Small Catechism is an example of his attempts to restore it to its original significance and central place in Christian worship. But here is where Luther's role is complicated and nuanced: though he wanted to remove superstitious misuse and distorted understandings of the sacrament, he resisted efforts to return entirely to New Testament models and restore the "communal meal" aspect of the eucharist as many of his contemporaries, who questioned Christ's real presence, did.

Instead of wading into the metaphysics of "real presence" or focusing on the outward forms of eucharistic practice, Luther goes to a deeper place and asks rhetorically in the Small Catechism what real purpose the sacrament of the altar has for believers. His answer is revealing: the miracle lies not in the transformation of the elements, but in Christ's promise to be present "under the bread and wine" and in their effect on the believer. The bread and wine the people receive are real mediators of grace: forgiving sin, giving life, promising salvation. Luther roots the whole purpose of the sacrament in the reconciliation of sinful humans with their loving God. To be forgiven is really to live.

Originally, the term *transubstantiation* was simply a means to explain that Christ was truly present in the bread and wine. The terminology, however, was quickly associated with Aristotelian metaphysics. Following the lead of several medieval theologians, Luther insisted on Christ's presence without recourse to an Aristotelian explanation (or that of any other philosophy). See more on page 165.

What is the benefit of such eating and drinking?

♥ The words "given for you" and "shed for you for the forgiveness of sin" show us that forgiveness of sin, life, and salvation are given to us in the sacrament through these words, because where there is forgiveness of sin, there is also life and salvation.

Here is the heart of Luther's theology of the sacrament of the altar: God's forgiveness, promised and now shown in the breaking of bread, signed and sealed in the eating and drinking. What sets the eucharistic meal apart from all other eating and drinking is the promise it contains: forgiveness for sin. Here Luther lifts up to a special importance the words of Jesus as recorded in the Gospel of Luke (although note Paul's use of "for you" for the bread and Mark and Matthew's use of "for many"). Among the other scriptural accounts, Luke specifically states that both the bread and the wine are given "for you."

"For you." This is crucial for Luther. This great sacrament, keystone of the church's worship and center of its devotion, is not primarily about an abstract appreciation of a marvelous priestly miracle of Jesus' physical presence. Nor is it a devotional ladder on which one can climb closer to God by gazing on Jesus in the form of bread. It is not something instrumental that we can use to please God through our respect and adoration. No—it is none of these things—it is a gift of God we can receive with confidence and gratitude. We can come as we are—burdened and fearful—and receive what we need: assurance, forgiveness, and love. It's not just about the eating and drinking, though those are important—it's about the sure promise of God that the eating and drinking make personal "for us." The physical reception of the bread and wine makes personal and individual what God has promised the whole church—the essential thing— that God accepts us and makes us children of God.

How can bodily eating and drinking do such a great thing?

> ♥ Eating and drinking certainly do not do it, but rather the words that are recorded: "given for you" and "shed for you for the forgiveness of sin." These words, when accompanied by the physical eating and drinking, are the essential thing in the sacrament, and whoever believes these very words has what they declare and state, namely, "forgiveness of sin."

Such a great thing! We have an unbreakable promise of love and acceptance from God, and a sacrament to keep the promise fresh

Starting in 1520, in his tract *The Babylonian Captivity of the Church* (TAL 3:8–129), and continuing throughout his career, Luther contrasted the "for you" of Christ's words to the late medieval understanding that at the altar the priest was offering up an "unbloodied sacrifice" of Christ's body and blood for the sins of either those present or (in the case of private masses said by a priest alone at an altar) those living or dead for whom the Mass had been purchased. This sacrifice was thus effective by the mere performance of the rite (Lat., *ex opere operato*) whether the person believed or not (or was even alive!). Over against this view of the Mass, Luther insisted that the Lord's supper consisted of Christ's promise, which, through the words "for you," inspired faith in the recipients. Thus, the point of the eucharist was not to watch a sacrifice but to receive a gift or treasure (two of Luther's favorite words for the supper in the Large Catechism).

In the defense of the Augsburg Confession (called the Apology), Philip Melanchthon, Luther's colleague at the University of Wittenberg, wrote about all of the sacraments: "For these rites have the command of God and the promise of grace, which is the essence of the New Testament. For surely our hearts ought to be certain that when we are baptized, when we eat the body of the Lord, and when we are absolved, God truly forgives us on account of Christ. And God moves our hearts through the word and the rite at the same time so that they believe and receive faith. . . . For just as the Word enters through the ear in order to strike the heart, so also the rite enters through the eye in order to move the heart. The word and the rite have the same effect. Augustine put it well when he said that the sacrament is a 'visible word,' because the rite is received by the eyes and is, as it were, a picture of the Word, signifying the same thing as the Word. Therefore both have the same effect" (Apology XIII.4–5 [BC 219–20]).

and strong in our hearts, simply by hearing the words and believing them, and eating and drinking together. And we become what we eat: the body of Christ we consume makes us together the body of Christ restored!

What does this mean? It means that we can see both God and ourselves more clearly through this gift. It means we can understand that our "worthiness" is not as important to God as it is to us. God, as our creator, loves us purely and completely; our inward focus on ourselves distorts our love into self-regard and self-criticism, neither of which is helpful and both of which get in the way of our joy in God's love and mercy.

So what, then, is the importance of the eating and drinking? They are real things, even if somewhat symbolically presented: even a wafer and a tiny cup of wine are tangible realities and allow us to receive the promise of God into our hands and mouths, experiencing through every sense that God is with us. We see and touch the bread; we hear the promise: "This is my body." We smell and taste the wine; the tingle on our tongues confirms in our mouths what our hearts already know: this is Jesus, God with us—and for us, not against us! Without faith in God's promises, we eat and drink in vain; with such faith, the forgiveness and grace we experience are as real as the bread and wine that touch our tongues.[1]

Who, then, receives this sacrament worthily?

> ♥ Fasting and bodily preparation are in fact a fine external discipline, but a person who has faith in these words, "given for you" and "shed for you for the forgiveness of sin," is really worthy and well prepared. However, a person who does not believe these words or doubts them is unworthy and unprepared, because the words "for you" require truly believing hearts.

To receive the sacrament worthily, one must need it truly. That means understanding your weakness and self-centeredness, and wanting to connect to a divine reality larger than yourself. It means wanting to

In the Large Catechism (par. 39–84 [BC 470–75]), Luther describes the attitudes of many different kinds of Christians toward the sacrament: those "who cherish and honor the sacrament" (par. 43); "the weak, who would like to be Christians" (par. 43); the "cold and indifferent" (par. 45–54); those who feel unfit (par. 55–74); and those who feel no need (par. 75–84). The same issue of who communes is reflected in Luther's preface to the Small Catechism.

In Luther's day, the supper was celebrated each Sunday, although few if any received it that often. Rejecting the idea that people had to receive the supper once a year, Luther wrote, "People no longer want to receive the sacrament, and they treat it with contempt. This, too, needs to be stressed, while keeping in mind that we should not compel anyone to believe or to receive the sacrament and should not fix any law or time or place for it. Instead, we should preach in such a way that the people make themselves come without our law and just plain compel us pastors to administer it to them. . . . For Christ did not say 'Omit this,' or 'Despise this,' but instead . . . 'Do this. . . .' He really wants it to be done. . . . If [those who do not hold the sacrament in high esteem] believed that they had so much evil and needed so much good, they would not neglect the sacrament, in which help against such evil is provided and in which so much good is given. . . . Instead, they would come on their own, rushing and running to it; they would compel themselves to come and would insist that you [pastors] give them the sacrament" (par. 21–25 [BC 350–51]).

---

1. To avoid turning "faith" into a work (and again losing God's mercy in this sacrament), it is important to keep in mind Luther's explanation of the third article of the Creed.

be there, wanting to be together with sisters and brothers who are as flawed as you are. These are "believing hearts": hearts that understand their own need. You don't need to be an expert in eucharistic theology or even really know what's going on—you need only know your hunger and thirst for God's love, and be ready to receive it.

When Luther says we need believing hearts, he doesn't mean perfect ones, but hearts like ours: hearts ready to love; bruised by loss and hurt; anxious in the face of uncertainty. Our minds are full of tricks: they ask, "Do I believe enough?" when the question really is "Do I need God's love?" Luther expands on this in colorful language in the Large Catechism: "Christ does not say, 'If you believe or if you are worthy, you have my body and blood,' but rather, 'Take, eat and drink, this is my body and blood.'"[2] It is the power of God and not the power of our faith that makes Jesus present for us and gives us forgiveness and strength in his promise.

This seems simple, but it is not. In our humanness, we strive for control to manage our hearts and our thoughts. It is so hard for us to give ourselves to anyone else, even to God, and to trust a reality that comes to us from outside rather than inside. Luther described this willfulness as the work of the devil, who attacks us with doubt and despair where we are weakest and when we are most vulnerable.[3] But the sacrament is always there: we can go again and again and hear the words anew and rejoice in the promise they contain.

It is this sense of human weakness and the profound consolation of relying on the truth of Jesus' words "This is my body" that makes Luther so fierce in his defense of the reality of Christ's presence in the bread and wine. It is not about logic or the strength of a theological argument, but an existential reality and necessity for Luther that we meet Jesus in the bread and wine. It's not about adoring the elements or marveling at the miracle that happens at the altar—it's about the miracle that God's promises are sure and Christ's sacrament is always available to us in its power and love.

This, in part, accounts for Luther's deep impatience with those who obsess about the "how" of Jesus' presence in the bread and wine instead of the "why." It doesn't matter when the "real presence" begins and ends; or whether a priest who distractedly looks out the church window at a bakery display just as he says the words of Jesus has

Aquinas on Transubstantiation

In the technical theological discussion on the nature and meaning of the eucharist, the term *transubstantiation* has come to refer to the change that occurs in the elements of bread and wine when they are consecrated to eucharistic use by the blessing of the priest in the context of the Mass. In this change, the entire nature of the bread and wine is replaced by the body and blood of Christ, and remains that way until consumed or naturally destroyed. How can this be, when no visible change can be perceived?

Theologians like Thomas Aquinas (c. 1225–74) used metaphysical categories derived from the writings of the ancient Greek philosopher Aristotle to separate out a thing's essential being (its "substance") from its outward appearance to the human senses (its "accidents"). In the action of the priest in consecrating the bread and wine, the substance is changed to the body and blood of Christ, while the accidents of bread and wine remain. Obviously, this is a complex way to explain an apparent inconsistency, and Luther rejected it as too complicated to be necessary— he did not believe it necessary to explain a divine mystery, and was satisfied to believe that the body and blood of Christ were present along with ("in, with, and under" is his formulation) the bread and wine.

The Roman Catholic doctrine of transubstantiation, first mentioned in 1215 and later more fully described by Aquinas, was reemphasized at the end of Luther's life by the Council of Trent. In modern ecumenical conversation, transubstantiation as a doctrine has been somewhat downplayed as itself an incomplete description of a holy mystery.

---

2. Large Catechism, Sacrament of the Altar, par. 17 (BC 468).   3. Large Catechism, Sacrament of the Altar, par. 26 (BC 469).

accidentally consecrated the whole inventory; or even whether a church mouse who happens to find and nibble consecrated wafers has actually consumed Jesus' body and blood.

Equally questionable to Luther are those on the other side, whose logic and physics keep them from being able to imagine how ordinary bread and wine can be bearers of the Divine. At a meeting in Marburg in 1529, Luther debated many aspects of sacramental theology with the reformer of the city of Zurich, Ulrich Zwingli, and his colleague from the University of Basel, Johann Oecolampadius. The two men disagreed fundamentally with Luther about what Jesus meant when he said, "This is my body," and "This is my blood." For Luther, the matter was simple: Jesus said what he said, and what was true then is still true now: in this bread and wine Christ's body and blood are present for us. But for Zwingli, this was illogical and irrational: only one thing can be in a place at a time—there was no room for the body and blood of Jesus within already existing bread and wine. To believe that, Zwingli said, was more than a reasonable God would expect of rational people, especially since Christ was seated at God's right hand.

Whatever the role of pride or ego may have been, the difference between them was significant enough to split the new reforming movement between those with an essentially traditional view of Christ's presence (Luther and his supporters) and those who saw the bread and wine as symbols and purely representative of Christ's body and blood. The latter, purely representational view is common among many Protestants today, and even some Lutherans may individually hold this view. But this is not Luther's understanding nor that of his colleagues or followers. He was quite consciously insisting on a more "real" real presence than Zwingli could tolerate. Later Reformed theologians

Saint Thomas Aquinas by Carlo Crivelli, 1476.

A depiction of the Marburg Colloquy of 1529, produced in 1557, with Landgrave Philipp of Hesse in the center, flanked by Zwingli (left) and Luther.

like John Calvin were able to develop descriptions of the mode of Christ's presence that reflected the Wittenberg Concord and mediated somewhat between Luther's view and Zwingli's, and today there is consistent agreement among the Protestant churches of Reformation heritage that Christ is truly present with the bread and wine. Other differences in theological emphasis, though real and enduring, do not prevent mutual sharing of the sacrament.

Strengthened by forgiveness; freed to serve

Though Luther preserved much of the Catholic view of Christ's real presence in the bread and wine of the eucharist, not only this reality but also the promise of the forgiveness of sins was most important to him. For without a sense of God's mercy, shown in forgiveness given freely and without preconditions, Luther believed Christians cannot escape their own fears and imaginings and become the kind of servants to their neighbors that God expects, indeed commands, them to be. The eucharist does not just strengthen and console and nourish believers: it gives them power to act in love, to show neighbor love, and to fight for justice for those too weak to advocate for themselves.[4]

In this regard, the eucharist may have its most important impact after believers have left the Lord's table and returned to the world, where it empowers and instructs and urges each of us to engage with the world, in love, for justice's sake. Luther understands this too: the eucharist is a symbol of strength and unity of Christians in the wider world. Witness the power of holy communion services celebrated in unusual places or places of special need: at the border fence that divides two countries; in the fields with farmworkers or in a factory; on the street at a march or a rally or a protest. Taking the sacrament to the streets is itself a kind of protest. Luther—we know—saw nothing but danger in that sort of protest in Wittenberg, when he criticized Karlstadt (see next page) for, in effect, taking the eucharistic celebration out of the church and into the market square. But his concern was for the faithful who might be shocked out of their faith by such radical change.

Zwingli and Marburg

The argument between Luther and Ulrich Zwingli (1484–1531) of Zurich (along with others) on the nature of Christ's presence in the eucharist caused a rift in reforming circles and by the end of the 1520s threatened to challenge the unity of the young movement. Landgrave Philipp of Hesse (1504–67), one of the rising leaders among the Protestant princes, convened a meeting in the city of his residence, Marburg on the Lahn, in October of 1529 to debate, hash out the differences, and seek an agreement on language with which all could live. Philipp believed that if he could simply bring Luther and Zwingli together, they could work out their differences.

The meeting (usually called the Marburg Colloquy) was constructive to some degree—the two antagonists were able to agree on fourteen out of fifteen points of doctrine, and reach substantive agreement on the fifteenth over the Lord's supper, but the sticking point continued to be the real presence in the eucharist. Zwingli would not concede any material presence of Christ in the bread and wine, which he believed to be symbolic; for his part, Luther insisted that denial of Christ's presence was a direct denial of Christ's promise ("This is my body").

Whether the ardent temperaments of the two men also contributed to the impasse is a matter of debate among scholars. But the division goes deeper than that: Luther simply believed, as with Christ's incarnation itself, that a suspension of logic and physics was necessary (and appropriate) to appreciate the eucharistic mystery, while Zwingli could not accept what he saw as an irrational and illogical belief at the heart of such an important Christian practice. So they left Marburg unreconciled, and both views still coexist among Protestants today, augmented and mediated by later teachers like John Calvin (1509–64).

In 1536, after the deaths of Zwingli and Oecolampadius in 1531, Luther did come to an agreement over the real presence with one of their supporters, Martin Bucer, and other south German pastors, in what became known as the Wittenberg Concord. This agreement, rather than using the terms "in" the bread or "under" [the form of] the bread, confessed that Christ is truly present with the bread. For the text, see the Solid Declaration of the Formula of Concord, VII.12–16 (BC 595–96).

---

4. Luther explained the communal aspects of the Lord's supper in his 1519 tract *The Blessed Sacrament of the Holy and True Body of Christ, and the Brotherhoods* (TAL 1:233–37).

Instead, we live in a world where everything our faith and our church can bring to bear is needed for our public witness; we live in a world full of fear and division, and we can face both by showing the world our trust in God—through this sacrament of trust and unity in and with Christ. In some deep way, every eucharistic celebration has an element of protest in it, defying all that keeps us from God. When we accept the bread and wine and receive it knowing what it really is—the body and blood of Christ, given for us—we defy the world's skepticism and hardness of heart and know a truth deeper than the world can offer. We can then offer ourselves back to the world in service, as Jesus himself did.

The eucharist is not just something we do in hiding, closed up in our churches or privately, but a public witness with a public welcome and a public impact. When it brings Jesus into a place of conflict and claims it for him and his eternal reign, the eucharist becomes a sign of defiance against the power of evil and death. Consider Sister Corita Kent's Vietnam-era pop art graphic: "God's not dead; he's bread." For example, when we have a street eucharist at a gay pride parade and take the holy meal to those who never expected to encounter it there, Jesus may work in us and the recipients, bringing reconciliation and grace. It seems so natural to be taking the eucharist to where it is needed, not just trying to convince the world to come to it at church. For the world needs to see and know Jesus, and the sacrament is the way we know him most intimately.

Jesus known in the breaking of the bread

We have already looked at the scriptural texts most closely associated with the eucharist, and which Luther cited and expanded on in the Small Catechism and elsewhere, trying to place ourselves and the practices of our church today both in relationship to our tradition and in the context of the challenges of Christian life in our own time. A gospel story Luther doesn't mention in the Small Catechism, but which can help illustrate his views, is the story of Jesus' two disciples on the road to Emmaus.

Karlstadt and the Invocavit Sermons

Andreas Bodenstein from Karlstadt in Franconia (1486–1541) was a colleague of Luther's at the university in Wittenberg, where he taught the theology of Thomas Aquinas. A highly educated leader in the community and an early supporter of Luther's reforms, he stepped into the vacuum created by Luther's confinement at the Wartburg Castle after the Diet of Worms in 1521 and promoted a rapid reform of the religious life of Wittenberg. He is credited with holding the first reformed eucharistic worship service, on Christmas Day of 1521, a service from which much of the liturgical language was removed and pared down to scriptural references in German and not Latin. Karlstadt conducted the service without vestments and in ordinary street clothes, and he pointedly did not elevate the bread or cup, nor did he distribute the elements but allowed the participants to take them on their own. This radical change in practice sent shock waves through the empire, and within three weeks a return to the old customs was demanded by the emperor and the pope, and Duke Frederick the Wise (1463–1525) ordered the resumption of the old Mass in Wittenberg as a consequence.

Upon Luther's return from the Wartburg in March of 1522, he preached a weeklong series of sermons now simply known as the "Invocavit Sermons" (the Latin name for the first Sunday in Lent when he preached the first one [TAL 4:7–45; LW 51:67–100]). In these sermons, Luther laid out his views about changes in religious practice—which he advocated—but made clear that changes needed to be gradual and done in ways that were considerate to those who were struggling to cope with change. This led to an estrangement from Karlstadt, who sought to carry out his reforming ideas in other cities instead. While engaged as pastor in the nearby city of Orlamünde two years later, Karlstadt explicitly denied the real presence of Christ in the eucharist, and he and Luther grew increasingly antagonistic from that time forward. Karlstadt was finally exiled from Saxony as a revolutionary by order of Duke Frederick in 1524. Despite these differences, Luther later housed the Karlstadt family for a time at his home.

Andreas Bodenstein (Karlstadt) (1486–1541).

Serigraph by Sister Corita Kent (1918–86). "There are so many hungry people that God cannot appear to them except in the form of bread." –Gandhi

A Lutheran bishop presides at a street eucharist before the Los Angeles Pride Parade in West Hollywood, California in June 2014.

> Now on that same day two of them were going to a village called Emmaus, about seven miles from Jerusalem, and talking with each other about all these things that had happened. While they were talking and discussing, Jesus himself came near and went with them, but their eyes were kept from recognizing him. . . .
>
> As they came near the village to which they were going, he walked ahead as if he were going on. But they urged him strongly, saying, "Stay with us, because it is almost evening and the day is now nearly over." So he went in to stay with them. When he was at the table with them, he took bread, blessed and broke it, and gave it to them. Then their eyes were opened, and they recognized him; and he vanished from their sight. They said to each other, "Were not our hearts burning within us while he was talking to us on the road, while he was opening the scriptures to us?" That same hour they got up and returned to Jerusalem; and they found the eleven and their companions gathered together. They were saying, "The Lord has risen indeed, and he has appeared to Simon!" Then they told what had happened on the road, and how he had been made known to them in the breaking of the bread. (Luke 24:13-16, 28-35)

This is a lovely and paradoxical story of the disciples who walked and talked with Jesus without recognizing him. Powerfully drawn to his personality and message, they remained unaware until the moment their eyes were opened by his breaking and giving them bread. The story is such a perfect companion to Luther's teaching on the sacrament, and so completely consonant with Luther's way of thinking that it seems strange he didn't use it as an example in either the Small or Large Catechism. It has all the parts: the two who listened to Jesus and ate with him, not knowing who he was but still drawn to him by their need for connection and solace; Jesus, deflecting attention from himself to the larger message of the world's need for God; then suddenly the recognition and the joy—and the renewed sorrow when (once again) Jesus is not with them anymore, except as a memory to be cherished and retold.

The text says Jesus had been made known to these two disciples "in the breaking of the bread." Were the actions and words of Jesus in that moment so evocative of the last supper that they opened the disciples' eyes? Was it the power of the message or the charisma of the speaker? How did the realization of Jesus' presence

Road to Emmaus by Duccio di Buoninsegna (c. 1255/60–1318/19), now in Siena's Museo dell'Opera del Duomo.

change these disciples and shape their lives moving forward? This is the power of a sacrament: to bring us into intimate connection with the Divine, to strengthen us in faith, and to point us to service and love in the world.

Augustine of Hippo (354–430) defined sacraments in general as outward signs of an inward truth, and helped the church understand the connection between baptism, the eucharist, and the growth of faith. His pervasive influence shaped the language we use even today. Particularly in regard to the union of Christ with the believer in the eucharistic meal, Augustine drew the connections Luther later would renew. Referring to the bread of the altar, Augustine portrayed a powerful connection between giver, receiver, and God's mission in the world: "Be what you can see, and receive what you are."[5]

A true sacrament transforms the one who experiences it through a personal, intimate connection with deep truth and divine reality. It changes the one it touches. It brings us into closer relationship with both God and our neighbor. It invites us into holy conversation and touches us with joy. *Taste and see that the LORD is good.*[6]

---

5. Sermon 272, in John E. Rotelle, OSA, ed., *The Works of St. Augustine*, part 3, *Sermons*, vol. 7, trans. Edmund Hill, OP (Hyde Park, London: New City Press, 1993), 300.   6. Psalm 34:8.

7

Daily Prayer and the Household Chart

Introduction

♥ In the morning, as soon as you get out of bed, you are to make the sign of the holy cross and say:

"God the Father, Son, and Holy Spirit watch over me. Amen."

With this little prayer, Martin Luther began his morning and evening prayers. It tells you that whether you are just waking up, getting ready for sleep, or somewhere in between, you can call on God all day for all you need: God, watch over me, you, us, them, everyone, and everything.

To help us see and feel that our entire life takes place under God's loving care, Luther also invited us to make the sign of the cross when we get ready to pray. Morning, evening, or anytime in between, we get to remind ourselves that we belong to Christ in body and soul through the promises given in baptism.

In the Large Catechism, Luther reflected on such prayer: "It also helps to form the habit of commending ourselves each day to God . . . for his protection against every conceivable need. This is why the [Table Blessings] and other evening and morning blessings were also introduced and have continued among us. From the same source comes the custom learned in childhood of making the sign of the cross when something dreadful or frightening is seen or heard" (Ten Commandments, par. 73–74 [BC 395–96]).

These simple words and actions show us how this final section of the Small Catechism gives concrete and creative ways to live out the liberating faith that Luther taught. With these prayers and Bible verses, Luther gave spiritual resources and practical guides for daily life. It is possible to read or experience this section in a very strict "do this, do that" way. However, that kind of interpretation would not fit with everything Luther taught earlier in the catechism about freedom, grace, and new life. More beneficially, therefore, we can meet these prayers and guidelines as Luther's way of sharing time-tested strategies for growing spiritually and living in harmony with the people around us.

Stories from Luther's life help show how truly fascinating this faith and spirituality can be. Luther knew the discipline of spending hours alone in study and reflection, as well as the benefit of reaching out to God, friends, and family for support. He valued time for prayer and worship, even as he embraced the holiness that surrounds us in daily life. By reading the Bible carefully, Luther learned what scripture says about how we ought to live as people of God. He also noticed that the Bible is not just a rulebook or answer book. Instead,

Martin Luther and his prince, Elector John Frederick, praying to the crucified Christ. A woodcut used for the edition of Luther's works published in Jena in the 1550s.

scripture comes alive when it serves as a companion on our faith journey, especially in hard and complicated times. In that way, Luther's experiences of prayer, struggle, family, and friendship give good examples of how we can navigate life's challenges in faith too.

This chapter, therefore, focuses on how faith in Christ transforms everything we do, from when we rise to when we rest. This part of the catechism shows how the Holy Spirit fills all our days and how life with Christ truly is an adventure full of spirituality and service, love and grace.

After all the teachings that came before it in the Small Catechism, this section sets a good model for what a Christian "day in the life" might look like. Following this "day in the life" theme, we will start with Morning Prayer and then discuss Evening Prayer at the end. In between, we will discuss the daily work and personal relationships that fill our day. We will even take a mealtime break. Along the way, many aspects of faith and spirituality will arise for discussion, showing how Christ walks with us every day.

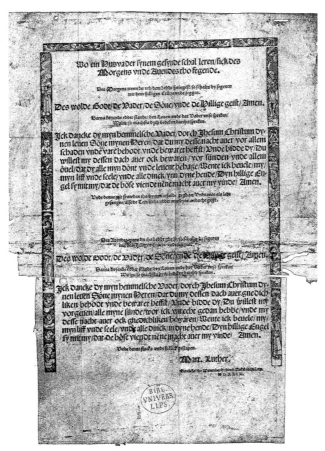

"Morning and Evening Prayers" in poster form from the 1529 Wittenberg edition of the Small Catechism.

Morning Prayer and the Sign of the Cross

The Morning Blessing

♥ In the morning, as soon as you get out of bed, you are to make the sign of the holy cross and say:

"God the Father, Son, and Holy Spirit watch over me. Amen."

Then, kneeling or standing, say the Apostles' Creed and the Lord's Prayer. If you wish, you may in addition recite this little prayer as well:

"I give thanks to you, heavenly Father, through Jesus Christ your dear Son, that you have protected me through the night from all harm and danger. I ask that you would also protect me today from sin and all evil, so that my life and actions may please you. Into your hands I commend myself: my body, my soul, and all that is mine. Let your holy angel be with me, so that the wicked foe may have no power over me. Amen."

After singing a hymn perhaps (for example, one on the Ten Commandments) or whatever else may serve your devotion, you are to go to your work joyfully.

In the early Middle Ages—a thousand years before Martin Luther's time—St. Benedict wrote a guide for monastery life that focused on prayer and work, *ora et labora*. Benedict's *Rule* organized the day by setting time for prayer, work, scripture readings, meals, sleep, and even bathroom breaks. It provided a standard guide for how people could live in Christian community by focusing on God's word, prayer, and service to those around them.

As a member of the Augustinian order centuries later, Luther practiced a similar pattern of prayer, study, and work. Even after the Reformation began and Luther left monastic life behind, he continued to pray throughout the day, take time for Bible study,

St. Benedict from an altarpiece by Andrea Mantegna (1431–1506). Benedict is shown wearing the black habit of his order. He carries his *Rule* and a bundle of sticks, symbolizing the strength of living in community. Benedict's *Rule* consisted of the basic regulations for monastic life and included specific instructions about communal prayer, so that every week a monk or friar would have prayed the entire Psalter. Lutheran services of Matins, Vespers, and Compline have always been modeled after Benedict's order.

and view his daily work as a primary way of living out his faith. Rather than abandoning the spirituality of the monastery, therefore, Luther invited all Christians to share in such spiritual dedication in a very simple way. To Luther, a spiritual life full of prayer and service belongs to all the baptized, not just a few spiritual professionals. This down-to-earth, prayer-filled approach to daily life starts as soon as we wake up with time for morning prayer.

Luther in his monk's habit.

Luther's guide to morning prayer starts with the sign of the cross. Making the sign of the cross reminds us that our bodies are holy, that we belong to Christ through baptism, faith, and the Holy Spirit, and that we live every moment under the care of our loving God. It is an ancient physical and spiritual way to remember that the cross of Christ gives us life. Even so, Lutherans do not believe that the sign of the cross has magical or supernatural power on its own. Luther himself criticized superstitions about this in his time, because some people believed that simply making the sign of the cross kept the devil away or was a good luck charm. Instead, Luther positively connected the sign of the cross with the prayers we say when we call on God in every time of need. As with so much of Luther's teaching, trusting in God in our hearts comes first and our actions come second. Making the sign of the cross in prayer can be part of how we physically show our trust in God's good care and claim the promises given in baptism.

In faith, the heart leads and the body follows. Luther's order for morning prayer then invites us to kneel or stand—both good postures for prayer. Kneeling is a sign of lowliness, repentance, and asking for help. Standing is a sign of resurrection and of being welcomed in God's presence, although in Luther's day it was also a sign of respect—similar to how people stand when the judge comes into his or her courtroom. Sitting could also work as a posture we use when listening, learning, and thinking. And if we can't quite get out of bed, the Psalms have words for that too: "When you are disturbed, do not sin; ponder it on your beds, and be silent."[1]

Although this action of tracing a cross over our bodies is not described in the Bible, it appeared already in the earliest centuries of Christian history.

After we get out of bed, make the sign of the cross, and ask God to watch over us, Luther recommended that we say the Apostles' Creed and the Lord's Prayer. With this, the day begins by confessing our faith in who God is and what God has done for us. We remember that we belong to the Lord of all creation who has freed us and continues to lead us in grace. That is the message of the Apostles'

1. Psalm 4:4.

Creed, as Luther taught. Then, in the Lord's Prayer, we use words given by Jesus himself to speak to God as our loving parent, placing before God all of our bodily and spiritual needs. This is the first of many times that Luther's guide for daily prayer encourages us to say the Our Father. For fun, count how many times Luther suggests we say the Lord's Prayer each day!

This personal reflection on the Commandments, Creed, and Lord's Prayer is what Luther meant when he talked about "learning the catechism." For him, the main part of the catechism was God's words, not his. The Commandments come from Exodus 20 and Deuteronomy 5. The Lord's Prayer appears in Matthew 6 and Luke 11. And Luther believed that the Apostles' Creed summarized the entire Bible, explained simply enough so that a child could learn it by heart. He offered his own explanations to these parts of the catechism as guides for how to understand these core Christian teachings. Including the Apostles' Creed and Lord's Prayer as part of our morning prayers shows how these great biblical resources can set a tone and framework for each day of our lives.

In addition to the spiritual practice of confessing the Creed and saying the Lord's Prayer, Luther added a prayer specific to the morning. He introduced it in a way that shows he did not believe his words were more important than God's words. "If you wish," Luther wrote, "you may in addition recite this little prayer as well." As in the rest of the catechism, the main thing is to learn and use God's teaching in the Commandments, Creed, Lord's Prayer, and sacraments. Luther's explanations are meant to supplement, not replace, those things. Moreover, this prayer was not unique to Luther but was probably borrowed from the fifteenth-century prayer book of Johannes Mauburnus with roots in the fourth century.

Even with his humble introduction of this "little prayer," we can still see how much Luther's Morning Prayer offers. It begins with thanks to our loving Lord for another day. While this may sound simple, being grateful for life itself is a deep spiritual practice. Life is precious! Our world is a different place and we are different people when we see what a beautiful gift it is to be alive in this wondrous creation. Such reminders of life's beauty awaken us to God, to goodness, to ourselves, and to compassion for other people and creatures who are just as miraculous as we are.

Commandments, Creed, Lord's Prayer
Luther began focusing on these three main parts of catechesis in his *Personal* or *Little Prayer Book*, first published in 1522. In that book's preface, he described how these three parts work together in this way: "Three things people must know in order to be saved. First, they must know what to do and what to leave undone. Second, when they realize that, by their own strength, they cannot measure up to what they should do or leave undone, they need to know where to seek, find, and take the strength they require. Third, they must know how to seek and obtain that strength. It is just like sick people who first have to determine the nature of their sickness, and what to do or to leave undone. After that they have to know where to get the medicine which will help them do or leave undone what is right for a healthy person. Third, they have to desire to search for this medicine and to obtain it or have it brought to them. Thus the commandments teach humans to recognize their sickness. . . . The Creed will teach and show them where to find the medicine—grace. . . . Third, the Lord's Prayer teaches how they may seek, get, and bring to themselves all this" (TAL 4:167).

After giving thanks, Luther's little prayer invites us to ask for protection from sin and evil. God knows we aren't perfect, but we can ask for protection from bad choices that might hurt us or those around us. Simply being aware of our capacity to hurt others is a step in the right direction. On the positive side, we pray that our actions show the love of God and care for our neighbors that the Holy Spirit has planted in our hearts. Instead of praying for a protective shield against sin and harm or pretending that we don't make mistakes, this prayer sends us into the world with our eyes open, mindful of our words and deeds, and ready to stand up for what is good and right.

As we have learned from other parts of the Small Catechism, Luther's little prayer continues by affirming that everything we have comes from God: "my body, my soul, and all that is mine."[2] Just as gratitude for life itself changes how we see the world, remembering that all things come from God turns our body, soul, and possessions into gifts to use with care. Instead of being free agents or sole proprietors of ourselves, we are stewards and caretakers of the sacred lives and gracious possessions that God has first given us.

The concluding line about God's holy angels being with us echoes several Bible verses about angels caring for people. Psalm 91:11-12 says, "For he will command his angels concerning you to guard you in all your ways. On their hands they will bear you up, so that you will not dash your foot against a stone." Speaking of care for children, Jesus said in Matthew 18:10, "Take care that you do not despise one of these little ones; for, I tell you, in heaven their angels continually see the face of my Father in heaven."[3] And in Hebrews 1:14, the apostle asks, "Are not all angels spirits in the divine service, sent to serve for the sake of those who are to inherit salvation?"

In the Bible, angels are messengers and servants of God, who assist with God's care for creation. Our word *angel* comes from the Greek word for "messenger."

At the same time, the Bible teaches that there are other spiritual forces between God and humans that are harmful. While good angels share God's grace and good news, evil spirits get in the way of faith and life. Although many people in twenty-first-century North America might not be used to blaming bad things on evil spirits, we do talk about powers that are stronger than us or bad for us. When someone makes a bad choice, we might say, "What possessed you to do that?" or "What got into you?" When people struggle with challenges like addictions or hurtful experiences in their past, we might say that they are "battling their demons." Mob mentalities similarly take over entire groups of people so that they no longer act like they normally would but go along with the crowd in hurtful ways.

---

2. From Luther's explanation to the first article of the Apostles' Creed.   3. In the Small Catechism, the word *angel* is in the singular and reflects Luther's conviction that God provides protection through what are sometimes called "guardian angels."

While Luther's language of the "wicked foe" might sound strange, we do know that people can be overcome by forces they cannot control to do things that are harmful to themselves or others. For this reason, it is good to pray for awareness about these kinds of harmful forces: for vigilance against evil in and around us and for gracious help in the face of strong opposition. Rather than leaving us to live in fear of hurtful powers, this little prayer sends us once again to God for help and courage in all situations, including the most frightening or perplexing ones.[4]

After maybe saying this little prayer, Luther's plan for morning prayer sends us to meet the day with a song. Luther loved music as a gift of God. Singing lifts our spirits, invites us to think in poetic new ways, and is itself a form of prayer. To build up people's faith, Luther and his coworkers wrote hymns based on the catechism, the Psalms, and other Bible stories. With these songs people could learn, feel, and share God's word by singing it. This is an example of how Luther used what we would now call "a variety of learning methods" to teach the faith. Through making the sign of the cross, moving our bodies into a posture of prayer, and singing songs, Luther suggested several ways to live out our faith with our hearts, minds, bodies, and voices.

Recalling the work and prayer—*ora et labora*—of his time in the monastery, Luther then sends us from prayer to work—"joyfully." In this way, our daily life follows the pattern set by the Ten Commandments and the Lord's Prayer: it starts with God and flows out into our relationships with others. The little word "joyfully" similarly reminds us that what we do in our daily life is holy and good, because life itself is a precious gift of God. Our family relationships, work, and time spent resting, learning, and playing all give us chances to give thanks to God for the gift of life and to see the holiness that surrounds us.

A printing of Luther's "Come, Holy Ghost, Lord and God" (Erfurt, 1524).

God used the Ten Commandments not only to reveal human sin but also to order this world and restrain evil. A person going to work could thus employ a song on the Ten Commandments (or Luther's explanations in the Small Catechism) to help them serve God and their neighbor out of faith.

---

4. For more on the forces of evil, see Luther's explanation to the seventh petition of the Lord's Prayer.

The Household Chart: One Baptism, Two Kingdoms, Three Estates

The Household Chart[5] of Some Bible Passages

> ❤ Through these verses all kinds of holy orders and walks of life[6] may be admonished, as through lessons particularly pertinent to their office and duty.

While Luther's reforms certainly borrowed from the medieval monastic experience that had shaped him, his theology of baptism resulted in a major point of difference: a concept often called "the priesthood of all the baptized." In medieval Christianity, people who had taken religious vows, such as priests, monks, and nuns, were thought to have a higher spiritual calling. They were on a different path to salvation than other Christians, doing works of holiness above what other Christians could do because of their extra prayers, good works, and vows of obedience, poverty, and celibacy.

Through his study of scripture and tradition, Luther believed that all Christians share the same spiritual status before God: beloved child. Noticing that God established marriage in holiness, Luther taught that celibacy (staying unmarried and avoiding sexual relationships) was not more or less God-pleasing than getting married. With respect to poverty, Luther noticed that Jesus and the disciples used money and financial resources for the good of others in the New Testament, so that possessions can be used in beneficial ways without vows of poverty. And while he continued to value the importance of good ministers and church workers, Luther valued the daily work of other Christians as equally full of godly service.

The Household Chart in the Small Catechism rests on this understanding that all Christians can fully live out their faith in the ordinary relationships that God has given them on earth. People do not need to enter a monastery, take ordination vows, or work in the church to become truly spiritual. Baptism already makes all Christians full children of God. While some will serve God and neighbors through church work, others serve in spiritually equal ways in their homes, jobs, studies, friendships, and communities.

This "priesthood of all the baptized" means that every Christian who shares through baptism in Christ's priesthood has equal access to God's grace through faith, prayer, the forgiveness of sins, the sacraments, and the support of the community. All Christians can pray to God, speak words of forgiveness to their neighbors, share the good news of Jesus, and serve the world in love and faith. In that, they share spiritual status with pastors, bishops, and deacons.

This one baptismal identity common to all Christians then shaped Luther's thoughts about the "two kingdoms." For him, the two kingdoms did not primarily mean a division between the church and state. Instead, they pointed to the difference between heaven and earth (that is, between the world to come and this world), with God as the ruler of both. Even though sin affects every part of life in this world—including

---

5. German: *Die Haustafel*. Sometimes translated "table of duties." 6. German: *Stende* (stations or walks of life).

our families, governments, and churches—God works for our good in each of these areas of life. Our Good Shepherd cares for us by giving us support networks not apart from our real-life communities but precisely in them. At the same time, God breaks into our lives through the gospel with forgiveness and the promise of eternal life.

This stands in contrast to some Christians—past and present—who have tended to think of church and state as the "two kingdoms" that are separate from each other. That model often ends up with one of two results: Christians needing to take control of political matters so that earthly life lines up with their heavenly ideals, or Christians believing they need to avoid the corrupting influence of secular society. Instead, Luther's view of the two kingdoms as the difference between heaven and earth plants the church firmly on the earthly side of the equation and gives positive ways for people of faith to engage the real world around them.

In this way, people who work in the church are just like everyone else. The only difference is that their role or office is to make sure the gospel is being shared and received publicly, just like other people might serve God and neighbor by providing food, housing, social services, medical care, legal protection, or education. Without confusing heaven and earth, the church's gospel witness makes a difference in this earthly side of life by letting people know we have a loving God who cares for us. People who know that message are then sent out to care for others with the same grace and love they have received from God. As 1 John puts it, "We love because he first loved us."[7]

The Household Chart section of the Small Catechism affirms this one spiritual status—baptized child of God—which we then put to work in all kinds of ways for the good of our neighbors in this world. In the Small Catechism, the full heading of this section is "The Household Chart of Some Bible Passages. Through these verses all kinds of holy orders and walks of life may be admonished, as through lessons particularly pertinent to their office and duty."

Remembering Luther's experience with monastic life, we might notice that Luther's phrase "holy orders" intentionally disrupts the idea that some Christians are holier than others. Before the Reformation, many people believed that priests, monks, and nuns lived holier lives because of their religious vows and status as church workers. From the Lutheran point of view, however, all believers live in the one "holy order" of being baptized Christians. They just live out their faith differently, in whatever "walk of life" God has put them in.

The phrase "two kingdoms" or "two realms" or "two governments" refers to Luther's conviction that God rules with two hands. With the left hand, God maintains order and restrains evil for the sake of life in this world, governing matters through the rule of law, households, and work. With the right hand, God is bringing in a new world through the gospel, the first fruits of which come in words of forgiveness and comfort and in the sacraments. The Christian lives in both worlds: trusting God for salvation on the right and caring for creation and the neighbor on the left.

In the Middle Ages, people viewed the world as divided into three separate walks of life or "estates": clerics, princes, and peasants, where the clerics and especially those under a vow (monks, nuns, and bishops) were considered on a higher spiritual plane.

---

7. 1 John 4:19.

A woodcut depicting a number of trades and tools, including agriculture, architecture, and armor making.

The phrase "walks of life"[8] refers especially to three key parts of life: household or family, government, and church. Luther believed that God created each of these for our good. The household is the primary source of personal nurture and relationships. In Luther's time, it was also the main economic unit, since families often farmed together or ran a business together (not unlike family farms today). To learn a trade, apprentices joined the household of a master craftsman. People who worked as servants were considered parts of the household they served too. In each of these cases, the household or family was the primary place where people received personal support, gainful employment, and physical nourishment.

While Luther's identification of the family as a God-given part of life may seem obvious, his pointing to government as another part of life created by God for our good may be less apparent. Here, however, Luther noticed from scripture and from history that as soon as people live together, they inevitably need to develop communal systems to help them keep peace, stay safe, protect the innocent, punish wrong, and make sure

---

8. "Walks of life" is a translation of the German word *Stende* (standings or estates) and the Latin word *status*.

people have what they need for daily life. Among other places, he explained this view of government in the Large Catechism's words about the fourth commandment and the petition for daily bread in the Lord's Prayer.[9] While our systems of government will be just as imperfect as we are, they are nevertheless key sources of peace, stability, order, education, and nourishment. For Luther, serving the common good through public office, law enforcement, or social work is just as holy and God-pleasing as being a parent or a pastor.

The third estate created by God for our well-being is the church. On this side of heaven, the church is an earthly institution with a heavenly mission. While we should never equate the church with the kingdom of God, the church on earth shares divine grace with this fallen world and in that way participates in the coming kingdom. The church needs good people to preach this message well, whose work revolves around making sure that God's grace reaches real people and teaching Christ's liberating and life-giving gospel across the generations.

Each of these "estates" has parts of life where one walk of life takes the lead and another plays a more supporting role. In the home, parents oversee both the physical and spiritual lives of members of the household. They, in turn, are spiritually fed and sustained through the gospel ministry of the church. Having heard the liberating gospel in worship, Christians fill their days by serving their neighbors in secular society, helping daily bread reach real stomachs. For their part, good political leaders help set conditions for spiritual growth by providing physical health and safety: after all, it is hard to provide sustained spiritual care when people first need to worry about where their food and shelter will come from.

Luther lived in a time when almost everyone in the community belonged to the same church. The church received legal and financial support from the state, and most members of society would belong to the local church simply because they lived there. We might rightly wonder whether such a model can work in the religiously and socially diverse realities of twenty-first-century North America. On this point, however, we might remember Luther's insistence that faith happens one person at a time. Your personal faith matters, regardless of whatever else is going on around you. You get to claim this faith, share it, and live it out with the people you are closest to. You get to work for the good of your neighbors, caring about them whether or not they believe or act like you. You get to contribute to strong communities and good governance because these things are godly ways to serve too. You get to receive grace in church, even as you claim your baptism and share good news with the people around you. As different as our time is from Luther's, all these ways of living out the "holy orders" of the three estates can still be true in today's diverse world.

One of Luther's colleagues at the University of Wittenberg, Philip Melanchthon, himself not ordained, pointed out that in church there are two offices or callings: the office of preacher and the office of hearer. Similarly, we could add that there are the offices of baptizer and baptizand or presider and communicant. In his view, neither office was somehow better than the other but rather necessary for the church. In the household, too, there are callings as parent *and* as child.

---

9. Large Catechism, Ten Commandments, par. 142 (BC 405–6); and Lord's Prayer, par. 73–75 (BC 450).

Four church steeples in Mahone Bay, Nova Scotia.

Blessing and Thanks at Mealtimes

The Table Blessing

♥ The children and the members of the household are to come devoutly to the table, fold their hands, and recite:

"The eyes of all wait upon you, O Lord, and you give them their food in due season. You open your hand and satisfy the desire of every living creature."[10]

Then they are to recite the Lord's Prayer and the following prayer:

"Lord God, heavenly Father, bless us and these your gifts, which we receive from your bountiful goodness, through Jesus Christ our Lord. Amen."[11]

Thanksgiving

♥ Similarly, after eating they should in the same manner fold their hands and recite devoutly:

"Give thanks to the Lord, for the Lord is good, for God's mercy endures forever. God provides food for the cattle and for the young ravens when they cry. God is not impressed by the might of a horse, and has no pleasure in the speed of a runner, but finds pleasure in those who fear the Lord, in those who await God's steadfast love."

Then recite the Lord's Prayer and the following prayer:

"We give thanks to you, Lord God our Father, through Jesus Christ our Lord for all your benefits, you who live and reign forever. Amen."

---

10. Luther translated the Hebrew as "satisfy all living things with delight," and he added a note: "'Delight' means that all animals receive enough to eat to make them joyful and of good cheer, because worry and greed prevent such delight" (Small Catechism, the table blessing, par. 8 [BC 364]). He echoed this same joy in the final comment following morning prayer.   11. Luther adapted these prayers from the Latin Breviary, a medieval collection of prayers for daily use.

Before continuing this discussion of how we can live out our faith in the various God-given roles that fill our daily lives, let's take a food break. You eat food throughout the day. Jesus did too! Much of Christ's ministry happened around the table. The customs and patterns may change: maybe we have a big meal around lunch and lighter meals before or after that; maybe we have a breakfast, simple lunch, and bigger dinner; or those who live with food insecurity might eat less regularly from day to day. But whatever the pattern, the Small Catechism gives guidance for how meals can be times of prayer, reflection, and gratitude. Giving thanks for the nourishment we receive can also open our eyes to the hunger of others in our communities, continuously transforming us into servants committed to the holy task of connecting people with their daily bread.

Notice first in Luther's mealtime prayers an assumption that people are eating together. In a time like today when our lives can feel rushed and scattered, taking a break to eat with others can be a refreshing pause. We get to reconnect with our bodies by paying attention to what we are eating and the people around us. And even if we take some or most of our meals alone, food reminds us that we belong to an incredibly rich web of creation. The spiritual practice of thankful eating provides opportunities to give thanks for all the ways we are connected to God and each other.

Second, Luther's guide for mealtime prayer sends us into the world of scripture, recalling Psalm 145:15-16. In this passage, we join with all creation as we look to God for life. Beyond that particular psalm, calling on God as our good creator might also remind us of the first commandment, the first article of the Apostles' Creed, and the petition for daily bread in the Lord's Prayer. Just as the word "joyfully" connected morning prayer with daily work, this psalm joins our hearts with the blessings and abundance of creation.

Third, Luther again recommended saying the Lord's Prayer. He certainly did not believe that this prayer loses meaning through overuse. Quite the opposite, Luther found endless grace and riches in this prayer. Different parts of it constantly strike us in new and invigorating ways as we say it throughout our lives and throughout each day. Asking for "daily bread," for instance, can remind us to give thanks for all the times this prayer gets answered for us and to renew our commitment that others receive their daily bread when it may be lacking. It can also inspire a midday reflection on how things are going, as we pray, "Forgive us our sins, as we forgive those who have sinned against us."

Luther's mealtime prayers assume that people are eating together.

A farmers' market.

Praying Hands by Albrecht Dürer, 1508.

A third-century fresco from the Roman catacombs. The figure in the center is praying with palms open and facing up, called the *orans*.

Finally, Luther provides a prayer asking God to bless us and the food we so graciously receive. This again connects us with the gift of life and the abundance of creation. While this gratitude may sound like a little thing, it can be terribly tempting to think of ourselves as the sources of our food, as if all we need for daily life originated in our kitchens, paychecks, shopping, or gardens. Not so. On a far deeper and truer level, God created the earth, everything that grows on it, every creature that lives on it, the sun that generates heat and energy, and the ability to develop and sustain sources of food. Praying in the name of Christ reminds us where our blessings come from.[12]

And with that, we eat. Far from being legalistic rules we need to follow for God to bless us, these words, actions, and prayers at mealtime provide many sources of nourishment. Through prayer, the simple act of eating becomes a moment for gratitude, community, recalling scripture, heavenly blessing, care for creation, and concern for those who do not have the daily bread they need. Whatever practices you develop around eating, these patterns of thankfulness and prayerful reflection will renew your spiritual life just as the food itself renews your body.

After the meal, Luther again invites those around the table to fold their hands and pray. Just as we spoke of postures for prayer earlier, this action of folding hands is worth noticing. While its origins are unclear,[13] folding our hands invites physical centering, slow breathing, and focused reflection. We might also place the fingers and palms together, as illustrated in the famous sketch of praying hands by the German painter Albrecht Dürer. Another way to pray is with palms open and facing up, which is a position of being open and receptive to God. Simply resting one hand in the other also fosters a peaceful, centering mood. Whatever your practice, this is another sign that prayer happens with our whole bodies.

---

12. For much longer lists of these blessings, see the Small Catechism's explanation of the fourth petition of the Lord's Prayer or the Large Catechism, Lord's Prayer, par. 71–84 (BC 449–52).   13. Some scholars trace its roots to a version of bound hands, showing one's dependence on God (similar to the open hands, which show vulnerability). In medieval ritual, the liege lord would place his hands over the vassal, showing lordship. See Luther's comments in the Small Catechism on the second article of the Apostles' Creed ("in order that I may belong to him").

In Latin the prayer after the meal is called the *Gratias*, because we return our thanks to God for the goodness we have just received. Again, Luther borrowed words from the Psalms,[14] connecting our meal and prayer with the faith and witness of the Bible. We are once again invited to say the Lord's Prayer, along with concluding words of thanksgiving for all the benefits we receive from God. This word, *benefits*, reminds us that God is not far away or only interested in telling us what to do. Instead, God loves to care and provide for us, just as loving parents care for their children.

Though Luther adapted monastic patterns, these prayers at mealtime belong to all the baptized. Parents can teach them to their children. Christians can practice them together, use other prayers of blessing and thanksgiving, or pray extemporaneously from the heart. These prayers connect us to creation and to other communities even if we are eating alone. They show the deep spirituality that can come with something as basic as eating. Mealtime prayers bring together bodily realities, daily nourishment, spiritual food, and God's great care for creation.

The Household Chart, with Stories from Luther's Life

These prayers in the Small Catechism show that all Christians share equal access to God in prayer, faith, and baptism. As described in the earlier discussion of the "holy orders and walks of life," Christians get to live out that faith in diverse ways in daily life.

With the Household Chart, Luther presented scriptural job descriptions for how people might live out their faith in God-pleasing ways in whatever roles they play: spouses, bosses or employees, parents or children, friends or neighbors, pastors or parishioners, the governing and the governed. Sometimes we can exercise more than one calling at once: bosses can be parishioners, neighbors can be friends, and parents were always children themselves first! In the priesthood of all the baptized, we put our God-given gifts to use—whatever they may be—for our daily realities in families, workplaces, friendships, communities, and congregations.

With the priesthood of all the baptized in mind, Luther's Household Chart is not as rigid as it may first appear. For starters, it is based on scripture verses, which themselves exist in larger contexts. Paul, for instance, could speak of being both entirely free in Christ and entirely bound to others because of Christ (as in 1 Corinthians 9:19), a paradox that formed the basis of Luther's great book *The Freedom of a Christian*.[15] The Bible knows that our lives are complex, that we frequently hold many roles at the same time, and that the same rules don't always apply to every situation. Scripture talks to scripture, creating more of a conversation about faith than a set of rigid laws. Jesus' teaching ministry often showed this when he debated points of the law with the religious leaders of his day.[16] Rather than burdening us with strict new rules of behavior, therefore, the Household Chart offers beneficial clarity from scripture about how we get to serve each other in real-life situations.

Stories from Luther's life help show how he himself navigated life's complexities, using gospel faith and Christian freedom as flexible yet reliable guides. For instance, the person whose Household Chart quoted Romans 13—"be subject to the governing authorities"—is the same person who defied the most powerful governing authorities of his time: popes, bishops, princes, and the Holy Roman emperor. By paying attention

---

14. Psalm 147.   15. 1 Corinthians 9:19: "For though I am free with respect to all, I have made myself a slave to all, so that I might win more of them." Cited in *The Freedom of a Christian*, LW 31:344 (TAL 1:488).   16. Among many other examples, see Jesus' encounters with religious leaders in Matthew 9 and 12.

Luther is shown as an Augustinian monk debating the pope, a cardinal, a
bishop, and another monk.

The Barber by Lucas van Leyden (1494–1533).

to situations like these in Luther's life, we learn to see the gospel-centered faith and values that informed how
the reformer dealt with the challenges and complexities he faced.

To this end, as we read the Household Chart we might follow some advice that Luther gave about praying
the Ten Commandments. In a 1535 work that he wrote for his barber, Luther said:

> I divide each commandment into four parts, thereby fashioning a garland of four strands. That is,
> I think of each commandment as, first, instruction, which is really what it is intended to be, and
> consider what the Lord God demands of me so earnestly. Second, I turn it into a thanksgiving; third,
> a confession, and fourth, a prayer.[17]

This approach to the Commandments provides a refreshing way to think about the roles we have in daily life.
First, we can remember why we are in such work in the first place: to guide, nurture, serve, protect, and so
on. Second, we give thanks to God for these opportunities to live out our faith in care for our neighbors, as
well as give thanks for those who have cared for us. Third, we confess where we have fallen short, asking for
forgiveness and for strength to turn things around. Fourth, we can entrust all of this to God in a prayer that
looks honestly at the actual reality we find ourselves in, the needs we have, and the grace and aid we need
every day in these important roles.

---

17. TAL 4:267; LW 43:200.

For Bishops, Pastors, and Preachers

> ❤ Now a bishop must be above reproach, married only once, temperate, sensible, respectable, hospitable, an apt teacher, not a drunkard, not violent but gentle, not quarrelsome, and not a lover of money.
> *1 Timothy 3:2-3*

Later editions of the Small Catechism, starting in 1540, also included a section titled "What Christians ought to do for their teachers and pastors [literally, carers of souls]." Bible passages for this section included Luke 10:7; 1 Corinthians 9:14; Galatians 6:6-7; 1 Thessalonians 5:12-13; 1 Timothy 5:17-18; and Hebrews 13:17.

The Reformation that Luther started in 1517 grew out of a deep concern that the church needed to refocus on the gospel. God's good news to a broken world belongs at the center of Christian worship, preaching, teaching, parish life, church structures, spiritual care, and daily service. Luther's reforms looked for ways to keep Jesus central to who Christians are and what they do, both in and out of church. While this Reformation mission may sound obvious enough, there were—and still are—many ways for Christians and church leaders to let other things block our focus on Christ.

Based on their study of the New Testament, the Lutheran reformers understood church leaders like pastors and bishops to be members of the community who are especially responsible for keeping this life-changing good news at the heart of Christian life. Their sermons announce Christ's word to "repent, and believe in the good news."[18] The sacraments they share physically connect believers with God's gifts of forgiveness, grace, and new life. Their teaching provides guidance for Christians, wherever people might be on their faith journey. Spiritual care serves people with heavenly medicine and personal assurance of God's love amid life's many aches and pains, hardships and doubts.

These qualities for church leaders are included in the traits Luther gathered together from 1 Timothy 3 and Titus 1. Remembering Luther's "garland of four strands" about how to pray the Commandments, these passages can provide a solid base for church leaders. Without assuming church leaders will somehow be morally perfect or more spiritual than any other Christians, these characteristics can keep church leaders grounded in God's mission, conscious of their own limitations, and aware that they too live by grace one day at a time. Good leaders in the church support Christ's mission by providing personal examples of the difference that a living faith can make in our lives.

Luther himself benefited from good pastoral care. The head pastor in Wittenberg was a man named Johannes Bugenhagen. One time in 1527 when Luther was deathly ill, Bugenhagen and a coworker named Justus Jonas stayed up all night

---

18. Mark 1:15.

with him. They prayed with him, heard his confession and the concerns on his heart, read the Bible together, and talked with Katie Luther, who was a new mother at the time. Beyond spiritual care, Bugenhagen and Jonas also worked with the town doctor to make sure Luther was getting good medical attention. Jonas even once dumped water on Luther's head to revive him! Later, after Luther's body improved, his spirits still suffered; it was a case in which physical illness had taken a toll on his heart and mind as well. About those days, Luther would later tell stories about how Bugenhagen said words of God's goodness and love that lifted him out of self-doubt and restored his spirits.[19]

While all Christians can minister to each other with prayers, scripture, and encouragement, good church workers are especially valuable for keeping individuals and communities focused on God's amazing grace publicly. Their role in the body of Christ is to make sure the gospel is being shared and experienced as clearly as possible. This is a role worth tending to and supporting with care, humility, honesty, joy, and thanksgiving.

Portrait of Johannes Bugenhagen by Lucas Cranach the Elder, 1537.

Concerning Governing Authorities

> ♥ Let every person be subject to the governing authorities; for there is no authority except from God, and those authorities that exist have been instituted by God. Therefore whoever resists authority resists what God has appointed, and those who resist will incur judgment. . . . It is the servant of God to execute wrath on the wrongdoer.
> *Romans 13:1-2, 4b*

Martin Luther is one of the most famous rebels in history. Beginning in 1517, his questions about the use of indulgences started a controversy that shook the church in Europe. During these debates, Luther refused to back down, even when he was confronted with the strong authority of bishops, popes, and princes. This led to his excommunication—or expulsion—from the Church of Rome, which took effect in early 1521. Luther's commitment to gospel theology meant that he was cast out of the only church there was in Western Europe.

Luther at the Diet of Worms, 1521.

---

19. Martin Lohrmann, "Bugenhagen's Pastoral Care of Martin Luther," *Lutheran Quarterly* 24 (2010): 125–36.

The crests or flags of the Holy Roman Empire are depicted in this 1510 hand-colored woodcut by Hans Burgkmair der Ältere.

After his excommunication, Luther stood trial before the highest political authority in Germany, the Holy Roman emperor Charles V. In addition to ruling over the German lands that formed the Holy Roman Empire, Charles was the king of Spain; moreover, he was a grandson of Ferdinand and Isabella, whose territories included Spanish claims in the Americas. Charles was also a member of the royal Hapsburg family who ruled Austria, Bohemia (now the Czech Republic), and Hungary. He remains one of the most powerful political figures in world history. In Luther's trial, Charles sided with the pope's decision and declared Luther's teachings to be illegal in the Holy Roman Empire. Despite this rejection by church and political leaders, Luther's ideas and reforms had taken root and continued to spread.

On one hand, Luther is a famous rebel who stood up to the most powerful people in his time. On the other hand, Luther was fond of pointing to Bible passages like Romans 13 which emphasize the importance of obeying authority. What gives? Did Luther hold other people to standards that he believed did not apply to him? How did his personal experience of being a rebel inform what he wrote in the Household Chart? This question of freedom and obedience is one of the more fascinating questions in Reformation history and Lutheran theology.

As we have seen in his explanations to the fourth commandment and the petition for daily bread, Luther's view of political authority emphasized making sure that people had what they needed for daily life and could live in safety. He was grateful to good rulers whose baptismal calls included preserving the peace, supporting fair economic systems, and carrying out just laws. By the same token, he was not shy about condemning political, church, or business leaders who used their authority to start wars or make life harder for regular people. He believed that such authority figures should be held accountable to basic standards of justice and honesty; we can challenge our leaders on that basis.

To be able to care for society in these ways, however, public leaders need the cooperation of their citizens. New Testament verses like Romans 13 emphasize that our political leaders have been given by God for the common good and public peace. For this reason, Christians are not free to ignore local laws, hurt their neighbors, disturb the peace, refuse to pay taxes, or disobey the authorities. Luther saw the great harm that could come when people used religion to justify their disobedience, most notably in the terrible violence that accompanied the Peasants' War of 1524–25. He described such upheaval this way: "For rebellion is not simple murder; it is like a great fire, which attacks and devastates a whole land. Thus rebellion brings with it a land filled with murder and bloodshed; it makes widows and orphans, and turns everything upside down, like the worst disaster."[20]

To the contrary, Christians can participate in God's care for all people by being good citizens: obeying the law, serving their neighbors through fair business practices, promoting public safety and education, and working for the public peace. Even if a leader or law is unjust, Christians in democratic societies have many opportunities to do the right thing and work for better solutions. They can speak against an unjust law, use legal systems to challenge it, or use other nonviolent forms of resistance, and, of course, they can pray to God for aid.

As with the preceding category, Luther here was addressing not subjects but rulers. He was reading the passage from Romans 13 as defining the divine limits of governmental authority. Thus, starting in 1542 someone added a section after this one titled "What subjects ought to do for the governing authority" and included references to Matthew 22:21; Romans 13:1, 5-7; 1 Timothy 2:1-2; Titus 3:1; and 1 Peter 2:13-14.

In comments on the fourth commandment in the Large Catechism, Luther limited governing authority in two ways. First: "If God's Word and will are placed first and are observed, nothing ought to be considered more important than the will and word of our parents, provided that these, too, are subordinated to God and are not set in opposition to the preceding commandments." Second: "For [God] does not want scoundrels or tyrants in this office or authority; nor does he assign them this honor (that is, power and right to govern) so that they may receive homage. Instead, they should keep in mind that they owe obedience to God, and that, above all, they should earnestly and faithfully discharge the duties of their office" (Ten Commandments, par. 116, 168 [BC 402, 409]).

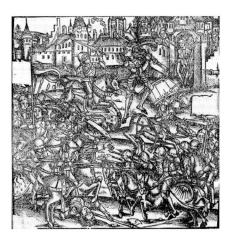

Peasants' War by Hans Baldung Grien, 1535.

20. LW 46:50.

In the relatively rare cases where Christians need to defy the law in order to follow God, the Lutheran reformers pointed to Acts 5:29: "We must obey God rather than human authority."[21] This scriptural conscience clause supports people standing up for what is right and faithful. However, in both Acts 5 and Lutheran theology, such resistance means that believers are willing to suffer for their beliefs. It does not give them the right to make others suffer for their beliefs.

This obedience to the gospel was the basis for Luther's resistance. In his conflicts with church authorities, Luther frequently asked for a public debate about his ideas and reforms. As a theologian and pastor, he believed that he and all Christians need to be accountable to the Bible and to the wider church. Though he was excommunicated before those debates could take place, he did not advocate violent actions against priests or church leaders. Similarly, although he disobeyed Emperor Charles by continuing to teach, Luther repeatedly emphasized his desire for peace. In the decades that followed, Luther and his coworkers often appealed to Emperor Charles for the legal right to reform their churches in peaceful, gospel-centered ways.

Citizenship remains a rich way to live out Christian faith. When we pay taxes, encourage good government and public service, work to curb injustice, and support fair living conditions for all, we are promoting public peace, helping people get their daily bread, and caring unconditionally for the neighbors around us. Such benefits begin by trusting that God is working in and through our secular communities and political institutions, imperfect as they will always be.

For Husbands and Wives

> ♥ Husbands, in the same way, show consideration for your wives in your life together, paying honor to the woman as the weaker sex, since they too are also heirs of the gracious gift of life—so that nothing may hinder your prayers. *1 Peter 3:7*
>
> Husbands, love your wives and never treat them harshly. *Colossians 3:19*

Civil rights march on Washington, DC, 1963.

Martin Luther, Ulrich Zwingli, and others debating in Marburg before Landgrave Philip of Hesse (center).

This section for husbands and wives is very difficult for us to understand because in our times the relation between men and women is understood differently than in Luther's day. For example, as a pastor in Wittenberg Luther was very concerned that husbands not mistreat their wives, thus he most likely understood the term "weaker sex" simply in terms of differences in brute strength. He also adds the reference to Colossians 3:19 to exclude any mistreatment of women and includes the last part of 1 Peter 3:6 to make it clear that women should not have to live in fear.

---

21. As in the Augsburg Confession, Article XVI.7 (BC 50).

♥ Wives, in the same way, accept the authority of your husbands, so that, even if some of them do not obey the word, they may be won over without a word by their wives' conduct. . . . Thus Sarah obeyed Abraham and called him lord. You have become her daughters as long as you do what is good and never let fears alarm you. *1 Peter 3:1, 6*

Though easily overshadowed by the many dramatic theological and political debates of the time, very basic questions of sexuality and marriage were central to the Reformation. Although celibacy—remaining unmarried and avoiding sexual relationships—had long been a common practice for priests in Western Christendom, the Church of Rome did not formally require priestly celibacy until about four hundred years before the Reformation. Luther's theology that people receive God's grace through faith alone—simply by trusting in God—challenged the idea that celibacy automatically makes people holier before God. If Christians are justified by faith alone in Christ alone, then "marital status" is not a category related to salvation. This not only challenged common ideas about personal holiness, but also went against powerful laws about who could serve as a church leader.

More than simply changing the rules about marriage for priests, Luther's reforms emphasized the positive place of marriage in Christian life. Studying what scripture says about marriage, Luther noticed that God created marriage as a uniquely intimate relationship. In contrast to church traditions about celibacy that developed over time, the Bible gives many positive examples of God blessing marriage. While recognizing that social customs surrounding marriage have changed over time—both in the Bible and across cultures—the basic values of trust, intimacy, and mutual care that take place in a good marriage are true blessings. Healthy marriages also provide stable homes for raising children and can have positive ripple effects across local communities.

1536 section title: "Marriage Booklet for Simple Pastors."

At the same time, Luther was realistic about the stresses and strains that can come with marriage. In the "Marriage Booklet" that was often printed with the Small Catechism, Luther recognized that asking for God's blessing in marriage implied awareness of the many trials and pains that can arise.

For all who desire prayer and blessing from the pastor or bishop indicate thereby—whether or not they say so expressly—to what danger and need they are exposing themselves and how much they need God's blessing and the community's prayers for the estate into which they are entering. For we experience every day how much unhappiness the devil causes in the married estate through adultery, unfaithfulness, discord, and all kinds of misery.[22]

As evidence of these hardships, people often wrote to Luther and his coworkers with complicated questions about marriage, engagements, and family difficulties. In considering these cases, the reformers combined their appreciation for the blessings of marriage with sensitivity to real-life hardships like infidelity, abuse, and discord.

A saying attributed to Luther shows that he viewed marriage through the theology of the cross: "Whoever enters into marriage enters a monastery full of trials." While this may sound negative or even sarcastic, we remember that the theology of the cross means experiencing God's power, grace, and love not only in life's good moments but also in its darkest valleys and hardest trials. This theology does not justify sin, pain, or abuse. On the contrary, the cross proclaims that God acts where our need is greatest.

In that sense, marriage can be a relationship in which two people who have gone through very hard times together can also find deep love, sympathy, forgiveness, and trust in each other. Martin and Katie Luther experienced life together that way, leaning on each other through both good and trying times. While we are not justified by how successful or healthy our closest relationships may be, the "holy order" of marriage can be a gift and source of blessing in many practical and profound ways.

When talking about husbands and wives, it is important to note that Luther lived in a time of gender hierarchies, with men alone taking formal leadership in matters of church and state. Even in the home, husbands were the head of the

Portrait of Katharina von Bora by Lucas Cranach the Elder, 1526.

Miriam's dance, miniature from the Bulgarian Tomic Psalter. Exodus 15:20.

---

22. Small Catechism, Marriage Booklet, par. 5 (BC 369).

household. In addition to such gender roles having centuries of cultural support, Bible verses about female weakness and male headship reinforced these views. At the same time, however, New Testament stories like the parable of the good Samaritan[23] and Jesus' welcome of tax collectors and sinners show that Christian faith does not force us to accept the cultural assumptions and prejudices of the past, including biblically based ones. Scriptural examples of female leaders like Miriam, Deborah, Huldah, and Mary Magdalene—who is sometimes called the apostle to the apostles—further challenge the idea that the Bible always and forever puts women in a lower role than men.[24] St. Paul, too, named women like Prisca and Junia as coworkers and valued Lydia as a leader of the church in Philippi.[25]

While Luther largely adhered to the male-dominated social views of his time, his relationship with his wife, Katie, also reveals an egalitarian outlook, as seen in his last will and testament.[26] In that 1542 will, Luther left the entire estate to Katie. This violated the laws of Saxony, in which a widow could not inherit property or income but had to depend on children or the children's appointed guardians, other male relatives, or a specified amount of money stated in the will as an allowance after the husband's death. Though frequently accepting the established gender roles of his day, Luther did not feel bound to custom for custom's sake. He could approach these issues through the twin lenses of freedom and service.

In that light, we can view the Household Chart's citations about husbands and wives (taken from 1 Peter 3 and Colossians 3) in a couple of helpful ways.[27] First, these passages stand in strong contrast to a monastic ideal that valued celibacy as being holier or godlier than married life. Against that claim, Luther often emphasized the personal, spiritual, and communal blessings that marriage can bring. Marriage and households are God-given "walks of life" in which we get to live out our faith as we receive love, share forgiveness, give encouragement, and graciously care for the people around us.

The Magdalen by Bernardino Luini, c. 1525.

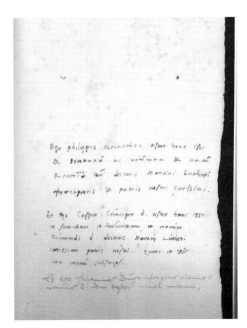

Martin Luther's last will and testament, written on Epiphany (January 6), 1542. The picture shows the signatures of Philip Melanchthon, Caspar Cruciger, and Johannes Bugenhagen, who served as witnesses.

---

23. Luke 10:25-37. 24. Exodus 15:20; Judges 5:4; 2 Kings 22:14; and John 20:18. 25. Romans 16:3, 7; Acts 16:11-15, 40. 26. LW 34:295–97.
27. Luther's use of these passages does not prevent our using others that emphasize equality among the sexes, such as Galatians 3:28; 1 Corinthians 7:3-4; and Ephesians 5:21.

Second, while Luther cited Bible verses about husbands and wives that affirmed traditional gender roles, a fundamental value of mutual respect exists at the heart of these relationships. Luther's Marriage Booklet, for instance, cites Ephesians 5:22-29, which includes the instruction that "husbands should love their wives as they do their own bodies." This applies the Golden Rule to married life: "In everything do to others as you would have them do to you."[28] Such a view of loving our partners as we love ourselves encourages couples to love and support each other in a way that does not automatically impose centuries of culturally defined gender roles on us. Moreover, by using biblical passages that reject harshness and fear, Luther was explicitly rejecting violence in marriage, as much a crisis in our day as in his.

For Parents and Children, Employees and Employers

♥ And, parents, do not provoke your children to anger, but bring them up in the discipline and instruction of the Lord. *based on Ephesians 6:4*

♥ Children, obey your parents in the Lord, for this is right. "Honor your father and mother"—this is the first commandment with a promise: "so that it may be well with you and you may live long on the earth." *Ephesians 6:1-3*

♥ You employees, be obedient to your bosses with respect and cooperation, with singleness of heart, as to Christ himself; not with service meant only for the eyes, done as people-pleasers, but rather as servants of Christ, so that you do the will of God from the heart [with a good attitude]. Imagine to yourselves that you are serving the Lord and not people, and know that whatever good anyone does, the same will that person receive, whether servant or free. *based on Ephesians 6:5-8*

♥ And, bosses, do the same to them. Stop threatening them, for you know that both of you have the same Master in heaven, and with him there is no partiality. *based on Ephesians 6:9*

In rendering Ephesians 6:5-9 for the Catechism, Luther does not translate the Greek literally as *slave* or *servant* but uses the familiar German words for the household servants, day laborers and workers (*Knecht, Magd, Tagelöhner, Arbeiter*). In our day, given that outside of family farms few people work and live in the same building, we could better render Paul's terms as *employee* and *employer*.

---

28. Matthew 7:12.

In addition to becoming a married priest, Martin Luther also became a father. Martin and Katie had six children together. Their sons Hans, Martin, and Paul and their youngest daughter Margaret lived into adulthood. One daughter, Elizabeth, died as an infant; another daughter, Magdalena, died of an illness at the age of thirteen (more about her later).

Luther's own parents—Hans and Margaret—seem to have been typical parents of the time, using physical punishment for discipline but also providing a stable and supportive upbringing. Martin kept in touch with them throughout his life, in a relationship that weathered even his decision to join the monastery without his parents' approval at age twenty-two. He later dedicated his book *On Monastic Vows* to his father, apologizing for his disobedience and giving thanks that God brought some good out of that dramatic life choice.[29] As the deaths of his parents neared, Martin wrote open letters of consolation to both of them.[30]

The fourth commandment provided the basis for Luther's teachings about parents and children, as well as for secular extensions of these relationships, for instance, those between bosses and employees, leaders and servers. Based on the importance of these roles, he could preach that "every father of a family is a bishop in his house and the wife a bishopess."[31] And in another place he wrote, "Most certainly father and mother are apostles, bishops, and priests to their children, for it is they who make them acquainted with the gospel."[32] Parents and other heads of households have key roles to play in not only the physical but spiritual lives of their children. It is a holy thing to care for the well-being of another out of sheer grace, share the love of God, and sow seeds of faith that will someday bear fruit in beautiful ways.

For children, Luther turned to Ephesians 6:1-3, which quotes the fourth commandment and the promise "so that it may be well with you" which accompanies that commandment.[33] Apart from whether our parents deserve it, honoring parents reminds us that we do not create ourselves but belong to the same biological processes as the rest of creation. If being a caretaker—as mentioned above—is a holy thing, then it is equally holy to know ourselves as people who receive care and love from others too. This is certainly part of what Jesus meant when he said, "Truly I tell you, unless you change and become like children, you will never enter the kingdom of heaven."[34]

To those whose daily work includes having an employer or boss, Luther commended Ephesians 6:5-8 and its conviction that our work for others is work performed "as to Christ himself." This leads to the helpful practice of asking: What kind of work do you do when no one is watching? This Bible reading makes the important point that our good service to others at work is as much a service to Christ as anything else we do. We serve God by serving our neighbors. This is the "priesthood of all the baptized" in action.

Of course, the command to obey does not give those in authority the right to be cruel. In the Household Chart, Luther points to the reminder in Ephesians 6:4 that people of all social status have the same God, who looks at everyone with equity. This reveals an often overlooked flip side to the fourth commandment about how people in authority are supposed to treat those in their care. On this point, Luther's Large Catechism spoke strongly against the abuse of authority.

---

29. LW 48:329–36. 30. LW 49:267–71 and LW 50:17–21. 31. LW 51:137. 32. LW 45:46. 33. Exodus 20:12 and Deuteronomy 5:16.
34. Matthew 18:3.

Everyone acts as if God gave us children for our pleasure and amusement, gave us servants merely to put them to work like cows or donkeys, and gave us subjects to treat as we please, as if it were no concern of ours what they learn or how they live. No one is willing to see that this is the command of the divine Majesty, who will solemnly call us to account and punish us for its neglect. Nor is it recognized how very necessary it is to devote serious attention to the young. For if we want capable and qualified people for both the civil and the spiritual realms, we really must spare no effort, time, and expense in teaching and educating our children to serve God and the world.[35]

This section of the Household Chart reminds people in positions of authority—whether in the home, church, business, or government—that they are servant leaders. Their power is not their own but exists for the good of those entrusted to their care.

Aware of the complexities of human nature and personal relationships, Luther knew that these issues of service and leadership are not abstract ideas but real-life questions that we face every day. As the child of Hans and Margaret, Martin experienced the ups and downs of life with parents with whom he did not always see

Nineteenth-century artists delighted in depicting Luther's home life. In this etching from 1867, he is playing the lute and singing with his children and wife, with Philip Melanchthon in the background.

---

35. Large Catechism, Ten Commandments, par. 170–72 (BC 409–10).

eye to eye. As a brother in the monastery, Luther knew the challenges of community life, including the challenges that come with both leading and serving. There are no perfect families or faith communities. That is precisely the point of the gospel: through his cross, Christ did not wait to save us until we got our acts together, but actively worked to reconcile and free us "while we were still sinners."[36] He goes to work right in the midst of our broken relationships and brings healing, one day at a time.

The Luther household itself was not always one of familial bliss. It had its share of hardships. For one thing, it was a busy place. The house—which had previously served as the Augustinian monastery—remained full of activity after it was given to the Luthers. Martin and Katie lived with many guests in their home, including students, servants, travelers, and relatives. For another thing, money needed to be carefully managed. Martin did not receive income from his many publications but continued to live primarily from his generous teaching salary. In that situation, Katie Luther became an extremely efficient manager of the household. She ran what we might today call a small business, which included gardens, farm animals, renters, property management, and beer brewing. Martin and Katie knew the daily challenges and blessings of family life and household work very well.

They also intimately knew the joys and sorrows of family life. The death of their thirteen-year-old daughter, Magdalena, in 1542 was especially painful for both Martin and Katie. In a letter to his friend Justas Jonas shortly after her death, Luther wrote:

> I believe the report has reached you that my dearest daughter Magdalen has been reborn in Christ's eternal kingdom. I and my wife should only joyfully give thanks for such a felicitous departure and blessed end . . . yet the force of our natural love is so great that we are unable to do this without crying and grieving in our hearts, or even without experiencing death ourselves. For the features, the words, and the movement of the living and dying daughter who was so very obedient and respectful remain engraved deep in the heart; even the death of Christ (and what is the dying of all people in comparison with Christ's death?) is unable totally to take all this away as it should. You, therefore, please give thanks to God in our stead![37]

Portrait of Magdalena Luther, c. 1540. Although scholars now dispute whether this is indeed Magdalena, this painting by Lucas Cranach the Elder certainly depicts someone of her age and social status.

Knowing the promise of resurrection and Christ's victory over death does not mean we do not grieve the absence of those near and dear to us. Jesus

36. Romans 5:8.   37. LW 50:238.

himself wept at the tomb of his friend Lazarus.[38] Our grief is a sign of our love. God has given us people who fill our lives in so many ways: in our homes, friendships, and close working relationships. We rightly grieve the loss of those relationships when they end.

In the meantime, we see how good it is to give thanks to God every day for surrounding us with such wonderful people. The love we feel in these relationships is a sign of God's incredible love for us. Observing the Luther family's grief at Magdalena's death, Luther's longtime friend and coworker Philip Melanchthon said, "The feelings of parents are a likeness of divinity impressed upon the human character. If the love of God for the human race is as great as the love of parents for their children, then it is truly great and ardent."[39]

For Young and Old

♥ In the same way, you who are younger must accept the authority of the elders. And all of you must clothe yourselves with humility in your dealings with one another, for "God opposes the proud, but gives grace to the humble." Humble yourselves therefore under the mighty hand of God, so that he may exalt you in due time. *1 Peter 5:5-6*

♥ The real widow, left alone, has set her hope on God and continues in supplications and prayers night and day; but the widow who lives for pleasure is dead even while she lives. *1 Timothy 5:5-6*

The Lutheran Reformation included a strong social concern for the needs of both younger and older members of the community. In 1524, for instance, Luther wrote an open letter to political leaders about supporting good public education. He identified three compelling reasons for these efforts: first, young people need to develop spiritually and intellectually, not just physically or economically; second, people should take advantage of all the new learning opportunities that had arisen in science, theology, and the arts in recent years (this was the era of the Renaissance, after all!); third, God has commanded that communities raise up their children in wisdom and strength.[40] Luther identified these points as matters of spiritual and public welfare, writing:

> It therefore behooves the council and the authorities to devote the greatest care and attention to the young. Since the property, honor, and life of the whole city have been committed to their faithful keeping, they would be remiss in their duty before God and man if they did not seek its welfare and improvement day and night with all the means at their command. Now the welfare of a city does not consist solely in accumulating vast treasures, building mighty walls and magnificent buildings, and producing a goodly supply of guns and armor. Indeed, where such things are plentiful, and reckless fools get control of them, it is so much the worse and the city suffers even greater loss. A city's best and greatest welfare, safety, and strength consist rather in its having many able, learned, wise, honorable, and well-educated citizens. They can then readily gather, protect, and properly use treasure and all manner of property.[41]

---

38. John 11:35. See also Romans 12:15.   39. LW 54:432.   40. TAL 5:247–53; LW 45:348–53.   41. TAL 5:255; LW 45:355–56.

Good schools are a primary way for communities to live out their care for the young. From this conviction, the early Lutherans not only talked about young people but built good schools for them. Philip Melanchthon, for instance, put his concern for young people and education into practice by dedicating one of the first modern German high schools (*Gymnasium*) in the 1520s. For this reason, he continues to be honored with the title *Praeceptor Germania*: the teacher of Germany.

Melanchthon Gymnasium (high school) in Nuremberg, founded in 1526, next to St. Aegidian's Church.

Similarly, Johannes Bugenhagen wrote "church orders" for lands around northern Germany that accepted the Reformation. These orders combined theological reform with practical instructions for how to build strong communities, including how to start local schools, hire good teachers, and teach boys and girls—regardless of their family's social status—the basics of reading, math, and faith formation. Bugenhagen explained the benefits of strong local schools by saying:

> In time there will emerge good schoolmasters; good preachers; good lawyers; good medical doctors; good, God-fearing, capable, honest, upright, obedient, friendly, learned, peaceful, not wild but joyful burghers [citizens] who will also take care of their children in the best possible manner in the future, and so on from generation to generation.[42]

The preface to Luther's Large Catechism concluded with an emphasis on care for young people by reminding church leaders such care belongs at the heart of what they do. "The reason we take such care to preach on the catechism frequently is to impress it upon our young people, not in a lofty and learned manner but briefly and very simply, so that it may penetrate deeply into their minds and remain fixed in their memories."[43] Children should not be an afterthought, either for congregations or for local communities. Instead, caring for children is a way to live out love for our neighbors today and support of the public good tomorrow.

Luther suggested that young people themselves learn to practice patience. This can be so hard! Being young brings with it the excitement of learning new things, testing new ideas, and finding your own voice. Who can be patient when so much exciting stuff is going on?

---

42. Johannes Bugenhagen, *Selected Writings*, vol. 2, trans. Kurt K. Hendel (Minneapolis: Fortress, 2015), 1215.
43. Large Catechism, preface, par. 27 (BC 386).

This is where Luther's words in the Household Chart show a realistic and sympathetic concern for young people. The passage he quoted from 1 Peter 5 reminds young folks to be patient. It is as if he were saying, "Your turn will come, so don't be in a hurry. Take time to grow, develop, and learn from your elders. You don't know everything right now, but someday soon it will be your turn to lead others in good paths. We will help you be ready when that time comes."

To Luther's words from 1 Peter 5, we might add the following from 1 Timothy: "Let no one despise your youth, but set the believers an example in speech and conduct, in love, in faith, in purity."[44] Advice like this is not meant to burden youth with demands to be perfect. Instead, it encourages them to grow daily in the promises and grace given in baptism. A young person who wonders if they are loved and valuable can always say, "I am loved and I am valued by God and the people around me. Baptism promises it. God the Holy Spirit is with me, and so is the community of God's saints who love me no matter what." This section of the Household Chart reminds us that the description of the young Jesus is a great image for all children: "The child grew and became strong, filled with wisdom; and the favor of God was upon him."[45]

Christ as a Boy by Bartolomeo Montagna (c. 1450–1523).

In addition to caring for the youth, communities also care for their elders. This was true in Luther's immediate household, which included the presence of Katie Luther's aunt Magdalena von Bora. This "Aunt Lena" lived with the Luthers before getting married to a professor. She moved back in with the family after her husband's death and became the subject of the Luther household's prayers as she approached death. This a personal example of the value the reformers placed on caring for older family members. And while responsibility begins with the immediate family, Reformation documents like Bugenhagen's Braunschweig Church Order explicitly name the fact that care for elders is a social concern belonging to the entire community.[46]

Cover of Bugenhagen's 1528 Church Order for the City of Braunschweig.

Speaking of Pastor Bugenhagen, he outlived his friend Luther by almost a decade. By then, he had a full head of white hair, recalling verses like these: "Gray hair is a crown of glory; it is gained in a righteous life" and "Even to your old age I am he, even when you turn gray I will carry you. I have made, and I will bear; I will carry and will save."[47] This latter verse was one that Luther himself clung to as a word of gospel promise throughout life.[48]

Portrait of an older Johannes Bugenhagen after Lucas Cranach the Elder, 1543.

---

44. 1 Timothy 4:12. 45. Luke 2:40. 46. Bugenhagen, *Selected Writings,* vol. 2, 1379. 47. Proverbs 16:31 and Isaiah 46:4. 48. LW 43:171.

At some point after Bugenhagen's death, the people of Wittenberg honored this esteemed senior pastor by placing a plaque over the door of his house. It ends with Hebrews 13:7, which says, "Remember your leaders, those who spoke the word of God to you; consider the outcome of their way of life, and imitate their faith." Honoring our elders includes giving thanks for all we have learned from their faithful witness, their wisdom, and their loving care.

The verses from 1 Timothy 5 that Luther chose for the Household Chart focus more, however, on how older members of the community can themselves remain dedicated to God through hope, prayer, and service. The setting of this New Testament letter suggests that Timothy's community was struggling to find roles for the widows in their midst. Because so much of social life revolved around family relationships, the question of whether these widows should remarry was important. The main conclusion was that women who felt called to remarry should remarry, while those who wanted to stay single should do that. In either case, the goal was to find the right combination of personal and communal well-being.

From that perspective, Luther's emphasis on hope, prayer, and service here provides positive roles for senior members of the community: they can use their wisdom, patience, and skills for the good of the people around them. Communities continually benefit from the wisdom of their elders. In turn, these wise souls get to share in the joyous testimony of Simeon and Anna who met the infant Jesus in the temple, singing, "My eyes have seen your salvation!"[49]

Presentation in the Temple (detail) by Lorenzetti Ambrogio, 1342. Simeon holds the infant Jesus, and Anna points to him.

For All in the Community

♥ The commandments . . . are summed up in this word, "Love your neighbor as yourself." *Romans 13:9*

First of all, then, I urge that supplications, prayers, intercessions, and thanksgivings be made for everyone. *1 Timothy 2:1*

Let all their lessons learn with care,
So that the household well may fare.

The final section of the Household Chart explicitly returns to the priesthood of all the baptized. In German, the heading for this final

---

49. Luke 2:30.

section is simply *Der Gemeine*; in Latin, *Omnibus in commune*. We could translate these headings in English as "for the congregation," "for the community," or "for all in common."

Each of these meanings says something important about our holy orders as baptized people. First, as congregations, we remember that we are gathered as equally beloved and redeemed children of God: all belong to Christ and serve him equally. Second, as community members in a diverse world, we get to claim the Golden Rule as a core value for who we are and how we will treat others; freed from everything that would keep us from God in body or soul, this common priesthood frees us to care for our neighbors with no strings attached. Third, as individual children of God, we are assured that we are valuable and loved, blessed to be a blessing to others.[50]

In the freedom of the gospel, the Household Chart is not a rigid list of rules to follow. Luther did not end his Small Catechism by sending us back to legalism or perfectionism. Instead, the Household Chart provides a reliable starting point for how all of us can live out the "holy orders" given to us in baptism through our daily lives. The little poem that ends the Household Chart offers a fitting finale to this journey of Christian life together. Luther seems to have written it himself. It connects faith and love, as it shows that the faith lessons we learn in our hearts shape the daily relationships that fill our lives. Being set free in the gospel does not keep us apart from each other but shows us how much we truly belong to each other. Learning to see the holiness of everyday life reveals the profound beauty and grace that God has given to all of creation.

Conclusion: Evening Prayer and a Blessed Rest

The Evening Blessing

♥ In the evening, when you go to bed, you are to make the sign of the holy cross and say:

"God the Father, Son, and Holy Spirit watch over me. Amen."

Then, kneeling or standing, say the Apostles' Creed and the Lord's Prayer. If you wish, you may in addition recite this little prayer as well:

"I give thanks to you, heavenly Father, through Jesus Christ your dear Son, that you have graciously protected me today. I ask you to forgive me all my sins, where I have done wrong, and graciously to protect me tonight. Into your hands I commend myself: my body, my soul, and all that is mine. Let your holy angel be with me, so that the wicked foe may have no power over me. Amen."

Then you are to go to sleep quickly and cheerfully.

Being baptized means returning to the goodness, mercy, and love of our God one day at a time. From that perspective, the Daily Prayer section and Household Chart in Luther's Small Catechism provide excellent

---

50. Genesis 12:2-3.

guidance for the journey. Luther's order for evening prayer is a great chance to review how rich a single day with God can be.

You awoke and immediately covered yourself in the sign of the cross, saying, "God the Father, Son, and Holy Spirit watch over me. Amen." Luther then invited you to start your day by reclaiming your faith through the words of the Apostles' Creed and to call on God for all of life's needs, using Christ's own words of prayer. This order for morning prayer sent you out with a song, ready to serve your neighbors in faith and love.

Taking time to pray at your meals connected your body with your soul, your physical food with spiritual nourishment. Giving thanks at mealtime also reminded you to give thanks that God has given daily bread and inspired you to see to it that your neighbors are getting what they need for daily life too. Between prayers at morning, night, and mealtimes, you have prayed and pondered the Lord's Prayer several times. You have also reflected on scripture and entrusted yourself repeatedly to God's good providing.

In this "day in the life" of a Christian, you started to notice all the different ways that people serve their communities as family members, parishioners, citizens, and neighbors. Each of these roles presents countless opportunities to live out our faith. People in positions of authority can practice servant leadership. Others contribute by being good team players. In Christ, the lowliest acts of service become sacred moments of love and grace. Through baptism, each of us belongs to the "holy order" of following the crucified and risen Christ, invited to share freely the grace we ourselves first received from God.

You go to bed at the close of the day, once again giving thanks to the Lord, entrusting your life to the Good Shepherd and praying for the abiding presence of the Holy Spirit. In faith, you ask for forgiveness, mercy, and support, confident in God's steadfast love. You pray, "God the Father, Son, and Holy Spirit watch over me. Amen."

Child at Prayer by Eastman Johnson, 1873.

Small Catechism of Martin Luther

Luther's Preface to the Small Catechism of 1529[1]

Martin Luther, to all faithful and upright pastors and preachers: Grace, mercy, and peace in Jesus Christ our Lord.

The deplorable, wretched deprivation that I recently encountered while I was a visitor has constrained and compelled me to prepare this catechism, or Christian instruction, in such a brief, plain, and simple version. Dear God, what misery I beheld! The ordinary person, especially in the villages, knows absolutely nothing about the Christian faith, and unfortunately many pastors are completely unskilled and incompetent teachers. Yet supposedly they all bear the name Christian, are baptized, and receive the holy sacrament, even though they do not know the Lord's Prayer, the Creed, or the Ten Commandments! As a result they live like simple cattle or irrational pigs and, despite the fact that the gospel has returned, have mastered the fine art of misusing all their freedom.

O you bishops! How are you going to answer to Christ, now that you have so shamefully neglected the people and have not exercised your office for even a single second? May you escape punishment for this! You forbid the cup to the laity in the Lord's supper[2] and insist on observance of your human laws, while never even bothering to ask whether the people know the Lord's Prayer, the Creed, the Ten Commandments, or a single section of God's word. Shame on you forever!

---

1. Here Luther advises pastors on how to teach Christian doctrine and use this book.
2. In Luther's day only priests received the wine in the Lord's supper.

Therefore, my dear sirs and brothers, who are either pastors or preachers, I beg all of you for God's sake to take up your office boldly, to have pity on your people who are entrusted to you, and to help us bring the catechism to the people, especially to the young. Moreover, I ask that those unable to do any better take up these charts and versions and read them to the people word for word in the following manner:

In the first place, the preacher should above all take care to avoid changes or variations in the text and version of the Ten Commandments, the Lord's Prayer, the Creed, the sacraments, but instead adopt a single version, stick with it, and always use the same one year after year. For the young and the unlettered people must be taught with a single, fixed text and version. Otherwise, if someone teaches one way now and another way next year—even for the sake of making improvements—the people become quite easily confused, and all the time and effort will go for naught.

The dear church fathers also understood this well. They used one form for the Lord's Prayer, the Creed, and the Ten Commandments. Therefore, we, too, should teach these parts to the young and to people who cannot read in such a way that we neither change a single syllable nor present or recite it differently from one year to the next. Therefore, choose for yourself whatever version you want and stick with it for good. To be sure, when you preach to educated and intelligent people, then you may demonstrate your erudition and discuss these parts with as much complexity and from as many different angles as you can. But with the young people, stick with a fixed, unchanging version and form. To begin with, teach them these parts: the Ten Commandments, the Creed, the Lord's Prayer, etc., following the text word for word, so that they can also repeat it back to you and learn it by heart.

Those who do not want to learn these things—who must be told how they deny Christ and are not Christians—should also not be admitted to the sacrament, should not be sponsors for children at baptism, and should not exercise any aspect of Christian freedom, but instead should simply be sent back home to the pope and his officials and, along with them, to the devil himself. Moreover, their parents and employers ought to deny them food and drink and advise them that the prince is disposed to drive such coarse people out of the country.

Although no one can or should force another person to believe, nevertheless one should insist upon and hold the masses to this: that they know what is right and wrong among those with whom they wish to reside, eat, and earn a living. For example, if people want to live in a particular city, they ought to know and abide by the laws of the city whose protection they enjoy, no matter whether they believe or are at heart scoundrels and villains.

In the second place, once the people have learned the text well, then teach them to understand it, too, so that they know what it means. Take up again the form offered in these charts or some other short form that you may prefer. Then adhere to it without changing a single syllable, just as was stated above regarding the text. Moreover, allow yourself ample time for it, because you need not take up all the parts at once but may instead handle them one at a time. After the people understand the First Commandment well, then take up the Second, and so on. Otherwise they will be so overwhelmed that they will hardly remember a single thing.

In the third place, after you have taught the people a short catechism like this one, then take up a longer catechism and impart to them a richer and fuller understanding. Using such a catechism, explain each individual commandment, petition, or part with its various works, benefits and blessings, harm and danger, as you find treated at length in so many booklets. In particular, put the greatest stress on that commandment or part where your people experience the greatest need. For example, you must strongly emphasize the Seventh Commandment, dealing with stealing, to artisans and shopkeepers and even to farmers and household workers, because rampant among such people are all kinds of dishonesty and thievery. Likewise, you must emphasize the Fourth Commandment to children and the common people, so that they are orderly, faithful, obedient, and peaceful. Always adduce many examples from the scriptures where God either punished or blessed such people.

In particular, at this point also urge governing authorities and parents to rule well and to send their children to school. Point out how they are obliged to do so and what a damnable sin they commit if they do not, for thereby, as the worst enemies of God and humanity, they overthrow and lay waste both the kingdom of God and the kingdom of the world. Explain very clearly what kind of horrible damage they do when they do not help to train children as pastors, preachers, civil servants, etc., and tell them that God will punish them dreadfully for this. For in our day and age it is necessary to preach about these things. The extent to which parents and governing authorities are now sinning in these matters defies description. The devil, too, intends to do something horrible in all this.

Finally, because the tyranny of the pope[3] has been abolished, people no longer want to receive the sacrament [of the altar], and they treat it with contempt. This, too, needs to be stressed, while keeping in mind that we should not compel anyone to believe or to receive the sacrament and should not fix any law or time or place for it.[4] Instead, we should preach in such a way that the people make themselves come without our law and just plain compel us pastors to administer the sacrament to them. This can be done by telling them: You have to worry that whoever does not desire or receive the sacrament at the very least around four times a year despises the sacrament and is no Christian, just as anyone who does not listen to or believe the gospel is no Christian. For Christ did not say, "Omit this," or "Despise this," but instead, "Do this, as often as you drink it . . ." He really wants it to be done and not completely omitted or despised. "Do this," he says.

Those who do not hold the sacrament in high esteem indicate that they have no sin, no flesh, no devil, no world, no death, no dangers, no hell. That is, they *believe* they have none of these things, although they are up to their ears in them and belong to the devil twice over. On the other hand, they indicate that they need no grace, no life, no paradise, no heaven, no Christ, no God, nor any other good thing. For if they believed that they had so much evil and needed so much good, they would not neglect the sacrament, in which help against such evil is provided and in which so much good is given. It would not be necessary to compel them with any law to receive the sacrament. Instead, they would come on their own, rushing and running to it; they would compel themselves to come and would insist that you give them the sacrament.

For these reasons you do not need to make any law concerning this, as the pope did. Only emphasize clearly the benefit and the harm, the need and the blessing, the danger and the salvation in this sacrament. Then

---

3. Luther's strong language reflects his ongoing struggle with the institutional church of his day.
4. In Luther's day all Christians had to commune between Easter and ten days after Pentecost.

they will doubtless come on their own without any compulsion. If they do not come, give up on them and tell them that those who do not pay attention to or feel their great need and God's gracious help belong to the devil. However, if you either do not urge such participation or make it into a law or poison, then it is your fault if they despise the sacrament. How can they help but neglect it, if you sleep and remain silent?

Therefore, pastors and preachers, take note! Our office has now become a completely different one than it was under the pope. It has now become serious and salutary. Thus, it now involves much toil and work, many dangers and attacks, and in addition little reward or gratitude in the world. But Christ himself will be our reward, so long as we labor faithfully. May the Father of all grace grant it, to whom be praise and thanks in eternity through Christ, our Lord. Amen.

The Ten Commandments

The First Commandment

You shall have no other gods.

What is this? or *What does this mean?*
We are to fear, love, and trust God above all things.

The Second Commandment

You shall not make wrongful use of the name of the Lord your God.

What is this? or *What does this mean?*
We are to fear and love God, so that we do not curse, swear, practice magic, lie, or deceive using God's name, but instead use that very name in every time of need to call on, pray to, praise, and give thanks to God.

The Third Commandment

Remember the sabbath day, and keep it holy.

What is this? or *What does this mean?*
We are to fear and love God, so that we do not despise preaching or God's word, but instead keep that word holy and gladly hear and learn it.

The Fourth Commandment

Honor your father and your mother.

What is this? or *What does this mean?*
We are to fear and love God, so that we neither despise nor anger our parents and others in authority, but instead honor, serve, obey, love, and respect them.

The Fifth Commandment

You shall not murder.

What is this? or *What does this mean?*
We are to fear and love God, so that we neither endanger nor harm the lives of our neighbors, but instead help and support them in all of life's needs.

The Sixth Commandment

You shall not commit adultery.

What is this? or *What does this mean?*
We are to fear and love God, so that we lead pure and decent lives in word and deed, and each of us loves and honors his or her spouse.

The Seventh Commandment

You shall not steal.

What is this? or *What does this mean?*
We are to fear and love God, so that we neither take our neighbors' money or property nor acquire them by using shoddy merchandise or crooked deals, but instead help them to improve and protect their property and income.

The Eighth Commandment

You shall not bear false witness against your neighbor.

What is this? or *What does this mean?*
We are to fear and love God, so that we do not tell lies about our neighbors, betray or slander them, or destroy their reputations. Instead we are to come to their defense, speak well of them, and interpret everything they do in the best possible light.

The Ninth Commandment

You shall not covet your neighbor's house.

What is this? or *What does this mean?*
We are to fear and love God, so that we do not try to trick our neighbors out of their inheritance or property or try to get it for ourselves by claiming to have a legal right to it and the like, but instead be of help and service to them in keeping what is theirs.

The Tenth Commandment

You shall not covet your neighbor's wife, or male or female slave, or ox, or donkey, or anything that belongs to your neighbor.

What is this? or *What does this mean?*
We are to fear and love God, so that we do not entice, force, or steal away from our neighbors their spouses, household workers, or livestock, but instead urge them to stay and fulfill their responsibilities to our neighbors.

What then does God say about all these commandments?

God says the following: "I, the Lord your God, am a jealous God, punishing children for the iniquity of parents, to the third and the fourth generation of those who reject me, but showing steadfast love to the thousandth generation of those who love me and keep my commandments."

What is this? or *What does this mean?*
God threatens to punish all who break these commandments. Therefore we are to fear his wrath and not disobey these commandments. However, God promises grace and every good thing to all those who keep these commandments. Therefore we also are to love and trust him and gladly act according to his commands.

The Apostles' Creed

The First Article: On Creation

I believe in God, the Father almighty, creator of heaven and earth.

What is this? or *What does this mean?*
I believe that God has created me together with all that exists. God has given me and still preserves my body and soul: eyes, ears, and all limbs and senses; reason and all mental faculties.

In addition, God daily and abundantly provides shoes and clothing, food and drink, house and farm, spouse and children, fields, livestock, and all property—along with all the necessities and nourishment for this body and life. God protects me against all danger and shields and preserves me from all evil. And all this is done out of pure, fatherly, and divine goodness and mercy, without any merit or worthiness of mine at all! For all of this I owe it to God to thank and praise, serve and obey him. This is most certainly true.

The Second Article: On Redemption

I believe in Jesus Christ, God's only Son, our Lord, who was conceived by the Holy Spirit, born of the virgin Mary, suffered under Pontius Pilate, was crucified, died, and was buried; he descended to the dead.[5] On the third day he rose again; he ascended into heaven, he is seated at the right hand of the Father, and he will come to judge the living and the dead.

What is this? or *What does this mean?*
I believe that Jesus Christ, true God, begotten of the Father in eternity, and also a true human being, born of the virgin Mary, is my Lord. He has redeemed me, a lost and condemned human being. He has purchased and freed me from all sins, from death, and from the power of the devil, not with gold or silver but with his holy, precious blood and with his innocent suffering and death. He has done all this in order that I may belong to him, live under him in his kingdom, and serve him in eternal righteousness, innocence, and blessedness, just as he is risen from the dead and lives and rules eternally. This is most certainly true.

The Third Article: On Being Made Holy

I believe in the Holy Spirit, the holy catholic church, the communion of saints, the forgiveness of sins, the resurrection of the body, and the life everlasting.

What is this? or *What does this mean?*
I believe that by my own understanding or strength I cannot believe in Jesus Christ my Lord or come to him, but instead the Holy Spirit has called me through the gospel, enlightened me with his gifts, made me holy and kept me in the true faith, just as he calls, gathers, enlightens, and makes holy the whole Christian church on earth and keeps it with Jesus Christ in the one common, true faith. Daily in this Christian church the Holy Spirit abundantly forgives all sins—mine and those of all believers. On the last day the Holy Spirit will raise me and all the dead and will give to me and all believers in Christ eternal life. This is most certainly true.

---

5. *Or,* "he descended into hell," *another translation of this text in widespread use.*

The Lord's Prayer

Introduction

Our Father in heaven.

What is this? or *What does this mean?*
With these words God wants to attract us, so that we come to believe he is truly our Father and we are truly his children, in order that we may ask him boldly and with complete confidence, just as loving children ask their loving father.

The First Petition

Hallowed be your name.

What is this? or *What does this mean?*
It is true that God's name is holy in itself, but we ask in this prayer that it may also become holy in and among us.

How does this come about?
Whenever the word of God is taught clearly and purely and we, as God's children, also live holy lives according to it. To this end help us, dear Father in heaven! However, whoever teaches and lives otherwise than the word of God teaches, dishonors the name of God among us. Preserve us from this, heavenly Father!

The Second Petition

Your kingdom come.

What is this? or *What does this mean?*
In fact, God's kingdom comes on its own without our prayer, but we ask in this prayer that it may also come to us.

How does this come about?
Whenever our heavenly Father gives us his Holy Spirit, so that through the Holy Spirit's grace we believe God's holy word and live godly lives here in time and hereafter in eternity.

The Third Petition

Your will be done, on earth as in heaven.

What is this? or *What does this mean?*
In fact, God's good and gracious will comes about without our prayer, but we ask in this prayer that it may also come about in and among us.

How does this come about?

Whenever God breaks and hinders every evil scheme and will—as are present in the will of the devil, the world, and our flesh—that would not allow us to hallow God's name and would prevent the coming of his kingdom, and instead whenever God strengthens us and keeps us steadfast in his word and in faith until the end of our lives. This is God's gracious and good will.

The Fourth Petition

Give us today our daily bread.

What is this? or *What does this mean?*

In fact, God gives daily bread without our prayer, even to all evil people, but we ask in this prayer that God cause us to recognize what our daily bread is and to receive it with thanksgiving.

What then does "daily bread" mean?

Everything included in the necessities and nourishment for our bodies, such as food, drink, clothing, shoes, house, farm, fields, livestock, money, property, an upright spouse, upright children, upright members of the household, upright and faithful rulers, good government, good weather, peace, health, decency, honor, good friends, faithful neighbors, and the like.

The Fifth Petition

Forgive us our sins as we forgive those who sin against us.

What is this? or *What does this mean?*

We ask in this prayer that our heavenly Father would not regard our sins nor deny these petitions on their account, for we are worthy of nothing for which we ask, nor have we earned it. Instead we ask that God would give us all things by grace, for we daily sin much and indeed deserve only punishment. So, on the other hand, we, too, truly want to forgive heartily and to do good gladly to those who sin against us.

The Sixth Petition

Save us from the time of trial.

What is this? or *What does this mean?*

It is true that God tempts no one, but we ask in this prayer that God would preserve and keep us, so that the devil, the world, and our flesh may not deceive us or mislead us into false belief, despair, and other great and shameful sins, and that, although we may be attacked by them, we may finally prevail and gain the victory.

The Seventh Petition

And deliver us from evil.

What is this? or *What does this mean?*
We ask in this prayer, as in a summary, that our Father in heaven may deliver us from all kinds of evil—affecting body or soul, property or reputation—and at last, when our final hour comes, may grant us a blessed end and take us by grace from this valley of tears to himself in heaven.

Conclusion

[For the kingdom, the power, and the glory are yours, now and forever.] Amen.

What is this? or *What does this mean?*
That I should be certain that such petitions are acceptable to and heard by our Father in heaven, for he himself commanded us to pray like this and has promised to hear us. "Amen, amen" means "Yes, yes, it is going to come about just like this."

The Sacrament of Holy Baptism

1: What is baptism?

Baptism is not simply plain water. Instead, it is water used according to God's command and connected with God's word.

What then is this word of God?

Where our Lord Christ says in Matthew 28, "Go therefore and make disciples of all nations, baptizing them in the name of the Father and of the Son and of the Holy Spirit."

2: What gifts or benefits does baptism grant?

It brings about forgiveness of sins, redeems from death and the devil, and gives eternal salvation to all who believe it, as the words and promise of God declare.

What are these words and promise of God?

Where our Lord Christ says in Mark 16, "The one who believes and is baptized will be saved; but the one who does not believe will be condemned."

3: How can water do such great things?

Clearly the water does not do it, but the word of God, which is with and alongside the water, and faith, which trusts this word of God in the water. For without the word of God the water is plain water and not a baptism, but with the word of God it is a baptism, that is, a grace-filled water of life and a "bath of the new birth in the Holy Spirit," as St. Paul says to Titus in chapter 3, "through the water of rebirth and renewal by the Holy Spirit. This Spirit he poured out on us richly through Jesus Christ our Savior, so that, having been justified by his grace, we might become heirs according to the hope of eternal life. The saying is sure."

4: What then is the significance of such a baptism with water?

It signifies that the old person in us with all sins and evil desires is to be drowned and die through daily sorrow for sin and through repentance, and on the other hand that daily a new person is to come forth and rise up to live before God in righteousness and purity forever.

Where is this written?

St. Paul says in Romans 6, "We have been buried with Christ by baptism into death, so that, just as Christ was raised from the dead by the glory of the Father, so we too might walk in newness of life."

How people are to be taught to confess

What is confession?

Confession consists of two parts. One is that we confess our sins. The other is that we receive the absolution, that is, forgiveness, from the pastor as from God himself and by no means doubt but firmly believe that our sins are thereby forgiven before God in heaven.

Which sins is a person to confess?

Before God one is to acknowledge the guilt for all sins, even those of which we are not aware, as we do in the Lord's Prayer. However, before the pastor we are to confess only those sins of which we have knowledge and which trouble us.

Which sins are these?

Here reflect on your place in life in light of the Ten Commandments: whether you are father, mother, son, daughter, master, mistress, servant; whether you have been disobedient, unfaithful, lazy, whether you have harmed anyone by word or deed; whether you have stolen, neglected, wasted, or injured anything.

The Sacrament of the Altar

What is the Sacrament of the Altar?

It is the true body and blood of our Lord Jesus Christ under the bread and wine, instituted by Christ himself for us Christians to eat and to drink.

Where is this written?

The holy evangelists, Matthew, Mark, and Luke, and St. Paul write thus:

"In the night in which he was betrayed, our Lord Jesus took bread, and gave thanks; broke it, and gave it to his disciples, saying: Take and eat; this is my body, given for you. Do this for the remembrance of me. Again, after supper, he took the cup, gave thanks, and gave it for all to drink, saying: This cup is the new covenant in my blood, shed for you and for all people for the forgiveness of sin. Do this for the remembrance of me."

What is the benefit of such eating and drinking?

The words "given for you" and "shed for you for the forgiveness of sin" show us that forgiveness of sin, life, and salvation are given to us in the sacrament through these words, because where there is forgiveness of sin, there is also life and salvation.

How can bodily eating and drinking do such a great thing?

Eating and drinking certainly do not do it, but rather the words that are recorded: "given for you" and "shed for you for the forgiveness of sin." These words, when accompanied by the physical eating and drinking, are the essential thing in the sacrament, and whoever believes these very words has what they declare and state, namely, "forgiveness of sin."

Who, then, receives this sacrament worthily?

Fasting and bodily preparation are in fact a fine external discipline, but a person who has faith in these words, "given for you" and "shed for you for the forgiveness of sin," is really worthy and well prepared. However, a person who does not believe these words or doubts them is unworthy and unprepared, because the words "for you" require truly believing hearts.

Morning and Evening Blessings

How the head of the house is to teach the members of the household to say morning and evening blessings.

The Morning Blessing

In the morning, as soon as you get out of bed, you are to make the sign of the holy cross and say:

"God the Father, Son, and Holy Spirit watch over me. Amen."

Then, kneeling or standing, say the Apostles' Creed and the Lord's Prayer. If you wish, you may in addition recite this little prayer as well:

"I give thanks to you, heavenly Father, through Jesus Christ your dear Son, that you have protected me through the night from all harm and danger. I ask that you would also protect me today from sin and all evil, so that my life and actions may please you. Into your hands I commend myself: my body, my soul, and all that is mine. Let your holy angel be with me, so that the wicked foe may have no power over me. Amen."

After singing a hymn perhaps (for example, one on the Ten Commandments) or whatever else may serve your devotion, you are to go to your work joyfully.

The Evening Blessing

In the evening, when you go to bed, you are to make the sign of the holy cross and say:

"God the Father, Son, and Holy Spirit watch over me. Amen."

Then, kneeling or standing, say the Apostles' Creed and the Lord's Prayer. If you wish, you may in addition recite this little prayer as well:

"I give thanks to you, heavenly Father, through Jesus Christ your dear Son, that you have graciously protected me today. I ask you to forgive me all my sins, where I have done wrong, and graciously to protect me tonight. Into your hands I commend myself: my body, my soul, and all that is mine. Let your holy angel be with me, so that the wicked foe may have no power over me. Amen."

Then you are to go to sleep quickly and cheerfully.

Blessings and Thanks at Mealtimes

The Table Blessing

The children and the members of the household are to come devoutly to the table, fold their hands, and recite:

"The eyes of all wait upon you, O Lord, and you give them their food in due season. You open your hand and satisfy the desire of every living creature."

Then they are to recite the Lord's Prayer and the following prayer:

"Lord God, heavenly Father, bless us and these your gifts, which we receive from your bountiful goodness, through Jesus Christ our Lord. Amen."

Thanksgiving

Similarly, after eating they should in the same manner fold their hands and recite devoutly:

"Give thanks to the Lord, for the Lord is good, for God's mercy endures forever. God provides food for the cattle and for the young ravens when they cry. God is not impressed by the might of a horse, and has no pleasure in the speed of a runner, but finds pleasure in those who fear the Lord, in those who await God's steadfast love."

Then recite the Lord's Prayer and the following prayer:

"We give thanks to you, Lord God our Father, through Jesus Christ our Lord for all your benefits, you who live and reign forever. Amen."

The Household Chart of Some Bible Passages

Through these verses all kinds of holy orders and walks of life may be admonished, as through lessons particularly pertinent to their office and duty.

For Bishops, Pastors, and Preachers

Now a bishop must be above reproach, married only once, temperate, sensible, respectable, hospitable, an apt teacher, not a drunkard, not violent but gentle, not quarrelsome, and not a lover of money.
1 Timothy 3:2-3

Concerning Governing Authorities

Let every person be subject to the governing authorities; for there is no authority except from God, and those authorities that exist have been instituted by God. Therefore whoever resists authority resists what God has appointed, and those who resist will incur judgment. . . . It is the servant of God to execute wrath on the wrongdoer.
Romans 13:1-2, 4b

For Husbands

Husbands, in the same way, show consideration for your wives in your life together, paying honor to the woman as the weaker sex, since they too are also heirs of the gracious gift of life—so that nothing may hinder your prayers.
1 Peter 3:7

Husbands, love your wives and never treat them harshly.
Colossians 3:19

For Wives

Wives, in the same way, accept the authority of your husbands, so that, even if some of them do not obey the word, they may be won over without a word by their wives' conduct. . . . Thus Sarah obeyed Abraham and called him lord. You have become her daughters as long as you do what is good and never let fears alarm you.
1 Peter 3:1, 6

For Parents

And, parents, do not provoke your children to anger, but bring them up in the discipline and instruction of the Lord.
based on Ephesians 6:4

For Children

Children, obey your parents in the Lord, for this is right. "Honor your father and mother"—this is the first commandment with a promise: "so that it may be well with you and you may live long on the earth."
Ephesians 6:1-3

For Employees

You employees, be obedient to your bosses with respect and cooperation, with singleness of heart, as to Christ himself; not with service meant only for the eyes, done as people-pleasers, but rather as servants of Christ, so that you do the will of God from the heart [with a good attitude]. Imagine to yourselves that you are serving the Lord and not people, and know that whatever good anyone does, the same will that person receive, whether servant or free.
based on Ephesians 6:5-8

For Employers

And, bosses, do the same to them. Stop threatening them, for you know that both of you have the same Master in heaven, and with him there is no partiality.
based on Ephesians 6:9

For Young People in General

In the same way, you who are younger must accept the authority of the elders. And all of you must clothe yourselves with humility in your dealings with one another, for "God opposes the proud, but gives grace to the humble." Humble yourselves therefore under the mighty hand of God, so that he may exalt you in due time.
1 Peter 5:5-6

For Widows

The real widow, left alone, has set her hope on God and continues in supplications and prayers night and day; but the widow who lives for pleasure is dead even while she lives.
1 Timothy 5:5-6

For All in the Community

The commandments . . . are summed up in this word, "Love your neighbor as yourself."
Romans 13:9

First of all, then, I urge that supplications, prayers, intercessions, and thanksgivings be made for everyone.
1 Timothy 2:1

Let all their lessons learn with care,
So that the household well may fare.

Image Credits

7, 9, 10, 11, 14 (bottom), 18 (top), 21, 22, 27 (bottom), 28, 30, 40, 48, 52 (left), 58 (bottom), 59, 60, 61 (bottom, both), 65, 66 (bottom), 68 (both), 71, 79, 81 (top), 82, 89 (top left; bottom), 90, 91, 95, 116, 121 (both), 123, 126 (top), 128 (both), 130 (top), 137 (right), 151 (bottom), 154, 155 (left; top right), 157, 159 (top), 166 (both), 169 (left), 170, 174, 178 (left), 180, 187 (right), 189–192, 194 (both), 198–201, 202 (center; bottom), 203, 205: Wikimedia Commons.

8: wikiart.org.

12: Classic Image / Alamy Stock Photo.

14 (top), 19 (both), 33, 35, 38, 52 (right), 78, 94, 100 (top), 103, 107, 129, 141, 143, 144, 175 (top), 178 (right), 181, 187 (left): Courtesy of the Richard C. Kessler Reformation Collection, Pitts Theology Library, Candler School of Theology, Emory University.

18 (bottom): Alinari / Art Resource, NY.

20: Ian W. Scott / Wikimedia Commons / GFDL.

25: akg-images / André Held.

26: Bernard Gagnon / Wikimedia Commons / GFDL.

27 (top): Prayitno Photography / Creative Commons.

27 (center): copyright © Heidi Fok. Used by permission.

31, 51, 53, 56, 58 (top), 61 (top), 64, 67, 70, 72, 73 (top), 81 (bottom), 87 (top), 92, 108–115, 117, 120 (top), 124, 150, 173, 193: public domain / scanned from facsimile of Otto Albrecht, ed., Der kleine Katechismus D. Martin Luthers nach der Ausgabe v. J. 1536 (Halle: Buchhandlung des Waisenhauses, 1905).

39, 195 (bottom): The Lutheran School of Theology at Chicago (Gruber Rare Books Collection). Used by permission.

41 (top): Courtesy ELCA Archives.

41 (bottom): Courtesy St. Luke's Lutheran Church, Park Ridge, Illinois.

44 (left): The British Museum / courtesy Art Resource, NY.

44 (right), 100 (bottom): copyright © He Qi. Used by permission. heqiart.com.

46: Foto Marburg / Art Resource, NY.

54, 73 (bottom): The Metropolitan Museum of Art.

62: map from Tim Dowley, Atlas of the European Reformations (Minneapolis: Fortress, 2015).

63: Thomas Doerfer / Wikimedia Commons / GFDL.

66 (top): Jwaller / Wikimedia Commons / GFDL.

69 (top): Mike Mozart / Creative Commons.

69 (bottom): David Shankbone / Wikimedia Commons.

80: 6wGagAS8xvs8Ng at Google Cultural Institute / Wikimedia Commons.

83: The Metropolitan Museum of Art / Gift of Harry G Friedman, 1961.

84, 131, 184 (left): Thinkstock / iStock.

85: Thinkstock / Purestock.

87 (bottom): The Metropolitan Museum of Art / Bequest of George D. Pratt, 1935.

89 (top center): National Gallery of Art.

89 (top right): Walters Art Museum / Wikimedia Commons / GFDL.

93: copyright © Hannah Joy Patterson / SilverWebForge.com. Used by permission.

101: The Metropolitan Museum of Art / Anonymous Bequest, 1984.

118: Alfredo Dagli Orti / Art Resource, NY.

120 (bottom): Deutsches Historisches Museum, Berlin.

126 (bottom): copyright © Birgit Korber / Dreamstime.com.

130 (bottom), 202 (top): Scala / Art Resource, NY.

135: Thinkstock / FlairImages.

137 (left): Reinhard Jahn / Wikimedia Commons / GFDL.

138: Rabanus Flavus / Wikimedia Commons.

139 (top): akg-images / Cameraphoto Arte.

139 (bottom left): ARISTIDIS VAFEIADAKIS / Alamy Stock Photo.

139 (bottom right): Courtesy of the Archbishop of York, York, England.

151 (top left): Robert Adamski / Wikimedia Commons.

151 (top center): KlausF / Wikimedia Commons / GFDL.

151 (top right): Misburg3014 / Wikimedia Commons.

155 (bottom right): Cameraphoto Arte / Art Resource, NY.

156: Erich Lessing / Art Resource, NY.

158 (top): Jean-Pol GRANDMONT / Wikimedia Commons/ GFDL.

158 (bottom): copyright © Steven E. Lawson. Used by permission.

159 (Nazareth): adriatikus / Wikimedia Commons / GFDL.

159 (communion trays): Allenscottwalker / Wikimedia Commons / GFDL.

159 (bottom): copyright © 2017 Kristin Tangen. Used by permission. kristintangen.com.

161 (left): KwEhdorc0CJJDA at Google Cultural Institute.

161 (right): The Metropolitan Museum of Art / Gift of J. Pierpont Morgan, 1917.

169 (center): The Corita Kent Art Center.

169 (right): copyright © James Boline, St. Paul's Lutheran, Santa Monica, California. Used by permission.

172: Collection Melanchthonhaus Bretten, Germany.

175 (bottom): robertharding / Alamy Stock Photo.

183: barrett&mackay / Getty Images.

184 (right): Thinkstock/ Photodisc.

185 (left): gwGj6BUX8D5Kug at Google Cultural Institute.

185 (right): REUTERS / Max Rossi.

195 (top): National Gallery of Art / Samuel H. Kress Collection.

Contributors

R. Guy Erwin (The Sacrament of the Altar) is bishop of the Southwest California Synod of the ELCA. He has served as a parish pastor, professor of Lutheran Confessional Theology at California Lutheran University, and, since 2004 as the ELCA representative to the Faith and Order Commission of the World Council of Churches.

Mary Jane Haemig (The Lord's Prayer) is professor of church history and director of the Reformation Research Program at Luther Seminary in Saint Paul, Minnesota. She specializes in the study of the Lutheran Reformation. Her interests include preaching, catechesis, and prayer in that period. She is also associate editor and book review editor of *Lutheran Quarterly*.

Ken Sundet Jones (The Ten Commandments) is Professor of Theology and Philosophy at Grand View University in Des Moines, Iowa. As a church historian, he specializes in Martin Luther and the Reformation. He has served as a pastor in South Dakota and Iowa.

Martin J. Lohrmann (Daily Prayer and the Household Chart) is assistant professor of Lutheran Confessions and Heritage at Wartburg Theological Seminary in Dubuque, Iowa. He is a pastor of the Evangelical Lutheran Church in America and has served congregations in Ohio and Philadelphia.

Derek R. Nelson (The Apostles' Creed) is professor of religion and holds the Stephen S. Bowen chair in the liberal arts at Wabash College in Crawfordsville, Indiana. He directs the Wabash Pastoral Leadership Program, and is a pastor of the Evangelical Lutheran Church in America.

Kirsi I. Stjerna (The Sacrament of Holy Baptism) is First Lutheran, Los Angeles/Southwest California Synod Professor of Lutheran History and Theology at Pacific Lutheran Theological Seminary of California Lutheran University and core doctoral faculty at Graduate Theological Union. She is also a docent at the University of Helsinki.

Timothy J. Wengert (Confession; additional sidebar material) is emeritus Ministerium of Pennsylvania Professor of Reformation History at the Lutheran Theological Seminary at Philadelphia. His translation of the Small Catechism is widely used throughout the church. He is a representative for the ELCA on the U.S. Lutheran/Roman Catholic Dialogue.

Hans Wiersma (The Story of the Small Catechism) is associate professor of religion at Augsburg College in Minneapolis, Minnesota. His main area of expertise is in the history of Christianity. He has served as a pastor in The Netherlands, California, and Minnesota.